THE HISTORY OF

AN ENGRAVING OF MEOPHAM CHURCH FROM THE NORTH-EAST, 1809

MEOPHAM CHURCH AND POND, EARLY 20TH CENTURY

The

HISTORY OF MEOPHAM

A KENTISH VILLAGE FROM SAXON TIMES

by

C. H. GOLDING-BIRD

B.A., M.B.(LOND.), F.R.C.S.

Senior Consulting Surgeon to Guy's Hospital

FONTHILL

Fonthill Media Limited
www.fonthillmedia.com
office@fonthillmedia.com

First published 1934
Reprinted 1990 and 2000
This revised edition published 2012

Published in association with Meopham Historical Society

British Library Cataloguing in Publication Data:
A catalogue record for this book is available from the British Library

Copyright © in additional material, Meopham Historical Society 2012

ISBN 978-1-78155-124-0

Printed and bound in England

TO THE MEMORY OF THE
Rev. LEWIS WOODWARD LEWIS
VICAR OF MEOPHAM, 1875–1900

SEAL OF SIMON DE MEOPHAM

FOREWORD TO THE 1934 EDITION

THE present book is based on an earlier one (in 1918) of the author, and entitled *The Story of Old Meopham*; it has, however, been out of print for years. This Kentish village not only had an interesting history in Saxon times, but is associated with two Archbishops of Canterbury and the Tradescants—father and son—and, especially in its church, has points of great archaeological interest.

C. H. GOLDING-BIRD

FOREWORD TO THE 2000 EDITION

IN times past, parsons with a scholarly turn of mind regularly investigated the history of their parishes, and left either memorable books and articles in print, or just a collection of notes recording their discoveries and insights. Such a one was the Reverend L. W. Lewis. He had assembled a multitude of papers, letters and copies of old documents, but he had used only some in articles written for his parish magazine before he died. We can picture it all! Fortunately, he had a good friend in C. H. Golding-Bird who was intent on guarding his memory. He carried on the work where Lewis left off, and completed a large canvas.

Every generation makes some contribution to its parish history, and it is appropriate in the year 2000 to be reminded of that fact. One hundred years after Lewis's death, we can welcome the success of today's local historians in making Golding-Bird's volume available again, and, we hope, spurring his successors on to make yet more investigations into the history of Meopham.

JOAN THIRSK

PREFACE

The late Vicar of this Parish, the Rev. L. W. Lewis, published in 1894-1900, in the *Parish Magazine*, a series of most interesting papers on Meopham, but his untimely and sudden death on Easter Day, 1900, left his work unfinished. These papers are now only in the hands of the few who have kept their old magazines; and all the labour he bestowed upon the subject threatens to be lost. His notes, and copies of old documents, etc., only part of which he had made use of, were, in 1914, unreservedly handed over to me by his widow, in the hope that some further use might be made of them; and in order that so much good material should not be lost, I have endeavoured, with their help, to give as complete an account of the old village as I possibly could. In what I have written will be found embodied the substance of all that Mr. Lewis published.

Mr. Lewis, a most earnest literary student, ransacked libraries and other available sources of information; but many of the old documents have clearly been copied by a professional hand, and often with valuable notes attached. Whether or not these are to be ascribed to the Rev. T. S. Frampton, of Platt, a well-known local archaeologist, I am not sure; but letters show that he provided much valuable information.

I shall be more than content if this History of Old Meopham remains as a lasting tribute to the memory of an old and valued friend.

Lastly, I desire to express my deep indebtedness to my friend, Mr. A. A. Arnold, of Cobham, who not only read the manuscript, but also supplied me with many valuable criticisms and references, of both of which I have made full use.

May 1916

The early exhaustion of the first edition and the repeated inquiries for copies have induced me to venture on a reissue, and I have less hesitancy in doing so, since many new facts have come to my knowledge in late years which are now embodied in this new edition.

C. H. GOLDING-BIRD *August* 1934

PREFACE TO THE 2000 EDITION

Meopham Historical Society thanks the Kent Archaeological Society for their permission to issue this further reprint of Golding-Bird's small classic in response to repeated requests. The text is a facsimile of the original 1934 edition and also contains the two pages of addenda and corrigenda thoughtfully inserted in the 1990 reprint by James Carley, President of the Society. Wherever possible the subjects in the original illustrations have been rephotographed for freshness and clarity. Where the subjects no longer exist the actual illustrations in Golding-Bird's 1918 book have been photographed. Maureen Arrowsmith and Keith Boxall are to be thanked for the hours of skilful work that this entailed. Six additional photographs have been included and thanks go to the Ashmolean Museum, Oxford, for permission to use the two reproductions of the Tradescant portraits. Michael Hughes has given considerable help with the jacket; the photograph on the front cover, taken by Maureen Arrowsmith, is of Meopham's Village Sign, erected in May 1998 by the Society; it depicts aspects of Meopham's history: the church, windmill, cricket bat, ball and stumps, Archbishop's mitre and trailing tradescantia. The photograph on the back cover comes, with permission, from the Wills Library, K.C.L., Guy's Hospital, and I am personally grateful to their librarian, Andrew Baster, for his patient assistance in my search for much of the background material incorporated in the short biography of "G.B." at the end of the book. The Society is particularly indebted to Doctor Joan Thirsk, C.B.E., F.B.A., for her interest and readiness to write a foreword to this special issue.

Joan O. Goodwins
Meopham Historical Society
February 2000

PREFACE TO THE 2012 EDITION

Meopham Historical Society is pleased to issue a third reprint of this classic. The contents of the text of this paperback edition are identical to those of previous issues but the quality of the original photographs has benefited from digitisation. We are particularly pleased now to give it its first much needed index and are grateful to Sarah Hilton for all the work that this has entailed and we hope that our readers will appreciate its help in their perusal of OUR STORY.

Joan Goodwins
President of the Meopham Historical Society

CONTENTS

Coffin and non-coffin burials—The winding-sheet—Burials "in woollen"; enactment of Charles II—Burials of a sixteenth-century Vicar; curious record—The "obit" and "moneths-minde" explained—The Meopham tombstones; their "evolution"—Old saying: "Meopham Churchyard's full of Buggs"—Number of burials *pages* 107–121

APPENDICES

LIST OF ILLUSTRATIONS

THE HISTORY OF MEOPHAM

CHAPTER I

SITUATION OF MEOPHAM AND ITS ANTIQUITY

THE village of Meopham lies on the northern slope of the North Downs, 480 feet above sea-level, and six miles due south of Gravesend. Its centre is immediately round the church, but the parish itself is extensive, nearly six miles from north to south, and contains several hamlets: that of Pitfield, one mile south of the church, is the most important, and contains one of the finest greens in Kent. In Lambarde's day (1570) it was known as a healthy site; and that author points out that the three contiguous parishes of Northfleet, Meopham, and Wrotham unite the Thames with Sussex.

The written history of Meopham is one not to be ashamed of, for it extends back, as I will shortly show, for 1,126 years!

The total written history of Britain can only—with an exception I will mention—boast of a period of just under two thousand years, so our village can claim for itself more than half that period.

Britain's history commenced with Julius Caesar's story of his invasion of our island on August 31, 55 B.C.; but I must not omit a short account of the visit of an adventurous Grecian traveller who reached our shores in the time of Alexander the Great, in the fourth century B.C. At that time there lived in the Grecian colony of Massilia (Marseilles) one Pytheas—a mathematician, a geographer, an astronomer; in a word, a scientific investigator and traveller—a Nares, a Nansen, a Scott of those days.

At that time the only known connection between Britain and the rest of the world was the traffic in tin, carried on by the Phoenicians, whose country was a strip of the coast of northern Palestine, where Tyre and Sidon are situated.

The metal mined in Cornwall—"the Cassiterides"—was cast into ingots or "astragali," and carried on the backs of horses to the isle of Ictis, the position of which is uncertain, and thence conveyed in ships to the north of Gaul (France), and so overland to Marseilles or elsewhere.

Why Pytheas ever ventured upon such a risky and dangerous voyage is unknown; perhaps from a spirit of adventure; but perhaps also at the instigation of the merchants of Marseilles, with a view to finding a route by sea for the carriage of tin, and so to be in a position to "break the ring" created by the Phoenician dealers.

Anyhow, it is certain that no better man could have been chosen, or one better fitted with scientific knowledge of the day to undertake the adventure.

He sailed through the Straits of Gibraltar, and along the peninsular coast to the mouth of the Channel, and landed first of all in Cornwall. He even reached the Baltic eventually; but we need not follow him so far.* The interest to us to-day in the country is this, that he made certain observations on the climate and habits of the inhabitants which hold good to the present time. He noted that the climate was so humid, uncertain, and foggy that corn could not be threshed out of doors on the hard ground, as in his own country, but that the ears of corn were gathered into barns and there threshed. He noted also that an intoxicating liquid—beer—was made by the natives from grain. Barns and the flail are now fast disappearing, not from any alteration in the climate, but from the use of more advantageous machinery; but the national beverage is with us still—the fogs likewise!

Over a thousand years now pass. In A.D. 788, in the reign of Offa, Saxon king of Mercia, who was defeated by the men

---

* His own writings are lost; Strabo [*ob.* A.D. 25] in the Fourth Book of his great geography, gives the best account of his works. If he intended circumnavigating our island he did not succeed; Agricola, a governor of Britain in the reign of Domitian, was the first to prove, by sailing round, that Britain was an island.

of Kent in A.D. 774 in a pitched battle at Otford, a charter*
was drawn up giving to St. Andrew's Church, Rochester, six
acres of land at Trottescliffe; and Meopham is given as one
of the boundaries of the property.

"Hujus autem telluris termini sunt isti: ab oriente et a
meridie Boerlingas: ab occidente Wrotaham: ab aquilone
Meapaham." *Anglice*: "The boundaries of this land are as
follows: on the east and south Boerling (Birling): on the west
Wrotaham: on the north Meapaham."

A hundred and fifty years later another reference to
Meopham is to be found in a charter† of King Athelstan
(925–941), grandson of Alfred the Great. After describing
himself as, by Divine favour, King of England and Ruler of
all Britain, he goes on: "I concede freely, by perpetual
donation, my right to a certain portion of land to my faithful
servant Ealdulph twelve 'mansas' in that locality popularly
and commonly called Meapham. Let him enjoy and continually
hold the property as long as he shall abide in this frail life . . .
and leave it to whomsoever he will as his heir in perpetuity"
(*v.* also Chapter IX).

This property, he adds, carries with it all its fields, pastures,
meadows, and woods, and then the deed of gift ends with
curses on anyone who would cross his will: "May he suffer
from icy blasts, and the winged tribe of evil spirits, until he
make amends with tears of penitence and true atonement. By
these terms the aforesaid land is seen to be protected."

The invocation of a curse was not unusual in olden times.
Somner (*History of Gavelkind*, 1726) quotes the will of Wolgith
of Stisted, a Saxon lady (1046), in which the following appears:
"And he that my testament bereaveth which I have now
ordained by God's testimony, bereaved let him be of these
earthly joyes, and the Almighty Lord which created and made
all creatures cut him off from all holy men's communion in
Domesday and be he delivered to Satan the Devil and all his

---

* *Textus Roffensis*, Hearn's ed., p. 86; original folio 131.
† The Meopham Charter, A.D. 939. Cott. Aug. ii. 28; K 377; B iii. 9.

cursed companions into Hell bottom and there perish with God's reprobates except he desist from molesting my heires."

The reader will be reminded also of the curse inscribed on Shakespeare's tomb.

The "mansas" mentioned stand for dwellings with all their belongings; and the property thus transferred formed eventually the Manor of Meopham.* Ealdulph left it in due course to Christ Church, Canterbury. The property reverted later to Queen Edwa, Athelstan's widow (the mother of Kings Edmund and Edred (A.D. 941–955), and she presented it once more to the monks of Canterbury. It remained in their possession till the dissolution in Henry VIII's reign, when it was handed over to the Dean and Chapter of Canterbury (see under "Court").

Byrhtric's Will

We owe a real debt of gratitude to one "William Lambarde, of Lincolnes Inn. Gent.," as he appears on the title-page of his book, called the *Perambulation of Kent*, and first published in 1576. The name is familiar still in Meopham, for his direct descendants till the other day were living at Ash, the late Rector being one of them; and the head of the family still lives on the estate near Sevenoaks.

The author of this work—who is familiarly known as the "Perambulator of Kent"—writes as follows: "It hath chaunced me to see one antiquitie of Mepham,† which both for the profit and pleasure that I conceived thereof, I think meet to insert"; and this he has done in Anglo-Saxon and in English: this translation I here transcribe:

This is Birtricks and Elfswithes his wyues last testament, which they declared at Mepham, in their kinsefolkes witnesse (hearing)

---

* A Manor was in origin a grant of land by the Crown to some baron or great man, for which he paid a rent or performed service. He had jurisdiction over the inhabitants, in some cases even the power of inflicting capital punishment; and his Court for this and other purposes was known (as it is to this day) as the Court-Baron. A Court or Hall for residence was an essential part of the domain, and often the parish church was included in the domain.

† *Textus Roffensis*, Hearn's ed., p. 110; original folio 144–5.

that was Wulstan Ucca, and Wulfsic his brother, and Syred Elfrides sonne, and Wulfsic the blacke, and Wyne the priest, and Elfgar of Mepham, and Wulfey Ordeys sonne, and Elfey his brother, and Birtwar Elfrices widowe, and Britric her cousine, and Elfstane the Bishop.

First, to his naturall Lord, one bracelet of foure score markes of golde, and one hatchet (dagger, hand-knife) of as muche: and foure horses, two of them trapped (i.e. harnessed): and two swordes trimmed, and two hawkes, and all his hedgehoundes.

And to the Ladie (Lordes wife), one bracelet of thirtie markes of golde: and one horse to intreate that this testament stande maye.

And for his soule, and his elders (auncestors) to Sainct Androes (Rochester) two plowland at Dentun.

And they bothe for their soules and their elders, 2 at Longfield (ploughlande).

And to the same place for them thirtie markes of golde, and one collar (neck bracelet) of fourtie markes and a Cuppe of silver, and a half bend gilden (headband covered with golde).

And everie yeere at their minde (yeeres minde) two dayes ferme of rent corne and victuall from Haselholte and two daies of (from) Watringbery: and two dayes out of Berling, and two days out of Hertesham.

And to Christes church 60 markes of golde, thirtie to the Bishop (archbishop) and thirtie to the Covent: And a necke bracelet (collar) of 30 markes: and two cuppes of silver, and the land at Mepham.

And to Sainct Augustine 30 markes of golde, and two cuppes of sylver, and halfe a bend gilt, and the land at Darnt to Byrware for his daies; and after his days to Sainct Androes, for us, and our elders.

And Berling to Wulfic, and he shall give a thousande pence to S. Androes for us, and our elders. And to Wulfsic Wateringbyrye, within that kinred.*

And to Syred Haselholt, within that kinred.

And to Wulfey, and Elfey his brother Hartesham, within that kinred, to Wulfee the inland, (demeanes) and to Elfey the outland (tenancie) & to Wulfstane Ucca, Walkenstede, within that kinred: And a hatchet (dagger) of three poundes, And those ten plough-

---

* "Within that kinred" (kindred) conveys no meaning. Somner (*History of Gavelkind*, 1726) translates "gecynde" as "of that nature," giving "cynde" the same meaning as "kind" in the word gavelkind: i.e. of the nature of gavel. This reading gives sense to the paragraph.

lands at Streiton to the mynster (church) at Walkenstede. And the land at Falcham, after Byrwares dayes, to Sainct Androes, for Elfrices soule their Lord, and his auncestors, even as their will was. And Brumley after Britwares daies to Sainct Androes, as Elfric their Lorde it bequeathed, for him and his elders, (auncestors). And Snodland also to S. Androes, after their daies, even as Elfere it bequeathed, being Elfrices father, & he afterwarde in the witnesse (presence, hearing) of Edgive The Ladie, and of Odo the Archbishop, and of Elfey Elfstanes sonne, and of Elfric his brother, and of Elfnothe filia, & of Godwine of Facham, and of Eadric of Hoo, and of Elfsie the priest of Croyden.

And to Wulfstane 60 markes of golde to deale for us and our elders: and other such (60 markes) to Wulfsie to deale, and have they with God together (between them and God be it) if they it do not.

And to Wulfsie, Titæsey, and the writing within that kinred: & 2 spurres of 3 pound.

And I pray for Gods love, my leefe (deere) Lorde, that he do not suffer that any man our testament doe breake.

And I praye all Gods friendes, they they thereto helpe.

Have they it with God together, that it do breake, and God be to them alwaies mylde that it holde will.

Byrhtric's position in Meopham will be understood if I mention that at that time and for long after all the land was nominally the king's, he parcelled it out to nobles or barons, and they were the king's tenants, rendering military service for their lands, called fiefs; but as one man might hold over a hundred fiefs all over the country he sublet them to subtenants, and their "rent" was service rendered to the Baron, or "Overlord." As time went on they to all intents and purposes became Lords of the various Manors, living in the village at the Manor-house, on the Demesne, near the church. Such a one was Byrhtric, and the reference in his will to his Lord or Overlord will be thus understood. There were further social grades in the village, but these will become apparent when we study the Domesday Book record. Byrhtric was a Theyn or Gentleman, his Lord an Eorl or Earl.

The will bore no date; but it is between A D. 955 and 995 that Aelfstane, one of the witnesses, was Bishop of Rochester.

so the approximate date can thus be fixed in the reign of either Edmund or Edred, the grandsons of Alfred the Great. We know, too, that Beorhtric and his wife were alive in 962, for Lewis has this note from *Privileges*, Edward, vol. 6, p. 3: "Beorhtric et Aelfswyth. 962, in villa quae vocatur Meapaham."

In commenting on the will Lambarde points out that it shows that in those days a husband and wife could make a joint will; how land could be devised; how the Lord's consent was necessary to the testament of his tenant, which consent was obtained by a legacy or gift of heriot; how land at Meopham and elsewhere was given to the Church; and, adds Lambarde, "that you may know also what weapons, jewels and ornaments were at that time worn and occupied."

The mention of Wine or Wina the priest proves the existence —if proof were necessary—of a village church at the time.

In a note on Longfield in the *Gravesend Reporter*, July 4, 1914, the land mentioned in the will, at Longfield, is said to have been given about 945 by Byrhtric's wife; this gift—two ploughlands—being now confirmed by testament. However, in 999 the Danes sailed up the Thames and ravaged Kent (*A.-S. Chron.*), and Longfield fell into their hands, but was eventually restored to St. Andrews and Gundulph, Bishop of Rochester, by Lanfranc, Archbishop of Canterbury (1077–1108); so the gift was for about a century in abeyance.

The mode of appeal at the end of the will for the keeping of the covenants it contains is of much older date. There is a deed of gift, for instance, drawn by Wulfere, King of Mercia, in A.D. 664, endowing Medhamsted (or Peterborough) Minster with land; and it ends: "And I pray all that come after me, be they my sons, be they my brethren, or Kings that come after me that our gift may stand."

Though unconnected with Meopham, there is a little story about this endowment worth relating. The Minster of Peterborough, a rich and very beautiful building, was entirely destroyed by the Danes in A.D. 870, and it lay wasted for a hundred years; then Abbot Athelwold of Winchester offered

King Edgar to restore it; this the king allowed, but, the poor Abbot relates, when he inspected the site he found nothing "but old walls and wild woods." In pulling down the walls he found secreted in a hole in the wall a document placed there for safety by Abbot Hedda, reciting what King Wulfere had done for the Abbey three hundred years before (*A.-S. Chron.*).

Byrhtric has no less than eleven witnesses to his will, in whose presence he drew it up, but no formality in signing it is recorded. In Wulfere's deed of A.D. 664, just quoted, the signing is formal and throws a light on present practices. A cross having been made on the deed, the king drew his finger over it, saying, "I, Wulfere, King, in the presence of Kings, and of Earls, and of Captains and of Thanes, witnesses of my gift, before the Archbishop Deus-Dedit I confirm it with the cross of Christ."

In this we see the meaning and origin of putting a cross to a paper by a man who cannot write, and someone else declaring in writing that it is, say, "John Smith, his mark"; and the cross is still prefixed to the signature of a Roman Catholic Bishop to this day.

"The mancus was a gold coin first introduced by Offa, King of Mercia (757–796), but in Anglo-Saxon times it was a silver one of the value of thirty silver pennies: and five silver pennies went to one shilling. *A propos* of 'bracelets' it may be mentioned that iron ring money was used by the ancient Britons, according to Caesar. He, however, does not mention rings in the more precious metals; but in finds of coins, objects in gold, usually taken to have been personal ornaments as bracelets or armlets, may have been employed for a similar purpose" (*Coin Collector*, by Carew Hazlett, pp. 252, 263, 268).

The mancus or mark had a purchasing value of 6/- in Saxon times, and of 13/4 in the thirteenth century.

The will incidentally gives the name of Byrhtric's "dear Lord," viz. Aelfric; and also of his "dear Lord's" father, which was Aelfere. Now both these nobles were of royal birth and kin to King Edgar (A.D. 959), Edward the Martyr (A.D. 975), and to Ethelred the Unready (A.D. 978). They were "Earles" and Governors of Mercia or Middle England, and Aelfric, the "dear Lord," sided with the Bishop of Rochester against King Ethelred when the latter besieged Rochester. Aelfric was, to say the least of it, an unsatisfactory person; he showed himself a coward and a traitor, for when the Danes in A.D. 992 were off the mouth of the Thames he "gave warning to the enemy; and on the night preceding the battle he sculked away from the army to his great disgrace" (*A.-S. Chron.*). Fifteen years later (A.D. 1007) he was sent to lead an army against the Danes in Wessex, but, as the old chronicler says, "he brought forth his old tricks," by pretending to be sick, and so his side was hindered and Sweyne the Dane defeated him. As in the same year a new Earl, or Governor, of Mercia was appointed, the "dear Lord" was perhaps killed in the battle.

It can only be hoped that, rascal that he proved himself to be, he had sufficient conscience to carry out poor Byrhtric's testamentary wishes.

Saxon Meopham has at least once found its way into romance. About forty years ago the son of the Rev. Charles Lane, Rector of Wrotham, published an historical tale, *The Rivals, a Tale of the Anglo-Saxon Church* (James Parker & Co.), in which part of the scene depicted lies in Meopham, where the hero's old mother lived.

Domesday Book

Many a village can carry its written history back no further than Domesday Book; we are, as we have seen, more fortunate.

Domesday Book, as every schoolboy knows, was a register, compiled by order of William the Conqueror in 1086, of the land and its value at that time (as well as in the time of Edward the Confessor) for the purpose of knowing how it was distributed, and what amount of tax it was to pay to the king's exchequer. (Landowners at the present time know too well that a second edition of Domesday Book—though called by another name—is in preparation!)

The entries in Domesday Book are in contracted Latin; but, expanded, the entry about Meopham reads as follows:

In Tollentreu Hd̃.

Ipse Archiepiscopus tenet Mepeham. Pro x solins se defendebat. T. R. E. modo pro vii. Terra est xxx carucarum. In dominio sunt iiii. Et xxv villani cum lxxi bordariis habent xxv carucas. Ibi ecclesia. Et xvii servi. Et xvi acrae prati. Silva x porcorum. In totis valentiis T. R. E. valebat xv libras et x solidos. Quando recepit xv libras. Modo xxvi libras. Ricardus de Tonebrige habet in sua leuga quod valet xviii solidos et vi denarios. Silvam xx porcorum.

Anglice:

The same Archbishop holds Mepeham. It answered for ten sulings in the time of King Edward (the Confessor): now for seven. There is (arable) land for 30 teams. In Demesne, there are four: and 25 villeins with 71 bordars have 25 teams. A Church there. And 17 servants. And 16 acres of meadow. Wood for ten hogs. In total value, in the time of King Edward, it was worth 15 pounds and ten shillings. When he received it, [it was worth] 15 pounds. Now 26 pounds. Richard de Tonebrige has in his lowy what is worth 18 shillings and 6 pence. Wood for 20 hogs.

Hundred of Tollingtreu

The division of a county into hundreds we owe to King Alfred. It meant originally an assemblage of families, probably a hundred, for military defence. Each hundred had its moot or local council (= Parish Council, more or less, though Parish is not the word to use in this connection, as "Parish" is purely an ecclesiastical term). Hundreds were united into Laths; and the Lath of Aylesford consisted of twelve hundreds, including those containing Meopham and Tonbridge.

The Hundred of Tollingtreu held six different places: Northfluet, Mepeham, Melestune (Milton), Lodesdune (Luddesdown), Gravesham (Gravesend), Notestede (Nurstead). Of these Northfluet and Mepeham were Church property held by the Archbishop and his monks, and were therefore well looked after and well farmed. These Manors, says an old historian writing in 1798,* were "more valuable than the four villages of Gravesend, Mylton, Ludsdown and Nutstead, which Earl Lewin and military tenants occupied under the Saxon Government."

The peculiar name Tol*l*ingtrew (Tollentreu in Domesday Book), Tol*t*yngtre in Edward I's time, and Tol*t*ingtrow in the sixteenth century, is due probably to the mote or moot meeting under some leaning or tilted tree, it being the custom to call the hundred after some notable object, out of doors, as a stone or tree, at which the people met.† There is Apple-tree Hundred in Derbyshire, Crowthorn Hundred in Gloucestershire, and many are so-named.

The following are some of the variations of the name of our hundred occurring in different documents:

Tollentreu	.	Domesday Book
Toltintre ⎱ Toltentre ⎰	.	1240–1254
Toltentr' .	.	1258
Toltyntr'	.	Edw. I.
Toltyngtre	.	1292
Toltyntre .	.	1313
Toltyngtrowe .		1523
Toltingtrow	.	1576

The first is the only one to have the double *l*, and is without doubt a scribe's mistake; the *t* in all the others is the correct reading; the "tre" or "trow" was the Anglo-Saxon word treow (= tree).

The *Suling* (Hide or Carucate) varied in amount in different parts of England. Generally in the southern districts it equalled 180 acres, and was tilled in this way; one part (60 acres) was tilled in the autumn, one (60 acres) in the spring at Lent-time, one (60 acres) was left fallow for one year. If, therefore, there

---

* Henshall, *History of County of Kent*, 1798.

† Toltentrough field (4 a. 1 r. 4 p.) exists in Major Edmeade's property at Nursted. No. 557 on the old map of Northfleet.

were 7 sulings at the time of Domesday, there must have been 1,260 acres under plough by the people.

The object of the suling (or *Sulin*, from *Suhl*, A.-S., Plough) was to have a basis, in Saxon times, for assessment for taxation, for Danegeld, the money paid annually to the Danish invaders. The tax was half a suling; Edward the Confessor took it off; William the Conqueror restored it, raising it to 6/- for his own purposes; it ceased finally in Stephen's reign. We see that Mepeham "se defendebat," i.e. paid for its share for defence 10/- in the Confessor's time, but only 7/- in 1086.

The ploughland in Meopham seems to have given work to twenty-five teams; and some authorities consider the amount a team could plough in one year to be enough to maintain a household for one year.

Four teams were occupied, besides, on the land of the Lord—called the Demesne—the rest of the Manor being the other land of the village, occupied by the villagers.

By comparing the ploughs or teams some idea of the size of a village at that time can be formed: thus, whilst Meopham had twenty-nine teams (25 + 4), Luddesdown had only four and Nurstead three teams.

Villeins—now a term of reproach (= a villain)—were the ceorls or churls in Saxon times, and were the direct tenants-in-villeinage of the Lord of the Manor. The villein was not a free man, but he tilled some thirty acres of land and thereby supported his family; he "could acquire no property and his Lord's consent was necessary for the marriage of his daughter" (Ditchfield). He rendered service for his land, working on the Demesne and even providing oxen for his Lord's team. Should he in some way (and there were many) become a free man, he could become a "copyholder," doing homage and paying quit rent for the land to his Lord.

The *Bordarii* or *Bordars* lived in wooden (boarded) cottages (Ditchfield), and came next to the villeins. They ploughed for themselves some five acres apiece, and rendered service for their land.

Next came the *Cottarii* or *Cottars*, who rendered domestic service to the Lord of the Manor; and last of all were the slaves, who were really bondmen, and their lot was not a happy one; but it improved in Norman times.

The *Servi*, literally "slaves," mentioned in connection with the church, probably meant ministers or servants in an ecclesiastical sense; and that number, viz. seventeen, is not surprising, as Meopham was an ecclesiastical possession. In Domesday generally where a church is named as being in any village, one or more of the servi or ministers is mentioned, and not where there is no church. At Trottescliffe, where the church is mentioned, there is one minister or servus.

The *Demesne* mentioned is that part of the village occupied by the Lord of the Manor; at Meopham it enjoyed the services, as we have seen, of four ploughs; and since the Church—the Abbot and monks of Canterbury—were the Lords of the Manor, it certainly contained the Parish Church, and the various manorial buildings that were connected with it, and which occupied the present site of Meopham Court.

No mention is made of a mill, but it is hardly likely that none existed at that time; mills (both water- and windmills) were valuable manorial property, and the people were not allowed to take their corn anywhere else to be ground except at the manorial mill.

Hogs.—Hogs are mentioned in the Survey, not only because they were the most important article of animal food—especially in the winter, since the feeding of cattle in the winter for food was then not known—but their number gives the size of the woods attached to the Manor.

Unfortunately, it is now quite unknown how many hogs went to an acre; perhaps it depended on the district, for it certainly depended upon whether the wood was largely made up of beech (A.-S. *boc*: hence our word bacon) and oak or not, for the hogs were daily driven to feed on the mast and acorns in the forest by the swineherd. Under these circumstances we cannot know the acreage of the Meopham woods; but we must remember that at that time Kent and Sussex were great forest lands, the various villages being of the nature of clearings in the forest—the run of the hogs was probably very extensive.

This pasturage for hogs, called "pannage," was greater in the weald than on the downs, as at Meopham; thus Wrotham supported five hundred hogs and Mereworth sixty, against our ten.

Richard de Tonebrige—in full, Richard Fitzgilbert de Tonebrige—was a relative of the Conqueror's and fought with him at the Battle of Hastings; he was one of the eleven nobles who shared Kent—"tenentes terras in Chent." He held his land immediately from the Crown and was a member of the royal council; his principal seat was Tonbridge Castle, which, with its surroundings and other properties, constituted his Lowy. A Lowy (from the Latin Leuca, a league) was a property with the land around it for a league or less. Property not strictly in the Lowy was included in it; hence that part of the forest round Meopham where his twenty hogs were fed was considered as part of his Lowy.* As a peer of the realm he also held Halling and Birling, besides parts of twenty-four other Manors in Kent; and in seven other counties he owned no less than 180. So, though only his swine lived in Meopham, he was a very important tenant there. He possessed so much land that, in one of the hundreds in Kent, of the arable land which had amounted to twenty sulings in the hands of ecclesiastical owners in Saxon times, only eleven sulings remained to the Church after William had satisfied his relative, Richard Fitzgilbert. The Castle at Tonbridge he took from the Conqueror in exchange for that of Brionne in Normandy, which he formerly held.

What our village was like in Saxon times, or at the date of Domesday Book, must be conjectured; but the ideal Saxon

---

* Woodland was always carefully estimated, because of the importance of beech-mast and acorns, a food indispensable for hogs among the Anglo-Saxons: therefore Kentish lands not provided with it, within the precincts of the estate, had "dens," "denu," "denbœro," feeding-places for the hogs, far away from the property itself (De Grey Birch, quoted by Clarke in his *Bermondsey*, p. 21).

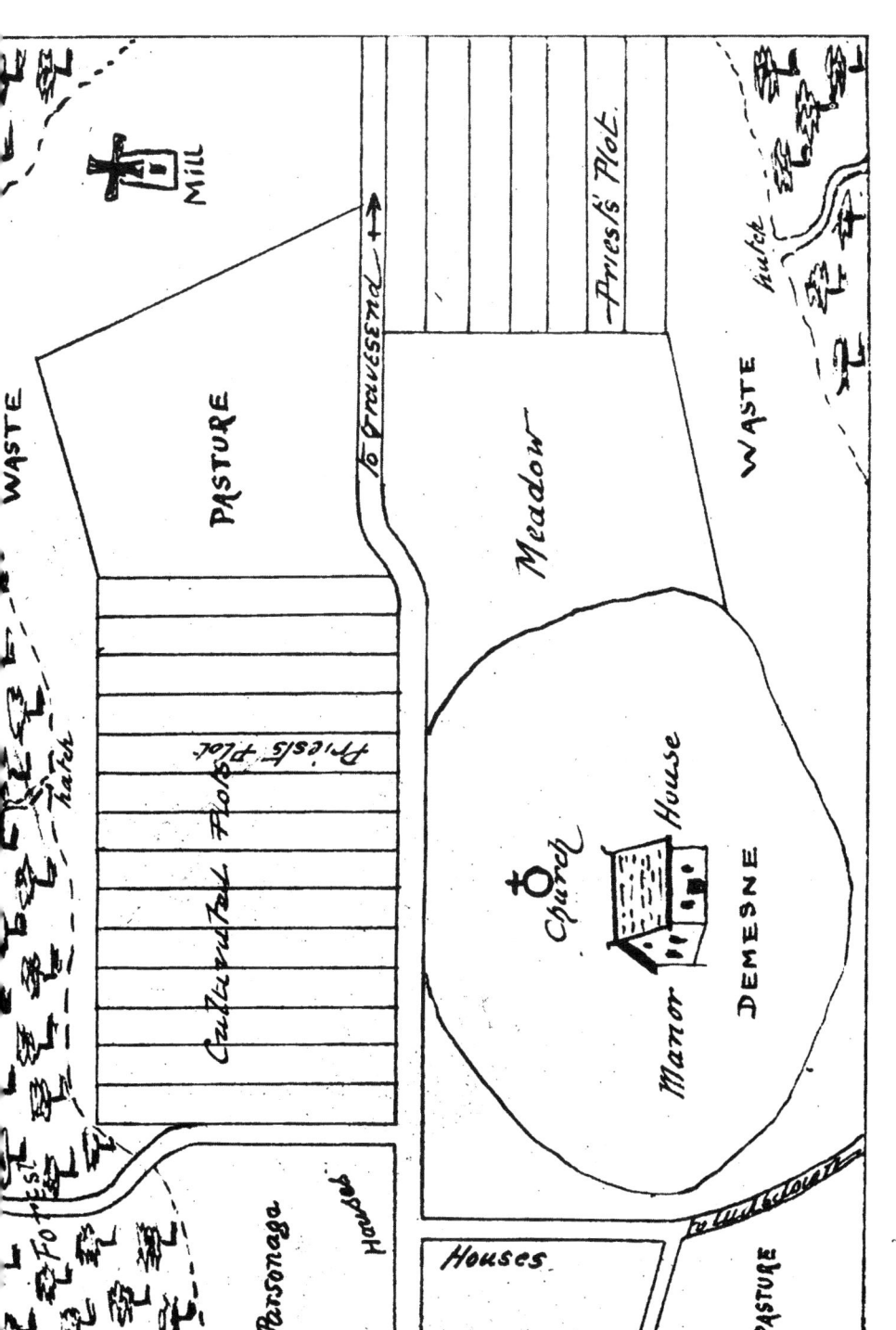

DITCHFIELD'S PLAN OF A SAXON VILLAGE ADAPTED TO MEOPHAM

NORTH-EAST CORNER OF THE CHURCH, SHOWING THE GEOMETRIC VESTRY WINDOW
AND THE OLD STONE WATER-DRAIN

village has been well worked out by the Rev. P. H. Ditchfield in his *English Villages*, and by adapting his general village plan to suit the topography of Meopham, some idea of what things were like a thousand years ago may be formed.

The Manor of Meopham, being held by the Archbishop and monks of Canterbury, we may be certain their Demesne or private property centred round the church, and contained the usual Manor-house, with farm buildings, etc., as already stated. The houses of the grades of free men, with the mud cabins of the poorest workers, were partly, no doubt, on their various holdings and partly along the road where the present street now is. Outside the carefully tended lands of the Lord's Demesne were waste and common pasturage lands and cultivated (arable) portions, not in fields as at present (these were a fourteenth-century introduction), but in strips side by side, a furlong in length, and a perch or two wide, separated from each other by balks of turf—resembling in appearance the modern garden allotments. Each villager had one or more strips, but not together; and every tenth strip was allotted to the priest; and once in three years each strip of land had to lie fallow. There are still places in England where this mode of agriculture has never died out; as, for instance, at Laxton in Nottinghamshire.

Hemming the village in more or less on all sides would be the forest clothing the hills and valleys, though nothing like as dense as that in the middle of the county—the weald. The early Saxon villages were settlements in clearings in the woods and forests; these were therefore easy of access for the hogs that pastured in them. The various picturesque lanes in our Parish, some hardly ever used now, doubtless are the same as in Saxon days when forest tracks united the various communities in the "hundred."

Before leaving Saxon Meopham we may offer an explanation of the name, its spelling and its pronunciation being a puzzle to most people; and we will take its earliest known form,

that in King Offa's time (A.D. 788), where it is spelt Meapaham.
There is no doubt that this means the "ham" or home of one
"Meapa," but who that was is a matter for conjecture.
Similarly, Bede (*Hist. Eccles.*) accounts for Rochester. He says:
"The city which the English nation named Rhofescestir, from
one that was formerly the chief man of it, called Rhof."
Meapa was no doubt a Saxon chieftain, and it must be
remembered that the Saxons, Angles, and Jutes arrived in
Britain under peculiar circumstances. They came at first by
the invitation of Wintgern, King of Britain (Vortigern)
(A.D. 447), to help him to beat back the Picts from the north.
This they did under Hengist and Horsa, then turned against
their hosts and settled themselves in Kent. Finding it even
then "the garden of England," they invited their friends over,
together with Angles and Jutes, "because of the worthlessness
of the Britons and the richness of the land" (*A.-S. Chron.*),
and seventeen shiploads came over and settled, and perhaps
Meapa was one who made the voyage (A.D. 447–450). In all,
during the next hundred years seven Saxon expeditions landed
in England, conquered the natives and established seven
Saxon kingdoms, forming the Heptarchy.

It is thus easy to understand that a Saxon chieftain would
give his name at once to the home he formed; and what the
Britons had called Meopham—if it had existed before and
were not a new settlement—we shall never know.

Variations in the spelling of Meopham from that time have
been numerous; they are:

A.D. 788 (time of King Offa) . . .	Meapaham
A.D. 939 (time of King Athelstan). .	Meapham
A.D. 950 (*cir.*) (Byrhtric's Will) . .	Meapaham
A.D. 961 (Queen Edwa's Deed of Gift)	Meopeham
A.D. 1086 (Domesday)	Mepeham
A.D. 1125 (Henry I)	Mappehame
(and later to John's reign)	{ Meepham / Meopham
A.D. 1236 (Chron. of Gervase)	{ Meapham / Mapeham

A.D. 1241 (Placita Roll) . . . . Mapham
A.D. 1284 (Eastry Letters). . . . Meapeham
A.D. 1344 (Papal Registers) . . . Meypham
A.D. 1345 (Papal Registers) . . . Mepham
A.D. 1348 (Canterbury Registers) . . Meepham
A.D. 1367 (Papal Registers) . . . Meffam
A.D. 1525 (Sprever's Will) *q.v.* . . Mepehm
A.D. 1666 (Church Register) . . . Meopam
A.D. 1667 (Burial Register) . . . Mepa
The Present Time . . . . . Meopham

The modern pronunciation, "Meppam," is explained in a letter to the Rev. L. Lewis in 1882 by the great etymologist, Professor Skeat. He points out that as late as the eighteenth century *ea* was often pronounced as *ay*—thus "Sea" was "Say." Thus Cowper in the eighteenth century wrote:

> I am monarch of all I survey,
> My right there is none to dispute,
> From the centre all down to the sea (say)
> I am lord of the fowl and the brute.

In olden times the long *e* and *ea* were both pronounced as the *ai* in the word "bait," so the Domesday spelling Mēpēham would be pronounced Māȳ-pā-hám; and in the twelfth century the long ē was often written as *eo* (but still pronounced as *ay*), and he adds: "This remains in the word 'people,' formerly always pronounced 'payple.' "

About the eighteenth century the long ē was again pronounced as *ee*, so "Māȳpham" became "Meēpham" in speaking; and in modern English this long ē became short ĕ, so Māȳpham became Mĕpham.

We have now gone back to the old spelling, but the pronunciation remains short, so Meopham is pronounced Mĕpham.*

* Yet it is curious to note that Deopham, a village in Norfolk, is pronounced either Deefam or Deepam.

CHAPTER II

EARLIEST CHRISTIANITY IN BRITAIN

IT has already been mentioned that in the Demesne of the Anglo-Saxon village the church was usually placed; and the Saxons, when not making an entirely new settlement for themselves by clearing forest land, may be assumed to have driven out the Britons and established themselves in their villages.

Some of the early Britons were undoubtedly Christian, though the origin of the British Church is obscure; and a Christian writer of Carthage, Tertullian, says that in A.D. 190 there was a part of Britain, unsubdued by Rome, that was Christian. Still, the mass of the people were heathen. The heathen Britons were accustomed to have special sites for religious purposes—we all know of the Druids' reverence for the oak and the mistletoe—and these sites were trees, rocks, and the like. As late as A.D. 601 Pope Gregory, when sending over Abbot Mellitus to assist St. Augustine in the conversion of England, most wisely instructed him that "the temples of the idols ought not to be destroyed; but let idols that are in them be destroyed. . . . For if these temples are well built, it is requisite they be converted from the worship of devils to the service of the true God; that the nation, seeing that their temples are not destroyed, may, adoring the true God, the more familiarly resort to the places to which they have been accustomed" (Bede, *Hist. Eccles.*). The letter from which the above is an extract is surely the wisest ever written to a missionary to the heathen!

That there was a Christian Church in England during the Roman occupation is clear from such facts as that in A.D. 314 two British Bishops attended the Council of Arles; and St. Alban was martyred for his Christianity at Verulanum— afterwards St. Alban's—in A.D. 365. It is therefore more than probable that many a country church stands on a site where worship—whether heathen or Christian—has been carried on from time immemorial.

Omitting for the present an account of the kind of building that was used as a church when the Romans held Britain, we may inquire what the churches of the Anglo-Saxon period were like; since one of these, we know, was at Meopham from the mention of Wina the priest in Byrhtric's will.

In A.D. 429 Germanus, Bishop of Auxerre, came to Britain to attend a Synod—a Church conference; and to refute the "Pelagian" heresy that had sprung up in England. Whilst he was here the Saxons, joining with the Picts from the north, began again to harass the poor native Britons, who, more or less Christianized, credited Germanus with miraculous powers. This was due, amongst other reasons, to the fact that having fallen down and broken his leg, as was thought, he was up and about again in so short a time that they considered he had cured himself miraculously. In fact, the thatched roof of the cottage in which he lay caught fire, and the poor Bishop had to flee for his life. The Britons begged him to help them in their danger and, says Bede, he "inspired so much courage into these fearful people that one would have thought they had been joined by a mighty army."

Germanus preached to the Britons and baptized many of the army, and, it being the end of Lent, A.D. 429, "a church was prepared with boughs for the feast of the resurrection of our Lord, and so fitted up in that martial camp as if it were in a city" (Bede). Then, leaving the church on Easter Day, and headed by Germanus, the Britons attacked and routed the enemy.

Such a church was but a temporary structure, but the record of a timber church—and many, if not most, of the early Saxon churches were such—is found in the reign of Edwin, son of Ella, king of the Northumbrians in A.D. 627. On Easter Day— April 12th—of that year King Edwin was baptized a Christian by Bishop Paulinus. Says the *Anglo-Saxon Chronicle*: "This was done at York, where he [the king] ordered a church to be built of timber, which was hallowed in the name of St. Peter." Later on a church of stone was erected in its place. Strange as it may seem, there still stands at Greensted, Essex (near Ongar), an ancient church, the Saxon part of which is made of the split trunks of trees, set upright and close together, with the rounded part of the trunk facing outwards. These are fastened with wooden pins to a wooden plate or beam at top and bottom. Into this church was the body of St. Edmund taken whilst on its journey from London to Bury St. Edmunds.

Old stone Saxon churches still exist in England, but it is impossible to say whether such a one, or one of wood, preceded our present church at Meopham. There is no trace of Saxon stonework in it, as is sometimes to be found in country churches.

Our present church is dedicated to St. John the Baptist; and in the will of "Hugo Chiddinstone de Mepeham" (v. Wills), dated June 9, 1460, comes the following: "Corpus-que meum sepeliendum in cimitio ecclie pochialis sancte Johannis Baptiste de Mepeham p̃ dic̃t:" He also asks his executors to arrange for prayers for his soul in the same church, without delay after his decease. I mention this as it has been thought that the church was really dedicated to St. Peter and St. Paul, whose Saints' Day was June 29th, as the fair is held still on St. Peter's Day (old style) (v. Fair), and chartered village fairs were often held on the patron saint's day. But the date of the will refutes this, as the fair was not granted till 1456—four years later. A writer in the Gentleman's Magazine for 1809, in support of the view that originally our church was dedicated to St. Peter and St. Paul, says, that "in one of the footways near the church which was ordered to be removed was found in good preservation a stone image of St. Peter, decollated, of the proportion of 16–18 inches. In his hands were a book, the back gilt, and his keys." No doubt the figure had once been in the church, but there is nothing to prove it represented the patron saint.

Everyone is familiar with the general shape of our country churches in this part of England; they consist more often than not of a central part, the body or nave, with or without side projections—the aisles or wings; at the east end is a projecting part of lower height than the body, the chancel, and at the west end a square tower. This is the type of church at Meopham; but there is one other that must be just mentioned as being specially English, which takes the form of the cross; the arms of the cross are the transepts, running north and south; the part to the east of these the chancel; and the longer part to the west the body or nave; and where the transepts and nave cross, there the tower of the church is erected. The earliest in England of these cruciform churches was that built by Edward the Confessor, and consecrated in A.D. 1065 on Thorney Isle, in the then marshy land of Westminster, the predecessor of our present Westminster Abbey.

The reason some churches should be built in the form of a cross is obvious; but that they should more often be like ours at Meopham requires explanation. As Christianity and Christian architecture spread over Europe from Rome, and as all churches in England date from the Roman *occupation*, which commenced in A.D. 150, under Claudius, just a century after Julius Caesar's *invasion*, it follows that the style of building was likely to have been on the Roman or Italian pattern, whether built by Christian Britons or Christianized Romans.

Now, when Christianity became the accepted religion of the Roman Empire in A.D. 313, the Christians had no further need to hold their services in hidden and secret places, such as the catacombs, but they naturally sought amongst the buildings of the time the one most useful for their purpose. They found to their hand the Basilica, or Hall of Justice. It had always a central hall or nave; sometimes at each side an additional part or wing separated from the main hall by pillars, between which the wing opened into the main hall. At one end of the hall was a smaller projecting part, generally rounded in shape, the apse, and here sat the judges and tribunal. At

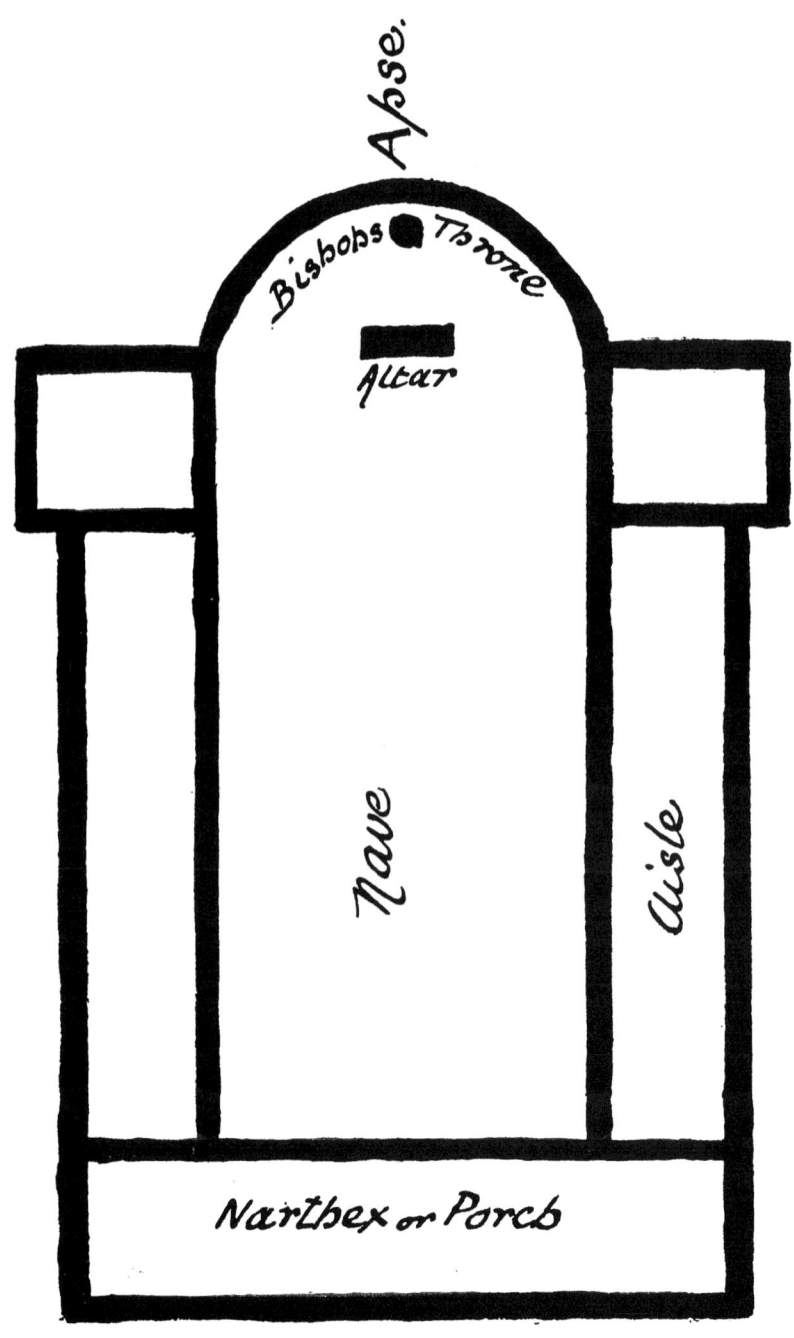

PLAN OF SILCHESTER CHURCH
(*Basilica*)

the other end was the entrance, protected sometimes by a narthex or porch, supported on pillars. When the Christians adopted such a building as a church, the Bishop had his "throne" in the apse, against the rounded wall at the end, and the priests were accommodated in the apse also; where the apse joined the main hall, and between the clergy and the people, stood the altar. As many of the Basilicas were built with the apse at the west end, the clergy, placed as described, faced the people, towards the east; that point of the compass being in the direction of Jerusalem, towards which Christian worshippers turned from earliest times.

In the Cathedral of St. Peter, in Rome, the Pope's throne is still at the end of the apse; and a marked distinction between the continental (French) Gothic cathedrals and the English to this day is that the apse or chancel in theirs is built round, whilst ours is generally square.

That the Roman Hall of Justice gave us the pattern for our early churches is seen in the fact that at Silchester, in recent years, the foundations of a little church, built during the Roman occupation of Britain, have been discovered of exactly the same shape as the Roman Basilica; and the Church of St. Paul, situated outside the walls of Rome, and built by Theodosius in A.D. 386, and still existing, is an exact Basilica. The church that St. Augustine built in Canterbury in A.D. 602, and dedicated to St. Peter and St. Paul, was also of this pattern, as also was that of Reculvers, which dates from Roman times.

Although there is nothing Norman about our church any more than there is Saxon, a word may be added on that style of architecture, both for contrast with the Gothic of our church and because Rochester, close by, affords such splendid examples of Norman architecture.

In a word, it was a heavy style; the walls were made very thick, often with flat buttress-like shafts, closely applied to them, running up their whole height at intervals, as anyone can see at Rochester Castle. There were two reasons, especially in North Kent, at any rate, for thick walls. First, the material about here is only "rubble," i.e. flints—and a high flint wall must be thicker than a stone or brick one, if it is to last; secondly, the Normans always built their window openings, doorways, and arches with half-round, barrel-like tops; and such a curve soon tends to flatten down under superimposed weight, unless very firmly supported on each side by a thick, strong wall. Rochester Cathedral, both inside and in the beautiful west entrance, is an example. Owing, too, to the thickness of the walls, the narrow Norman window with its round top had to be splayed considerably towards the interior of the building it lighted; and on this smooth splay Biblical pictures were very commonly drawn, as a means of education. A few years ago an old painting was revealed on the splay of a Norman window in Kingsdown Church near here: the subject of the picture is the sacrifice offered by Cain and Abel; and as their costume is that of a labourer of the twelfth century, this may be taken as its probable date.

The next style of architecture is known as the Gothic, and our church belongs to an early form of it, known as "Geometric" and "Early English." The one great character of the Gothic style is a pointed and not a rounded arch; it can be carried to any height, and not exerting the lateral thrust of the round arch it does not require massiveness in the walls it pierces; and as a matter of fact the walls of many of the Gothic cathedrals are more window than wall. Instead, therefore, of narrow lancet windows, as with the Normans, windows were now made large, often by combining as it were three or more lancet windows with pointed tops together; and ornamental stone tracery of various kinds was introduced into them; the simplest was the Geometric tracery, because it could be described with a pair of compasses, such as circles, trefoils, quatrefoils, etc., with soffit-cusping, which are to be seen in our chancel, and Lady Chapel, or vestry. The Early English Decorated is a more advanced style of tracery and ornament, of which our large east window and the west doorway afford examples. The various styles met with will receive detailed attention in describing the various parts of the church, which is essentially a thirteenth to fourteenth century one.

It must have struck the most superficial observer how many of our country churches, to speak of Kent alone, seem to have started into life in the twelfth to fourteenth centuries, as shown by architectural details that remain even when the bulk of the building is of later date, whilst our best cathedrals all date from A.D. 1000 to 1300. The reason is in part this: immediately before A.D. 1000 the churches were allowed to get out of repair, from the universal belief that A.D. 1000 would see the end of the world, a view held by the early second-century fathers and based on a misinterpretation of Rev. xx. 2. When, however, it was found that things went on as before, money was lavished upon building churches, doubtless largely from a feeling of thankfulness that the crisis was past; whilst the introduction of the Gothic style of architecture allowed builders scope and freedom they had never known before. It is stated that in the three centuries above given no less than seven thousand new churches were erected in Britain; and perhaps the old Meopham church may have been one of them, replacing a still more ancient Saxon one.

Our church, as already stated, was reconstructed between 1320–1328, and Simon de Meopham is credited with the work; and if this were so, he must have done it when Rector of Tunstall, as he only became Archbishop in 1327. I think this is due to the following statement by Lambarde, but I have found no proof that he really built anything; he was not, like some, a building prelate. Doubtless his influence bore upon the work and may have been its initiative, but beyond this we have no facts to go upon. There is no proof he built even the chantry of St. James de la Dene; he endowed it, that was all. Lambarde's remark is as follows: "Probably he [Simon] also builte the Church of Mepham for the use of the poor which William Courtenay [one of his successors] repaired fower score yeares after, and annexed thereunto fower new houses for the same ende and purpose."

Whilst our church, as already stated, is of early Gothic character, it is obvious at once that the nave is of somewhat later style than the rest of it, and the want of alignment (*q.v.*) between the chancel and the nave is taken by the highest architectural authorities as a proof of their having been constructed at different times.

That the reconstruction of our church must have been extensive we are certain, for it had to be rededicated, the commission for which was issued in May 1325, "for the dedication in canonical form of the Parish Church of Mepham in the immediate jurisdiction of the diaconate of Schorham (Shoreham) newly constructed (de novo constructam)," which reads in English thus:

Walter, etc., to the venerable brother in the Lord [Peter] by the grace of God Bishop of Corbavia, health and brotherly love in the Lord.

To dedicate in canonical form the Parish Church of Mephm in our immediate jurisdiction, in the Deanery of Shoreham, newly constructed; and to do all other things known to pertain to the pontifical office in this behalf, by the tenor of these presents we commit unto you full authority. In witness whereof, etc. Given at Mortelake ii Id. Maii, Anno Dni milliocccmo xxvto (*May* 14, 1325).*

Now when Archbishop Courtenay, at the end of the fourteenth century, "repaired" the church, no second dedication was called for, so his alterations clearly were not so extensive as "the beginning of the century," but were of subsidiary character, as will be presently mentioned.

Judging by what Phillpot says in his *Villare Cantianum* (ed. 1659, p. 235), the church must have suffered in the eighty years since Simon's time: "Courtenay rebuilded the church, which by the onsets of time was shrunk into Delapidation and Rubbish: and he erected likewise some almshouses for the support and maintenance of the poor of this Parish."

* *At Lambeth. Commission from Walter Reynolds, Archbishop of Canterbury, to dedicate the Church of Meopham. Ex Register Abp. Reynolds, folio* 135*b, at bottom of left-hand page:* Comm. ad dedicand eccliam de Mepham. (*Marginal note.*)

This may be explained by Stow's statement that "on May 31, 1352, there was a great earthquake, and it sunk churches and threw them down, especially in Kent."

The only thing in the body of our church of still later date than the early fourteenth century is the aisle windows, which are in the Perpendicular style (*v.* windows); and these were put in without doubt by Archbishop Courtenay in 1386. For reasons given presently it is architecturally certain that the aisles are of the same date as the nave itself. Courtenay almost certainly put in the beautiful coloured glass into the church (*v.* Coloured Glass, also Courtenay).

Why our church required such extensive repair in the *early* fourteenth century, and why so many village churches, in large part at least, are of the same period, may perhaps be explained by the fact that from 1208 to 1214 the country lay under Papal interdict, no religious services were held; the churches were shut or fell out of repair; and though when the interdict was taken off the churches were again made fit for public service, they well may have received such damage as to require eventually substantial repair or even partial rebuilding.

We may assume, however, that our church as we now have it, in the main, is as Simon de Meopham left it early in the fourteenth century (*v.* also Simon de Meopham).

Exterior of the Church

The walls are built of rubble; the walls, therefore, are very thick, and the window openings well splayed within.

The *Tower* has let into it at intervals string courses of freestone to add to its stability—a very common practice, and said to represent also the beams of wood that used to be built into rubble walls for the same purpose in still older times. This is not quite a true Kentish tower; these are square, as ours is, but have also an outside turret running up the full height (as at Wrotham), and containing the spiral staircase leading to the belfry and roof; our staircase is contained within one of the angles—the south-eastern one. The angles of the tower are alternately long and short work of "ashlar quoin" stones, i.e. squared and dressed corner-stones, whose use clearly was to give strength and sharpness to the angles; and though always employed in Norman work, and in England dating from that period, they are continued for the same reason to the present day by builders. An interesting exception to this is to be seen in Kingsdown Church, where the tower, constructed also of rubble, has no dressed quoin stones, larger rubble stones being worked into the four corners.

In Trottescliffe Church, in the east and north-east walls, which are beautiful examples of Norman rubble work, the original quoin stones are in perfect preservation and are of tufa, a porous, calcareous stone the Normans often used.

Usually in these old churches the tower was no higher than the roof-ridge of the nave, a wooden "pepper-box" spire being placed on the top, where there were bells, to accommodate them. This was so in our church until 1837, when an addition of 20 feet was made to the tower to contain a bell chamber, at the cost of £215. The new work was finished off at the top with battlements, a style not belonging to the date of the tower but to the much later period of Perpendicular architecture. Each western angle of the tower has a pair of buttresses at right angles to each other—an early English characteristic; buttresses of later date were single and stood straight out from each angle, thus forming an obtuse angle with the tower walls; and they were frequently decorated with additional carved stonework. In 1821 the buttresses were repaired in many places with red brick—an eyesore surely at first, but now, by the softening hand of time, not unpleasing. In 1928 the ivy covering the tower was removed, and the buttresses were found seriously damaged. These, with the tower itself, were repaired at a cost of £500 (v. Appendix R).

For many years, and up to 1870, the large west door in the tower was blocked up, only a small door existing for the use of the bell-ringers; it was then reopened by Mr. Hooper and the Churchwardens, a new stone doorway in Early English style and new oak doors being fitted at a cost of £76. The deeply cut mouldings and the delicate pillars are characteristic of the style.

In the south wall of the tower is a weather-beaten lancet window with soffit-cusping, of the same date as the older windows of the chancel and Lady Chapel.

Church towers were as much, at first, look-out places for defence as to hold bells; indeed, Ogilvie derives the word Belfry, not from bells, but the Celtic Bereffreid—*ber*, to carry, and *freid*, alarm—hence Latin Belfredus, a movable war-tower used by besiegers of walled towns. The Saxons highly valued a tower to a church, and a landowner having in his Demesne a church with a tower was by law entitled to be called "Thane" (Sydney Heath). That universal genius St. Dunstan, Archbishop of Canterbury in the tenth century, is said to have cast the first bell in England for Reading Abbey in A.D. 950, though Pope Leo I in 458 is credited with the introduction of bells for church purposes. Our tower may have answered both purposes in old days, though it has not the outside turret already mentioned, and as may be seen in many churches around; one use of these being to hang an iron fire basket or "cresset" from, to give an alarm in times of danger.

There still is another use for towers situated at the west end of churches like ours. I have already mentioned the tendency of arches to spread out under the weight they have to support; this thrust, as it is termed, must be met by counter-thrust, and this is provided for in such churches as ours, where we have a series of arches supporting the main roof, by the chancel at one end and the tower at the other. In Kingsdown Church there are no aisles and no arches; the tower there is on the south side, not at the west end. A similar arrangement obtains at Trottescliffe. The very latest use of towers is to carry clocks, and ours was presented by Mrs. Robert Barnett in 1879; but the old sundial still remains on the south face of the tower; it was put up in 1809, for which "Mr. Assiter, the Stone mason", was paid £8 13s. 6d.

The dry area on the south side of the church existed before 1851, but in that year the Archdeacon, at his visitation, drew attention to the dampness of the chancel and suggested the area should now be carried round the chancel, and the stone-work of the chancel scraped and cleaned; and this was done. At that time there was not proper drainage from the roof; the rain simply ran off and soaked into the foundations.

A south porch in a country church is very common; we have a north one as well. Originally designed as shelters, they became places where even baptisms were sometimes performed and vestries held; but there is no record of such use at Meopham. Seats, however, used to be provided, as the following shows: "1717. Paid for seats in the porch 4/1." The two small foliated lancet openings in the sides of the south porch are filled with painted glass, the work of Mrs. Lawson of Cobham, and inserted in 1868.* The coloured window in the west tower wall is by the same hand.

The right (east) pier of the external arch of the south porch, as well as the voussoir above, as also the west pier of the inner or doorway arch, show mason's marks, discovered by the late Rev. T. S. Cogswell in 1930. Each is $4\frac{1}{4}$ inches long, representing an Archbishop's pallium, with an incised cut across the pendant part of the pallium, thus combining the crest of the See of Canterbury with the cross. These marks certainly date from the fourteenth century, and may express the fact that the church belonged to the monks of Canterbury. The added cross suggests the Archbishop's own sign.

One other external feature that few know the existence of is the curious water-drain at the east end, in the angle between the Lady Chapel (vestry) and the north chancel wall. From the gutter above will be seen descending in an oblique direction a course of freestone let in flush with the flintwork of the wall. This stone course ends over a cistern for water beneath the east window of the vestry, and until some ignorant mason

---

* Now, however, replaced by stained glass as memorials to Mrs. Sarah Jane Russell (*ob.* 1922) and her daughter Ethel Maria Hammond (*ob.* 1921).

closed the opening with cement a few years ago it was possible to insert one's hand into the opening that was on the face of the lowest stone, and feel that it led up into a channel hollowed out in the course of stones above. This ancient drain is no longer of use, an ordinary iron pipe doing duty for it; but it is doubtless as old as the church. The joints seen on the faces of the alternate stones suggest that each stone is channelled on the inside, and when placed against its neighbour makes the cylindrical hollow required to form a pipe.

CHAPTER III

INTERIOR OF CHURCH

OUR church is a noble building, measuring fully 140 feet by 50 feet, and in studying its interior it must be imagined empty of all seats; and it then presents a nave communicating with the tower at one end by a fine archway, and at the other in a similar manner with the chancel. The nave roof is supported on each side by an arcading of five pointed arches, forming five bays which lead into the north and south aisles. The south aisle ends level with the chancel arch, but the north aisle opens by a wide archway into the present vestry, formerly the Lady Chapel, as is shown by the will of Richard Adene in 1542: "My body to be buryed in the chapell of our Lady w^tin the pyshe churche of Seynt John Baptist in Meopham."

It will be also seen that the chancel is not in line with the nave, but inclined somewhat to the south. Various reasons have been given for this peculiarity, which is found also in some other old churches in the country; and whilst some regard it as representing the inclination of the Saviour's head upon the Cross, the more probable explanation is that it is due to false alignment on the part of the builders, and especially in those cases, as here, where the chancel and body were separately constructed, it being the custom to erect one part first where service could be held, and not to wait till the whole were constructed, and the part thus utilized was screened off from the work that was proceeding. Mr. Hooper, a former Vicar, consulted the celebrated architect, Mr. Pugin, on this subject; the reply was short and unequivocal, and was that the false alignment was a "mere blunder of the architect."

Windows

As these largely determine the style of architecture, and therefore to some extent the date of an old church, I will take them first.

We have no example of the simple lancet window, which succeeded the narrow, slit-like Norman style of window; the difference between the two being that the former or Early English is a narrow, slit-like one with a pointed top—hence called a lancet window; whilst the similar Norman one had a rounded top. On the south side of the tower may be seen a very old lancet window, already referred to, with a projection or cusp of stone from each inner side of its curved top—a stage in window development next after the plain lancet.

As such windows gave but little light it was customary to put two or more together side by side, especially at the east end; and where there were three or more the centre one was often the largest, and, surmounting these, on the outside wall, an arched hood or "drip stone" would be let in, projecting a few inches from the wall, as a protection from rain and also for ornament. The bare wall between this drip stone and the window-tops being very ugly, at times a circular opening as an additional window would be cut, the style being called "plate tracery"; and thus originated the idea of the exquisite stone tracery in church windows. Just such a window as I have described, though of modern make, may be seen in the east wall of Strood Church.

The north window in the chancel is an instance of the Geometric style already mentioned. It consists of two plain lancets, without cusps, topped with a plain stone circle, which, however, is not cut out of a slab of stone, as in "plate tracery," but is a true circle of stone built in, the outer border of each lancet being joined as an arch to complete the window.

By degrees the Gothic style became much more elaborate, and the plain Geometric window tracery gave place to tracery with beautiful curves; and by the fourteenth century the most elaborate Gothic architecture and window tracery had reached its zenith. The east window in the vestry exhibits three cusped lancets side by side, the middle one being the widest and tallest. On the top of this lancet is a circle with five cusps projecting from its soffit or inner flat surface, forming a cinquefoil. It is known as soffit-cusping, a style in use as early as the middle of the twelfth century. It is so called because the cusps spring from the flat inner side of the stone circle, and could even be cut away without affecting the circle itself. This was not the case later on, when the inner surface of the circle was channelled and not flat and became part of the cusp. Above each lateral lancet of this window is a circle with similar cusps, but three instead of five, forming a trefoil. On the outside the whole is surmounted by a drip stone. This window till 1874 was partly bricked up, and has lately been "restored"—to its detriment. It has often been figured and quoted in architectural works as a perfect example of the early Decorated style—that is, a stage beyond the pure Geometric.

The larger windows in the south wall of the chancel are similar in style, with two lancets surmounted by a quatrefoil. There is no drip stone. The quatrefoil is not good; it is certainly an attempted copy of what was there before, and is evidently not the original tracery.

The great *East window* was inserted in 1874, but its stonework is said to be an exact replica of what was there before, and this is confirmed by a sketch of the church made in 1807. It represents a further decorative stage in tracery, and is a combination of lancets of various sizes, the total result being that the two chief mullions have a flowing or bent appearance, and hence, though still of the Early English Gothic or Decorated type, it is sometimes spoken of as curvilinear tracery. An almost similar window is in St. John's Hospital Chapel in Northampton. The delicate side pillars belong also to this type of work. Actually eight lancets can be traced in it, and it contains triangles, quatrefoils, and trefoils.

Considering the simplicity of the other chancel windows, it

MEOPHAM CHURCH (*vide* p. 46)

SOUTH-EAST CORNER OF THE CHURCH (*vide* p. 60)

THE HAGIOSCOPE IN 1884 (BRICKED UP) (*vide* p. 61)

THE HIGH SIDE WINDOW (*vide* p. 55)

is not likely that this window (or rather the original of it) was the first there; very probably it took the place of three or five lancets side by side, which was, as I have said, a common way of forming the east "window" and may still be seen in many Kentish churches.

High Side and Low Side Windows.—The window, with square-headed bay on the inside, next the chancel arch, is a cusped lancet one, but peculiar in that it has the ogee form of curve—a very early pattern, though more used in Tudor times, but also in late Decorated. The stone tracery is clearly also not the original; it may not be a copy of what was there before, though the drip stone outside is the original one. This window—a supplementary one, for it is touching a still larger one—is of a kind of which there are a few examples in our churches. They are always found in this situation in the chancel, and are called "High Side Windows." A popular name for ours here is the leper window; but it would neither afford a view of the priest at the altar for anyone outside, nor were so-called lepers allowed in the church precincts at all. In the fourteenth century Pope Alexander III promulgated a canon forbidding lepers even to enter the churchyard; they were required to have chapels and priests of their own. The numerous hospitals or lazar houses about the country bear testimony to this. *The Antiquary*, June 1881, reports a meeting of archaeologists, when "Mr. J. T. Micklethwaite read a paper upon a subject which, he said, appeared hitherto to have escaped the notice of ecclesiologists, and which, for want of a better name, he called the 'High Side Window.'" He adds that he had found only eleven examples of it, but offers no solution of their meaning, save in one church at Addlesthorpe, Lincoln, where tradition says a lantern was hung up in the window to guide people over the fens. This view, however, does not help us at Meopham.

Beneath this window is to be seen from the inside a deep square recess rather over a foot wide. It has always been something of a mystery in the village; it much resembles the aumbry in the north chancel wall, but I feel certain it represents a "Low Side Window" such as exists in Dallington Church, Northamptonshire, and is figured by Ditchfield; and if the recess I speak of opened outside through the wall, the resemblance would be complete. These small windows, which were closed by shutters, were ordered to be closed up in Henry VIII's reign, for they were used certainly on occasions for the priest to hear the confession of a penitent kneeling in the churchyard. Whether that was their original use is uncertain: some think they were solely for the purpose of ringing the Sacring bell, for people to hear outside the church, at the celebration of the Mass (Gasquet). Owing to the thick growth of ivy on the outside it is not possible to see by external marks if the aperture ever pierced the wall; but the presence of certain marks on the inside in the stonework round the square opening seem to indicate where a shutter hinge may have been. Another use for them mentioned by Ditchfield is that they were for the Anchorites, who not infrequently lived in the churches (as well as in buildings erected against the church walls). Our former Vicar, Mr. Hooper, also held this view (though we have no real facts in support of it here), because at the repaving of the chancel (1859) the foundations of an old wall, 16 feet long, were uncovered, running parallel with the south chancel wall and a few feet from it, opposite this window. It seems to me more likely that this was the south wall of a former smaller chancel, of which we know nothing now. Dr. Gasquet, however, offers the most likely explanation of these little windows; he says, Archbishop Peckham (1281) in his "Constitution" ordered that "at the time of the Elevation of the Body of the Lord, a bell be rung on one side of the church, that the people who cannot be at daily Mass . . . may kneel down, and so gain the indulgences granted by many bishops." It was through the little "low side window" the bell may have been rung—the Sacring bell above-mentioned—and its size and position would seem to be well adapted for this purpose.

The Aisle Windows.—These are of a later type than any in the church—the Perpendicular Gothic—and were no doubt put in by Archbishop Courtenay towards the end of the fourteenth century. They consist of three cusped and trefoiled lancets below; but the mullions between them are carried straight up to the top of the window arch; short mullions run also straight up from the heads of the lancets, thus forming three lights above with trefoil heads. The straightness of the mullions—quite unlike our east window—and the general effect of parallelism gives the name to this style. The tracery thus forms a series of panels, which lend themselves peculiarly to the grouping together of several figures to form one picture in stained glass.

Later on this style of tracery was placed in square windows, the heads of the lights being flat and not arched, and this formed the characteristic window of the Tudor period. Such windows may be seen to perfection in Cobham Hall.

Clerestory Pillars, etc.

Above the arches on either side of the nave the wall is heightened to maintain the main roof, and it is pierced with four circular splayed windows, each with a quatrefoil cusping and containing tinted glass. The splayed openings are original, but the stonework and glass are recent, the sum of £21 19s., being paid in 1868 for both, the cusping costing £12 and the glass £6. This wall above the arcading called the clerestory is found generally in churches of the Meopham character. It is probably the only way in which ancient Grecian temples were lighted; for these were built in quadrilateral form without any windows in the side walls, and it is from them the idea of the Roman Basilica, and subsequently Christian churches, was obtained.

The wall between the chancel and nave, and pierced by the great arch, is at the level of the clerestory unsymmetrical, the spandril being much wider on the north side than the south. The reason is obvious, for the north spandril is pierced with a doorway which communicates with a stone staircase, in the thickness of the wall, that starts in the south-west angle of the vestry. This was the way to the rood loft, above the screen, that once stretched across the chancel arch at the level of the top of the pillar at each side (*v.* Rood Loft). Until Mr. Hooper's time, when the pulpit was much higher than at present, the preacher obtained access to the pulpit through this doorway. Above the arch the wall is pierced by a window-like opening; a similar one, now closed, exists over the western arch.

The arches separating the nave from the aisles are supported by pillars; and this is specially to be noted because it has been suggested that, as the windows in the two aisles are of later date than in other parts of the church, the aisles must have been added at the same time. Against this is the important architectural fact—besides historic *evidence* to be mentioned presently—that where aisles were *added* to a nave the thick walls of the church were cut through to form the bays or communications, piers of the old walls being left to support the roof. This is not the case at Meopham, where we have strong stone pillars built up of half "drums," afterwards cut into octagonal shape. It will be observed that the under-surface or archivolt of all our arches has been chamfered square (and not curved or channelled as the mullions of the aisle windows are), a mode of treatment that Ruskin lays stress on as a character of early northern Gothic work.

The Roof

The present open roof was put in in 1859, at a cost of £315, when the old pews were swept away and the other radical changes made. Prior to this the church was ceiled, as the aisles are still; they were done in 1830. Access to the roof could be obtained by the tower and through the opening already mentioned above the western arch and so through the corresponding one above the eastern arch; and a late aged parishioner, Mr. Ashdown, told me many years ago he recollected as a boy making his way along the rafters above the ceiling and walking about one Sunday during service! As much of the church was whitewashed in the past, the white ceiling would not have appeared so objectionable as it would now; and this use of whitewash was in early medieval times ordered both for the inside and outside of churches, and from its external whitewash St. Alban's Abbey is said "to have shewn like the wings of an Angell when seen from a distance." It has been attributed also to an attempt to purify our churches after the plague; but without doubt it was employed also in Tudor times to obliterate the religious pictures that used to be painted on the walls. Entries in the Churchwardens' books bear on the above remarks:

1662. Whiting the church 2/–.
1760. John Raysell whitewashing the beams in the church 13/–.
1761. Paid towards ceiling the church £1.1.0.

It will be noticed that the stone corbels supporting the chancel roof are quite in keeping with the general architecture; they are of early English pattern, though put in in 1859, the characteristic being that the flowers and their stalks are placed in an upright position and not wrapped round the "capital" horizontally.

It is mainly to Mr. Robert Barnett that we owe the present condition of the chancel, which he undertook to repair in 1859, when the body of the church underwent its great alterations by the Parish. Writing in 1871 the then Vicar, Mr. Hooper, speaking of the state of the church generally before Mr. Barnett's time, says, "The condition of our church was such as to repel rather than encourage any desire to linger within its walls!" Mr. Barnett tiled the chancel floor, provided the present oak stalls and oak benches, removing the two great square pews that blocked the chancel up, removed the ceiling, and put in the open roof; and it was largely by his influence that the great changes were made in the body of the church and in its fittings.

Before the chancel was tiled the floor was composed of flag memorial stones (now in the nave); but some part of the church must have been tiled before: thus, "1717. Paving tyels for the Church £5.15.0."; but some of the floor seems to have been only of beaten earth as late as 1763, for in that year is this entry: "Levelling the earthen floor of the Church."

It may be here remarked that the Rector was always the freeholder of a Parish Church, on account of which he could sue or be sued; but the custom that he, as the holder of the tithes, should look after the chancel, and that the Parish through its Churchwardens should be responsible for the rest of the church structure, became universal in the thirteenth century; and when in later times a lay impropriator took the tithes (there being then a Vicar and not a Rector) it devolved on him to repair the chancel (Gasquet). Now Mr. Barnett *purchased* part of the Manor lands, with the Court Lodge (all previous occupants having been merely lessees), so the great tithes apportioned to the part he bought fell to him as lay impropriator, and also the responsibility of maintaining the chancel. The Dean and Chapter of Canterbury, as Lords of the Manor, retain the great tithes on the rest of the Manor property, the lesser tithes going to the Vicar.

The Priest's Door

The Priest's Door in the south wall of the chancel is unique in pattern in our church; it is also known as a "Shouldered Door," as well as a "Carnarvon Door," from its frequent use in Carnarvon Castle. Technically it is described as "flat-headed, having the angles corbelled with the square-headed trefoil, with [scroll] moulding carried round." Unlike a Gothic archway it does not depend upon the *pointed* arch for the support of the wall above, but on a flat and moulded stone slab resting on the corbels on either side. This beautiful doorway is perfect on the outside, but within it has been mutilated; and thereby hangs a tale. It is recorded in the Parish books that in 1829 the then Lessee of the Court—Rev.

W. Mansfield—was asked, as lay impropriator, by the Vicar, Rev. John Thompson, and the Churchwardens to put up guttering and spouting round the eaves of the chancel to prevent the rain—which up till then dripped off the roof anywhere—from running into the church underneath this particular door, the sill of which was lower than the ground outside. The Lessee declined, and began to brick up the doorway as the readiest means of abating the nuisance. The Vicar thereupon made application to the Dean of the Court of Arches, who promptly stopped this act of vandalism and had the doorway reopened. But already the mason had begun to cut away from within the shoulders of the arch, and the damaged stonework remains to the present time.

Originally this doorway was—as were all at one time—secured by a beam sliding in holes in the side walls; and these can be still traced.

Hagioscope

In the north chancel wall, and communicating with the chantry, is a large square aperture, but set obliquely, the hagioscope or squint, to enable those within to see the priest officiating at the altar; and it is peculiar in having a coarse iron grill to prevent access from chantry to church, and though squints are to be found in many old churches, it is not usual to find them protected in this way. For a long time it had been bricked up, but when the Rev. W. Crookes owned the Court he had the brickwork taken down in 1889 and a sheet of plate glass substituted.

Piscina

A piscina with arched hood and surrounded with a moulding of "scroll" pattern, and retaining its drain aperture, is in the usual place in the south chancel wall. These piscinae were introduced in the thirteenth century, and soon became common; they were for the ceremonial cleansing of the sacred vessels. The front part of an ancient piscina has just been dug up in the Vicarage garden (1934). May it not be the remains of one discarded at the repairs in the fourteenth century?

The *scroll moulding* just mentioned, it will be observed, runs as a string course round the chancel, and belongs to the thirteenth to fourteenth centuries. It is so called as it represents a roll of parchment manuscript, the free end of which is shown as a line running along the face of the stone; also the string course is marked into lengths, like rolls placed end to end. It is confined to the chancel.

Aumbry

Nearly opposite the piscina in the north chancel wall is a square recess, once closed with a wooden door, and locked; and the iron hasp into which the lock-bolt passed can still be seen. These in old times were the church's safes, and were used for keeping the sacred vessels or papers of importance; they were in fact cupboards, hence their name.

Close to the north door, in the nave wall, what remains of the *Holy Water Stoup* can be seen. The recess for it is in the form of a cusped lancet opening.

The Reredos and Chancel Walls

The present reredos in Decorated Gothic style with crocketted pinnacles was presented in 1874 by the late Mrs. R. Barnett in memory of her husband, together with the new east window and coloured glass (*v.* Court).

The handsome dado of encaustic tiles in the chancel was the gift of the late Mrs. Tweddell in 1897 in memory of her husband; and the inscription on the inserted tablet runs:

To the Glory of God and in memory of Ralph Hart Tweddell, C.E. of the Court. Died Sept. 3, 1895, aged 52. Psalm xv.

Before these changes the Lord's Prayer, Ten Commandments, and the Creed, now cut in the marble panels of the reredos, were painted upon framed panel boards. The following entry refers to them:

PISCINA WITH SCROLL MOULDING AND
REMAINS OF ALTAR CANOPY
(*vide* p. 61)

FOUR-LEAVED FLOWER CARVING ON OLD ROOD BEAM (*vide* p. 64)

VESTMENT PRESS IN VESTRY, MADE
FROM THE OLD READING DESK
(*vide* p. 67)

THE FONT (*vide* p. 66)

1830. Writing the Lord's Prayer, the Creed and Decalogue £6.0.0.

There are other entries in the Churchwardens' old books showing at one time that texts of scripture or "sentences," as they were called, were written up on the church walls—a common practice until recent times. Texts on church walls as well as paintings are of very ancient origin: it was in Elizabeth's time that the latter were generally defaced, texts being instituted for them. This is said to have been due to a dispute between Her Majesty and Dean Nowell of St Paul's on November 1, 1561, on the subject of a prayer-book containing illustrations. So strongly did the Queen express her disapproval of pictures in churches as well as in prayer-books that a general destruction of them in churches at once followed (see Hone's *Every Day Book*, vol. ii, under date November 1, 1827).

1759. Writing the sentences in the Church £3.19.0.
1830. Writing various sentences from the scriptures upon the church walls, W. Elliott. £3.10.0.

Altar Canopy

About 4 feet from the east end of the chancel and within the altar rails, against the north and south walls, are the truncated remains of two stone supports or pillars in Decorated Gothic style, with crocketted pinnacles. It has been suggested that these are the remains of an old stone reredos; but if so, the east wall must have been moved some feet from its original position, and there is nothing to prove this. What is more probable—in fact, a certainty—is that these are the remains of the supports for a stone altar canopy, from which hung the pyx. In an illustration, apparently from an old missal, given by Cardinal Gasquet in his *Parish Life in Medieval England,* such a canopy is figured with its supports, almost identical in pattern and position with the remains in our church. His words are: "If we may judge from existing illuminations the altar in English churches stood a little way from the eastern wall of the church, and had over it a canopy supported on pillars, between which curtains were suspended on rods and drawn during the celebration of the sacred mysteries."

The Rood Screen

The chancel of a church was before 1548 always separated from the nave by barriers of some sort ("cancelli," hence the name "chancel"); and whilst barriers are still often erected nowadays, the old ones were lofty and often most elaborate architectural structures in stone or wood, forming a screen pierced by a doorway in the middle. These screens, whether of stone or wood, were of openwork, allowing worshippers in the nave to witness everything in the chancel or choir. On the top of the same was a beam or platform supporting the Rood or Crucifix, having generally the figure of St. John on the one side and that of the Virgin on the other.

All that remains of our screen and beam is a part of the latter, now lying on the floor of the tower, but once worked into the front of the musicians' gallery; it is carved with the four-leaved flower, a pattern of the fourteenth century.

As late as 1819 there was still old oak in the church, as in that year W. Hodsoll, carpenter, is paid for cutting away in all "80 feet of old oak rail" in different lengths; and the same man the year before presents a bill for "work done for the desk and pulpit." It looks as if in 1818–1819 work were being done at the chancel arch where the "three-decker" pulpit and desk stood, and suggests the possibility that the "oak rails" cut away may have been remnants of an old screen. This, however, is pure conjecture.

Screens were often provided with a passageway or "rood loft" across the church, in front of the rood, and access was obtained to it by either a wooden stairway or a stone one; and where the latter remains it is a proof of there having been a rood loft. The rood loft stairway in this church has for years been bricked up, but in 1930 reopened. The entrance to it in the vestry has a sloping head of stone slabs, like an old Norman fireplace, as now may be seen in Luddesdown Manor-house.

The removal also of some plaster near by has exposed the well-shaped chalk "bricks" of which the inner wall of the chancel is built.

Where a loft existed it was customary to burn candles before the rood, and money was often bequeathed by the pious for this purpose, the necessary candlesticks being fitted in the rood beam. A bequest in the will of William Sprever of Dartford in 1525 runs thus: "Also [I bequeath] to the lighting of Saint Kateryn in the same [i.e. Meopham] Church xii pence" (v. Wills); but whether this refers to a figure of St. Catherine on the rood beam or not is uncertain. It is more probable that it refers to a figure of the saint in some other part of the church. St. Catherine seems to have been a favourite saint here,* and there is a fine figure of her amongst the old painted glass, so ruthlessly destroyed in the last century. There is also lying in the tower part of a stone figure, showing the drapery and part of an arm which may have belonged to a stone effigy of this saint, and be the one before which the candles were to be lighted.

The general destruction of screens or roods was largely owing to Archbishop Cranmer's influence; and on February 21, 1548, an Order in Council was issued for the destruction of all roods and images. In many instances the removal was only partial, the rood and all above the beam being taken down and the screen being left.

The earliest existing screen in Kent is in Northfleet Church (fourteenth century); and there is documentary evidence of one at Kingsdown in 1421, and also of one at Ash, where in 1449 one William Hodsoll makes a bequest for "our Lady upon the Beam." These bequests were sometimes for candles and sometimes for a veil to be thrown over the rood in Lent.

* This may be explained by the fact that Meopham is situated between the many pilgrim ways leading from the West to Canterbury; and the duty of the Knights of St. Catherine was specially the protection of pilgrims. That pilgrims often went a little out of the way to visit Meopham Church is certain, since Simon de Meopham—as is mentioned later—offered certain indulgences to such devotees.

At Gillingham the rood was at one time regarded as miraculous, and became the object of pilgrimages; but tradition says that one day a strange sailor's body was washed ashore, but having been a bad man (I know not on what authority), his burial at Gillingham "so provoked our Lady" that the rood at once lost its virtues!

It has been often stated that the Gospel and Epistle were read from the rood loft, but it is now known that this was only done on exceptional occasions. The only rood loft still existing in Kent is at Shoreham Church.

The Font and Lectern

The font has been described by an architect as an "octagonal font of the Perpendicular period, raised on a plinth." This would give its date as the end of the fourteenth, or early fifteenth, century; and, being of the same period as the windows of the nave, is it possible it may have been the gift also of Archbishop Courtenay? It shows evidence of more recent repair, and from the slots on the top it would seem to have had a cover at some time. Till Mr. Hooper's time it stood in the middle aisle at the chancel step.

The handsome modern brass *lectern* was given by the parishioners in memory of the late Rev. Lewis Woodward Lewis, Vicar (1875–1900), who passed to his rest Easter Morn, 1900.

The Pulpit, an exceptionally beautiful piece of work for a village church, was formerly in St. Margaret's Church, Westminster, the old parish church of the Houses of Parliament, and was obtained for the Parish by the Rev. W. Smedley, who was Vicar from 1786–1816. His connection with Westminster appears in the account given of him later (*v.* Smedley). The pulpit was in part at least bought by subscription, as the following shows:

1801.   For part of the pulpit above subscription £7.15.2½.

Hexagonal in shape, its panels were originally all filled with beautiful inlay work, but from one this has quite disappeared, whilst that in the door now bulges and is threatened by the same fate. The panel now facing south-west (for the pulpit has been turned round from its original position, the entrance then being towards the north) is perfect and bears the inlay I.H.S. with the date 1682. The woodwork is everywhere elaborately carved, and some think that it may have been done by that greatest of wood-carvers, Grinling Gibbons. I do not myself think so, though the strings of flowers and leaves and the horizontal representations of looped drapery show his influence; perhaps it was executed by one of his pupils. I may mention that Gibbons (1648–1721) flourished in the reigns of Charles II, James II, William and Mary, Anne, and was master carver to George I at the exorbitant wages of 1/6 a day! Not long ago some of his work sold for £30,000!

The central stem supporting the pulpit was originally much higher, and entrance to the pulpit was from the vestry by the old rood staircase (*q.v.*); and beneath the pulpit was room for the "minister's desk" from which the service was read, and still lower a desk for the Clerk, forming the well-known "three-decker" of a generation ago. The Clerk, it may be mentioned, was an important person, saying the responses aloud as well as the alternate verses in the psalms, thus leading —when not drowning—the congregation! He too had to start the tune where no music was provided by the aid of a pitchpipe or tuning-fork; and all this I can recall in my young days in various churches.

Here is an entry bearing on the Clerk: "1798. A Common Prayer Book for the Clerk's desk 14/-"; the previous entry for the same was in 1752. But to return to the pulpit.

In 1859 the desks were removed and the pulpit lowered, and out of the desks was made a cupboard or wardrobe for the church vestments, and still used for the purpose; it stands in the vestry. The panelling of it is in Jacobean style, and the desks could hardly have been in artistic harmony with the carved pulpit. When Mr. Hooper became Vicar in 1854 the pulpit was heavily draped, and therefore partly hidden in heavy hangings; they were usually velvet or cloth, and resembled the heavy hangings or hammer cloth with which the coachman's box was in former days always hung in the private carriages of the rich, but now only seen in State coaches. I may quote Ruskin's scathing remark on these hideous pulpit hangings—often covering, as at Meopham, a really exquisite work of art; he says, speaking of pulpit furniture, "pompousness without grace and meaning, and dependent merely on certain applications of upholstery." Mr. Hooper got rid of the "upholstery," except the big cushion and its tassels, which still remain with us!

The following entries explain themselves:

1709.   Pulpit Cloth £7.12.0.
1798.   New Velvet cushion for pulpit and cover £6.0.0.

The pulpit in Trottescliffe Church, with its sounding-board above, is an outcast from Westminster Abbey. It does not possess one redeeming artistic feature. Shoreham Church has also a pulpit from the Abbey.

In a letter received in 1914 from Miss Hooper, the daughter of our former Vicar, she writes:

I remember the late General Gordon and his father coming over from Gravesend to see our church, and he got up into the pulpit, why I do not know. I and one of my sisters happened to be in the church at the time, and we thought what a "little man" he looked; little we thought what a great man he would become . . . Dean Farrar when a young man preached from our pulpit, he being a great friend of the great-uncle of the Smith-Masters.

Another great man occupied our pulpit on October 20, 1859, when Archbishop Bird Sumner preached on the occasion of the reopening of the church after the renovation of the interior had taken place.

CHAPTER IV

CHURCH SEATING, MUSIC, AND FITTINGS PAST AND PRESENT

The Seating and Heating of the Church

UNTIL the fourteenth century the only seats in our churches, if any, were stone benches against the walls, the floor being strewn with straw or rushes, the charges for which appear in some old church accounts; and it was about the time when Archbishop Courtenay repaired the aisles of our church that wooden benches were introduced, exactly like the one now under the church tower; and from its style as well as from the evidences of age that it bears I have no hesitation in dating it from that period, i.e. the end of the fourteenth century. In 1392, when Rochester Bridge was rebuilt, the surplus oak timber was sold: some was used to make seats for Aylesford Church (*Rochester Bridge*, Becker, 1930). May not the seats in our church have like origin and date?

At this time also seats for the people were allowed only in the nave; it was forbidden to the laity to be in the chancel, which was reserved for the clergy and the choir.

Between 1649 and 1660 the old "family" pews were introduced into our churches.* They were large square enclosures, with high panelled sides, so that when standing only the tops of the occupants' heads were visible. They were furnished more like a room, with carpets, seats all round, and often with fireplaces, and, both for privacy and for comfort, were also often curtained round the top; in fact, they were comfortable places for the congregation to sleep in unobserved in the sleepy days of the Church of England. Until 1858–1859 two

---

* High pews were, however, clearly not unknown in the fourteenth century, as the following lines from *Piers Plowman* show:

> Among wives and widows I am wont to sit
> High fenced in the high pews in Church.

such pews, one on each side, filled up the chancel for the accommodation of the occupants of the Court Lodge. The square pew in the south-east corner of the south aisle was occupied by the family at Camer; but when the Rev. A. Smith-Masters came he had the whole structure removed, open seats, facing north, taking its place. The hooks, however, which supported the curtain rods are still to be seen on the walls of the church.

The nave and aisles were also filled with the same kind of pews, but only some were curtained. They were all removed in 1859 and the present open seats put in.

Up to this time also the heating of the church was by means of an open stove at the crossing of the nave and transept, an iron pipe for a chimney passing straight up through the nave roof. One old inhabitant of Meopham has expressed her regret to me at its disappearance, the open fire being "so cheerful"! It was followed by a system of hot-water pipes, and this again in 1884 by the present "Grundy" furnace, at a cost of £140. A hot-water system is now being introduced (1934).

The Musicians' Gallery. The Organ

Before the introduction of organs into country churches an orchestra—of sorts—was provided when possible; such a one was here till Mr. Hooper's time, and was accommodated in a gallery approached by some twenty steps, and situated in front of the western arch, which at that time was closed up. The gallery was occupied by the singers and musicians responsible for the musical part of the service, and according to old Mr. James Smith, my informant, who remembers them well, they were not always in harmony either musically or socially; for, to use his own words, "the Psalm Singers (as they were usually called) on one occasion fell out and would not sing, so the Clerk, William Wells, left his desk, went into the gallery, and sang like a bird"! In Mr. Thompson's time as much of the service as was permitted Wells often read, and not infrequently the lessons. His successor, Smith, was the last

THE PULPIT FROM ST. MARGARET'S, WESTMINSTER
(*vide* p. 66)

THE MECHANICAL ORGAN NOW IN TROTTESCLIFFE CHURCH
(*vide* p. 72)

THE "CROMWELL" TABLE IN VESTRY (*vide* p. 74)

of the "Clerks"; the Sexton for the future represented that official.

The Parish Clerk was in earlier times a "lay reader"; he could read part of the service, the lessons, etc., and it was essential that he should have such knowledge of music (!) as to enable him to pitch the note (with a pitch pipe) and start a hymn tune, and, where there were musicians, to direct them as to what they were to play. His office was a freehold; he could not be dismissed without appeal to the Bishop, and then only for something very serious. An entry in the old Churchwardens' book, under date 1623, shows the appointment of Henry Reeve as Parish Clerk, he "being sufficient and allowable by the Canons," in place of his father John Reeve, whom the vestry pensioned off at 13/4 per annum by quarterly payments of 3/4 for the rest of his life. The memorandum is signed by Thomas Pigott, Vicar, John Taylor, Robert Balcher, Henry Haslen, William Warren (apparently the son of the benefactor who died in 1618), and others.

The giving of the pension may mean only a recognition of past services, but it may mean that being a life office the younger man could only be appointed by the voluntary surrender of the post by the father, and that may have been brought about by promise of a pension!

In 1818 W. Mungeam was Parish Clerk, he being the first to combine the offices of Clerk and Sexton, for which he was paid £9 per annum; and when in 1827 Wells was appointed, notice of the fact was "duly proclaimed during divine service."

The musicians at this time (c. 1854) were:

Tom Hills, flute-player; he lived on the Green in the old house next the Inn, behind the walnut-tree.

Robert Hills, his brother, played the clarinet; he at one time kept the George Inn.

—— Waterman was bass viol; he was the miller at Luddesdown.

The violinist was Wells, the Camer butler.

The "Psalm Singers" had their "Choir Treats," as is shown by this entry in 1829: "Psalm Singers' Feast 1£."

In the last years of Mr. Thompson's Vicariate a difference, above referred to, arose between himself and the musicians, with the consequence that they ceased to play; this was about 1852-1853; the following year Mr. Hooper became Vicar, and in 1855 a mechanical organ was presented by Mr. W. Masters-Smith, M.P., of Camer. It stood at the west end of the nave in front of the gallery, on a raised platform, and was in use until 1865; since then it has done duty at Trottescliffe Church to the present day. It is a handsome instrument, standing some 10 feet high, with pipes in front. By a side door a chamber is entered where the organist can stand and turn the handle to revolve the barrel. There are several of these on one spindle, and by a very simple mechanism the requisite barrel and tune can be at once brought into action. It plays sixty hymn tunes, but some are worn out; the "Old Hundredth" seems to have been a favourite tune, but now is not to be depended on! Less used tunes are still really good, as is also the tone of the instrument. A mechanical organ also formerly existed in Cobham Church, as this extract, dated September 6, 1812, shows: "The Churchwardens have lately had a barrel-organ put up in the loft, the gift of Lady Darnley, adapted to play sundry tunes or portions of the Psalms" (*Diary of Robert Pocock*, by G. Arnold, 1883, p. 84).

The gift of this new organ was most opportune, and, without detracting from the generous spirit of the donor, it may be said to have been brought about by circumstances. For Mr. Hooper desired something better than the "sackbut and psaltery" in the gallery, and at a vestry on April 19, 1855, it was proposed to raise a church rate to supply an organ. Evidently much dissatisfaction arose, for at the next meeting the gift of an organ from Mr. Masters-Smith was announced, and the vote of thanks accorded had this rider appended: that there be "expressed to him their objection to the Church rate being used for such a purpose as had been suggested in April." Mr. Masters-Smith had saved the situation!

The School Children in Church

The seats for the school children were, in the middle of the last century, at the west end of the nave on either side of the organ; and the children were kept quiet by the presence of "Old Tomlin", as my informant, Mr. Smith, terms him, who during service perambulated in front of them armed with a cane, with which he administered such correction as he thought well.

Strange though this sounds nowadays, yet from old times this was one of the duties of the Parish Clerk, or of a person specially appointed with the title of "bobber" or "sluggard-waker," and many are the tales told of them by Ditchfield in his exhaustive account of the "Parish Clerk." One other duty for the Clerk was to keep dogs out of church, and even legacies were left to maintain "dog-whippers" for this purpose.

I can well remember as a small boy being much afraid of the beadle in full uniform keeping the youthful part of the congregation of Tonbridge Church quiet in Tomlin's fashion.

During Mr. Hooper's time the Clerk, who hitherto had been Sexton as well, ceased to act in his quasi-clerical position and became Sexton only; and this still holds good.

Moral and religious persuasion rather than the cane is now relied on to maintain order; but old Tomlin was only doing his duty according both to custom and law. In a manuscript note by the late Mr. Lewis I find the following: "By Act of Parliament, 1 Elizabeth, ch. 2, which deals with attendance at the Parish Church, etc., the Churchwardens were to see that People behaved reverently, and that they did not keep their hats on; if they did the Churchwardens were to remove them for them; they were also to chastise boys who behaved badly in church"!

The Sunday school used to be held, as at present, in the National School (as it was then called), and two ladies, the

great-aunts of Mr. W. A. Smith-Masters, taught the children—
Miss Charlotte and Miss Fanny Masters-Smith.

The parish and church became still further indebted to the
family of Mr. Masters-Smith when his niece by marriage,
Mrs. Smith-Masters, in 1865, partly by her own generosity
and partly by subscriptions that she collected, provided the
church with the very good organ—with two manuals, by
Walker—which we possess at the present time; and she was
herself the honorary organist for many years. To keep the
school children under her eye, they were removed from the
west end of the nave to benches under the windows of the
north aisle, the organ being then so placed at the east end of
the aisle that the keyboard faced west. In 1916, when the
instrument was substantially repaired, it was turned round,
that the organist might be in touch with the choir in the
chancel; the Sunday school children now for many years have
had their seats in the south aisle.

The Cromwell Table: Parish Chest, etc.

In the vestry stood a table of plain oak, which has a history;
it is now in the south transept.

From 1640, in the reign of Charles I, and shortly before
the outbreak of the Civil War, fixed stone altars at the east end
of our churches were ordered to be replaced by movable
tables,* which were not infrequently placed in the middle of
the church, and not against the east wall, though their position
at the east end, as at present, was later brought about again
by Archbishop Laud. The oak table I have referred to was
the one then used here; its pattern is of that period. They are
generally known as Cromwell Tables. Here and there stone
altars still remain. In this neighbourhood, at Maplescome, in
Kingsdown Parish, there is one remaining *in situ* in the ruined
church; it is an old "Sarsen Stone," and the remains at least

---

* The removal of stone altars and the substitution of wooden tables was
first ordered during the protectorate of Edward VI (1552).

of one are still underneath the present "movable" Holy Table in Wrotham Parish Church. An old altar stone, with five crosses, is still in Lydd Church.

Old Communion Table

Another table, formerly in the vestry but now in the transept, thought by some to have been a former altar table, is beautifully carved and very substantial, with a heavy oaken top. The legs represent those of a lion, ending in bold claws. On the front and back, carved as pendants between the legs, are lions' heads, and at the ends cockle-shells. The whole, in its depth of carving, general character, and decoration, is exactly in Chippendale's style (1735–1770). Except the top, the table is carved in some light-coloured wood, not, as far as can be seen, oak, but probably pear; the dark, almost black colour of the whole is due to colouring painted over a thin wash of white plaster. The period suggested for it above would agree with an entry in the parish books under date 1800, "Carriage of the Communion table 5/-." This date also being that of the introduction of our carved pulpit, it seems clear that both pulpit and the table just described came together from London, and both perhaps from the same church. I might add that, according to Allen (*County Churches*), the table described is of seventeenth-century work; and if this be so, both pulpit and table are of the same period.

Cromwell's name having been mentioned above, some events of his time that concerned our church may here be mentioned.

Directory of Public Worship. Civil Marriages

In 1643, the year of King Charles I's defeat at Newbury, the Parliament forbade the use of the Book of Common Prayer, under penalty; and a book called the Directory of Public Worship, drawn up by a body of divines at Westminster, was issued in its place in 1644; but it was not employed in our church till a year later (1645) (Smetham's *History of Strood*).

In Cromwell's time (1655) the Prayer Book was forbidden to be used even in private.

Just before this, in 1653, it was enacted that marriages were to be regarded only as civil contracts and to be performed by Justices of the Peace, and the banns published, not in church, but in the market-place. The following extract is from the Parish Register of Addington:

1657. John Kindon of Stanstead and Mary Woollett of Meopham were married the 15th day of September, 1657, having three several market days their Banns published in Rochester.

Canterbury Christmas. The Petition of Kent. General Fairfax at Meopham

This prohibition against the Prayer Book in 1643 gave rise to the *Canterbury Christmas* in 1647, when, the observance of Christmas having already been forbidden, the Rev. —— Allday of Canterbury on that Christmas Day held a Church of England service, using the Prayer Book. The Puritan authorities were down on him, but the Mayor got the worst of the riot that ensued, and was left on the ground! Whereupon Kent rose, sending in a petition to Parliament on May 11, 1648, i.e. about four months later. The petition asked that the King be "admitted in safety to consult with Parliament for the peace of the Realm and Church." This was the celebrated *Petition of Kent*; a further declaration followed, which was a determination of the Men of Kent and Kentishmen to resist the present tyranny—in fact, a declaration of war. Promptly the Parliament's General, Fairfax, marched into Kent, by Deptford, Shooter's Hill, Eltham, Dartford, Rochester, *Meopham*, East Malling, East Farleigh, to *Maidstone*. It was night when he reached Meopham, having crossed the North Downs after reconnoitring Rochester "by roads concealed entirely from the sight of the enemy" (from Goodman's *History of the Great Civil War*). The Luddesdown-Cuxton road would almost seem to be indicated by this description; any-how, Fairfax occupied Meopham for the night, and tradition says he stabled his horses in the church—what damage they did we do not know; we know our brasses are gone, but we can *prove* no damage. Meopham itself is said to have been deserted by its men, as practically all had gone to join the Royalist Kentish army on Barham Heath. Mr. Lewis notes it as a curious fact that the church bells were all recast soon after the army's visit; it suggests they had smashed up the bells—and they hated church bells! The Vicar at the time was the Rev. William Gibson, in place of the sequestered Piggott, and amongst the Royalists was one Francis Cour-thorpe, who had up to ten years before occupied Meopham Court. On their way into Kent, Fairfax's army had a skirmish at Gravesend, but soon swept away the opposition of the Royalists, and then, to quote the official account of the event: "Major Husbands advanced with a party two or three miles beyond Gravesend and afterwards had orders to march to Maulin [i.e. Malling], towards which the army marches this morning from Mapham, a very small village (where the Lord General quartered last night [May 31, 1648] and his forces about it in the fields) and will make a halt near Maulin, where orders will be given out. There are very few men to be seen in the towns through which we march, but only the women making sad moan, fearing the ill success their husbands are likely to have."

The final battle was fought the next day—June 1, 1648—and the Royalists were hopelessly defeated.

The Royal Arms

On the Restoration of Charles II it was ordered that the Royal Arms, painted on an escutcheon, should be set up in the parish churches (1662). Ours, now relegated to the vestry, used to be in front of the musicians' gallery. The names of the Churchwardens, Henry Masters of Camer and William Swift of the Court, are inscribed upon it, but time and dirt have rendered the painting very indistinct. The following Churchwardens' entries are interesting:

1662.   Paid to Mr. Clarke for deals for frame for the King's Arms £1.1.0.
1662.   For painting the Kings Arms £2.15.0.

The Parish Chest

The old oak chest with its three different locks, the keys being held by the Vicar and Churchwardens, still exists in the vestry, and no doubt is the actual one ordered to be placed in every church in Elizabeth's reign for storing the parish archives. For this purpose, however, now we have an iron box purchased in 1814.

Iron chest, 1814 £7.10.0.
Carriage of the Iron chest from London 6/–.

Church Glass

At one time our church contained beautiful stained glass, but it was taken out about the middle of the last century. I think there is little doubt that most, if not all of it, was put in by Archbishop Courtenay in 1386, in the north and south aisle windows: fragments of the old glass still existing are of that date.

In the fourteenth century all coloured glass was what is known as "pot metal"; that is, the ingredients to make the glass were, with the colouring matter, largely blue or red, mixed together in the crucible and melted, and then poured out on to a flat surface and cooled. Glass thus made was thick, $\frac{3}{16}$ to $\frac{1}{4}$ inch, often very uneven (of which advantage was taken to produce special light effects); of intense colour; and the colours, though the ingredients might be the same at each melting, often came out of different depths and tints; whilst, being of uneven thickness as well as of uneven surface, one piece would be very often lighter in one part than another.

Only one means of *staining* was then known, discovered early in the fourteenth century. It consisted in painting on the surface of the uncoloured glass a solution of a salt of silver; the glass then was again fired, and the silver imparted a yellow tint of varying shades, whilst the glass still remained transparent. Thus a figure with a face of white glass could have yellow (or golden) hair imparted to it.

The outline of features, wavy lines of hair, shadow effects, cross-hatching, and the like were produced in another way, which was true *painting*. A mixture of finely powdered glass with iron and manganese was made up with water and used as an opaque brown paint; the glass was then fired, and the paint became permanent on its surface. Our old glass is of the kind just described; of coloured "pot metal" or of "white" glass, silver-yellow stained or painted with the brown opaque paint. Some of it is ¼ inch thick, and its age is further attested by the deep serpentine or dendritic channelling on its outside, from the growth and erosion of a peculiar fungus or lichen, some of which can still be seen.

Further, the method of manufacture only allowed small pieces of glass to be made that were flat enough for the glazier's purpose; and in consequence, as well as because each piece was self-coloured, the leads in which each piece was held to build up a figure were very numerous; and even in a face or on a robe of one colour numerous lines of lead crossed. The resulting effect, however, was not bad; for the deformity to the picture which the dark lead lines produced was amply compensated for by the brilliant colouring of the glass which the dark lead lines showed up so well, producing not only a pictorial but a brilliant mosaic effect.

This latter was lost when transparent colours were discovered, and larger pieces of glass employed, allowing two or more colours to be painted on one large surface of glass.

Great waste occurred in making old coloured windows, for diamonds for cutting glass were not introduced till the seventeenth century, and the only way the old glaziers had was to crack the piece of glass as nearly as they could to the required shape with a hot iron, and then chip its edges, reminding one of the work of our flint-working forefathers. This peculiarity our glass also shows.

A common shape employed was more or less square or diamond, and such a piece in its lead was called a "quarry"; and where whole windows were thus made up (like the modern one on the south of the chancel) of white or very slightly tinted glass, with perhaps some pattern drawn in brown paint, they were known as "Grisaille" windows; they were employed when light had to be admitted. A similar treatment of stone in bas-relief, i.e. a pattern of small squares with some tracing cut on them, such as form the panels of our present reredos, was known as "Diapering."

Many years ago the late Mr. Lewis, our Vicar, told me of the old glass which had been lying in the roof of Meopham Court. He obtained possession of it and tried to piece it together; but it had been taken out of its lead; so the labour of discovering even one figure was enormous. What he accomplished I do not know; but at his death the broken glass in two or three boxes was consigned to my care.

Fortunately, I also obtained at that time some tracings on paper of three panels: one said to be of Simon de Meopham, one of St. Catherine, and one of some angels blowing trumpets —all about 20 inches by 6 inches. After considerable difficulty and with much patience, with the help of these pictures, I have recovered the above three panels more or less perfectly, and trust one day to see them again in the church.* The shape of these three panels suggests their having been in the Perpendicular windows of the aisles, but there is no record of any coloured glass having been there in recent times, whilst there is evidence of the east window having been coloured. In Glynne's *Churches of Kent* (1877, p. 27), in an account of Meopham Church, is the statement that in 1831 "the east window is an elegant one of three lights containing some very

---

* This was accomplished in 1923, *vide infra.*

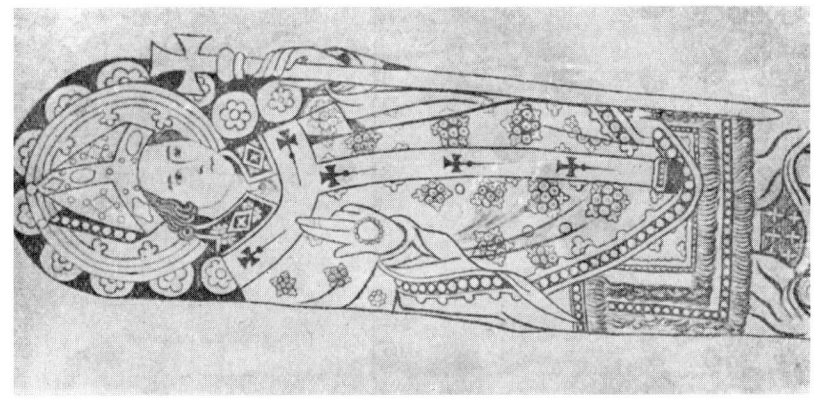

ST. CATHERINE

ST. THOMAS OF CANTERBURY

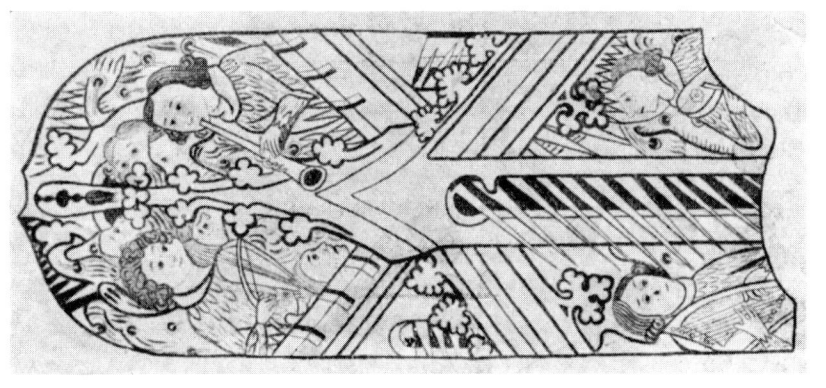

PANEL OF ANGELS

COPY OF JUDITH MARKLAND'S WILL (1665)
(vide p. 95)

THE FOLSHAM BRASS (*vide* p. 110)

fine stained glass." No mention is made of stained glass elsewhere. In the end window of the south aisle a few pieces of the old yellow (silver) glass have been worked into the modern glazing. The Churchwardens' book contains this entry for May 20, 1848, written by Archdeacon King at his visitation: "I found several windows in the church stopped up, and also a handsome eastern window of coloured glass totally unprotected on the outside. This window should be protected with wire, and the other windows restored." At this date, therefore, the window was intact.

I think that there can be little doubt that the old glass of the east window was removed to avoid the expense of protecting it with wire, for when Mr. Hooper came six years later the east window was quite plain except for the small round discs mentioned below.

Miss Hooper, the daughter of a former Vicar, told me that when her father came (1854) there were only two small leaded round panels or discs with the words "Ladie" and "Helpe" in the east window, the rest being plain glass; and this is confirmed by the recollection of both Mr. and Mrs. Oliver of this village. The round panels in their leads still exist.

The drawings of the three larger panels previously mentioned are clearly by a trained hand; and under the one supposed to be Archbishop Simon is written: "Portrait of Archbishop Simon de Mepham in the East window of Meopham Church in Kent. T.W. 1855." (? Thomas Willement of Davington.)

There can, however, be no question that this panel represents *not* Simon but Thomas à Becket, for the reason that though it is undoubtedly an archbishop, with his pall, there is a corona or halo represented round the head, which shows the wearer to have been canonized; and this Simon de Meopham certainly was not.

The remainder of the glass is broken into thousands of pieces, and fragments of figures, canopies, borders, etc., can be distinguished, but are too minute to be again properly assembled; the most that can be done with them is to make an "omnium gatherum" window, and this, I trust, may one day be accomplished.

Since the above was written the broken glass has been assembled, and it now forms a memorial window in the south aisle in memory of Florence Marion Golding-Bird. The work was undertaken by Messrs. Powell of Whitefriars, London. Three figures only are perfect—St. George, St. Thomas à Becket, and St. Catherine. The two discs above-mentioned are also inserted, with a similar disc of the Royal Rose (v. Appendix S).

Besides the modern east window there are other coloured windows of recent date. The north chancel window was put in by the Rev. J. Hooper in memory of his wife, the old stone tracery being renewed at the same time, in 1884. Opposite to it is a memorial window to General Elwin, father of the late Rev. L. Lewis, Vicar; in this also the tracery has been "restored." The two perpendicular windows at the east end of the south aisle are of richly coloured glass and to the memory of members of Mr. Smith-Masters' family, the one to the Rev. Allan Smith-Masters, the other to his daughter, Edith (v. also Appendix P).

Church Plate

The following is Mr. Lewis's account of the plate in Meopham Church:

Cup 7¾ in. high.
　　diam. 4¼ in.
Inscribed "Bought by ye Parrish." William Swift, Francis Britt then Churchwardens 1680.
Engraved with a rich ornament of marks and conventional foliage or flowing curves, forming alternately large and small pendants from a narrow belt around the mouth.
Weight 10½ ounces.

Paten Cover 5 in. diam. to match.
        Maker's mark, A R in shaped shield.
        Weight 2¾ ounces.

Flagon 12½ in. high.
        diam. of mouth 4¼ in.
        diam. of foot 7¼ in.

Engraved with IHS *en soleil*. On the base is this inscription: "The gift of George Masters to the Parish of Meopham 1757." Maker's mark T.W. in script capitals.

Paten. Inscribed, "The gift of the Revᵈ. Daniel Francis Warner, A.M., curate of this Parish, A.D. 1825."
    IHS *en soleil* with the words, "Take, eat, this is my body."
        Weight 1 lb. ½ oz.

1679. Paid towards Silver Cup £3.0.0.
     „   „   „   „ £1.3.0.
For marking cup   1/6
1740. A putter (pewter) plate for the Church 1/6.
This refers presumably to an almsdish.

In 1685 a flagon was purchased for 8/6—probably, at this price, of pewter; and there is an entry of its repair in 1693.

In 1873 Major Edwards presented the silver sacramental vessels to the school church at Culversole.

The present massive almsdish is of brass, and was a gift in November 1884 from the Rev. Geo. Cuff, Rector of Fawkham, and the letter with it says: "For perpetual use in Meopham Church as a trifling acknowledgment of much kindness received from friends in the latter parish." Previous alms-dishes—which were usually held at the door to receive contributions as the congregation passed out—were at times of pewter.

Our church books show that until Mr. Hooper's time (1854) the Holy Communion was administered only four times in the year, and several entries show that the bread and wine were bought for each occasion; for instance:

1663. Muskadine 6/–.
1692. Bread and wine for the Communion 7/8.
1693. Bread and wine at Whitsuntide 2/8.
　　,,　　,,　　,,　　,, Xmas 5/1.
　　,,　　,,　　,, on Palm Sunday 7/8.
　　,,　　,,　　,, at Easter 5/2.
1697. Bread and wine at Easter 5/10.
　　,,　　,,　　,,　　,, Xmas 3/–.
1741. Bread and wine 4 times 6/8—£1.6.8.

It was Mr. Hooper who first administered the Holy Communion eight times a year, and then every month.

CHAPTER V

THE CHURCH REGISTERS

OUR old church registers, with entries from 1561 to 1812, are contained in four vellum-bound volumes with vellum leaves, and show on the whole great care in the way they were kept; there are but few places where gaps appear. Their contents are:

Vol.	I.	1561–1727	Baptisms.
		1575–1680	Burials.
		1575–1743	Marriages.
Vol.	II.	1728–1812	Baptisms.
		1743–1812	Burials.
Vol.	III.	1754–1795	Marriages.
Vol.	IV.	1796–1812	Marriages.

The gap between 1680–1743 (burials) is broken in 1709 by four entries of burials; otherwise there are no burial entries for about sixty-two years.

Church registers were first ordered to be kept in 1536, in Henry VIII's time, at the instance of Thomas Cromwell, the Vicar-General; and from that time forwards these registers have become the official diary of all principal events both ecclesiastical and parochial, though originally intended only for the entries of weddings, christenings, and burials. It was enacted that every Sunday in the presence of the Church-wardens the Vicar should make his record of the various events above-mentioned during the previous week; failure to do so meant a forfeiture to the church of 3/4.

In 1554 the names of godparents were to be added when a baptism was recorded; but the first mention of these in our books is on July 30, 1575:

Año 1575. Baptized Nicholas Tailer the s of Richard Tailer, the xxx^th of July. His godfathers, Nicholas Baaker of Northfleet and Willm̃ Browne of Southfleet.

The last entry with the names of godparents is on September 27, 1601. In the sixteenth century godparents were also called "Borrowes"* and entered as such.

In 1597 Queen Elizabeth ordered that the registers should no longer be paper books, but parchment ones, into which first of all the entries of the old paper ones were to be copied; and a chest or coffer was also to be provided for their safe custody, with three locks, and the three keys were to be kept by the Vicar and Churchwardens, each holding one. Access to the contents, therefore, could only be obtained in the presence of all three officers at one and the same time.

During the Commonwealth, amongst other enactments against Church practices, it was ordered in 1653 that a register of vellum should be provided for the entries; and the entries were to be made, not by the parson of the parish, but by a "Register," or, as we should now say, a registrar, who was to be a layman and chosen by the parishioners. Mr. Lewis points out that in Meopham this order seems not to have been obeyed, since the same handwriting appears through these years as formerly—that of the Vicar, the Rev. William Gibson, who held office from 1646 to 1670. During the six years that followed this order, viz. 1653–1659, there is the entry of but one marriage; it seems as though the Meopham people declined to comply with another of the oppressive Commonwealth orders, which was that weddings should not be held in church but before a Justice of the Peace, and that the banns should be published in the market-place. In 1660 the offensive order came to an end, and an Act was passed legalizing the marriages of the last six years contracted before a Justice. "We believe," says Mr. Lewis, "that the marriages

* "Borrowes," der. A.-S. Borgian, to give a pledge. The godparents were "pledges" for the infant. Thus, in A.D. 1175: "Heore Godfaderes and heore Godmoderes scullen beo in borges," etc.

Similarly, godparents were also called "Gossips" = God-sib = kin to God. Thus Evelyn's *Diary*, A.D. 1649: "The parents being so poore that they had provided no Gossips."

in 1663, which amounted to nine, were more numerous than in any other year down to 1872."

Our register contains the following entry, in 1698 and again in 1700: "I gave the Collectors a list." It is explained by the fact that in 1694 all entries in the register were taxed to raise money for the French war, and a tax collector regularly visited the churches to inspect the books and to obtain his "list" and collect the tax.*

1784. Paid licence for registering births, marriages and deaths.

With a view of still further augmenting profits, it was also enacted in the same year that every *birth* in the parish should be entered in the church register, whether the child were a baptized member of the Church or not. On conscientious grounds many clergy refused to comply, and had in many instances to face ruin thereby, the fine for not obeying the order being £100. For about ten years these promiscuous births were duly registered in our register, and then ceased to be so recorded.

One register was kept for all purposes until 1812 (George III), when separate registers for births, marriages, and deaths, printed by the "King's Printers" on a uniform plan, were issued; and this use is still followed.

Thirty-three years after registers were first used, viz. in 1569, our first register and other books were stolen from the church. Our earliest one now dates from that year, but as the first entry in it is a baptism in 1561, it is evident that this, and some other early entries, were copied from some other documents then extant.

At the commencement of our earliest register appear the following:

Christ'ninges collected out of the old Book from the year 1561 with the names of as many as can be found untill the year 1599.

---

* "No sermon at Church: but after prayers the names of all the parishioners were read in order to gathering the tax of 4/- for marriages, burials, etc. A very imprudent tax, especially this reading of names, so that most went out of the Church" (Evelyn's *Diary*, July 14, 1695).

A true Register of all marriages Christninges and Buryings from the sixt day of Aprill 1595, with the names of all such as are to be found registered from the yere 1570 unto the said yere 1595. The first that can be found are in the yere 1561.

You shall understand that the anncient Register was stolen out of our church with Divers other bookes Año Dñi 1569.

From these it is clear that the book or document in which the registrations were made after 1569–1570, when the old register was stolen, until April 1595, when our present Volume I was commenced, must have been imperfectly preserved, since the implication contained above is that many leaves or papers were missing.

Another note runs:

Further you shall understand that in the Daies of Mr. Jeames Day Vicar of Meopham for five years space none were registered.

Mr. Day was Vicar 1576–1593.

The disappearance of registers and parish books from old parish churches is a most serious loss, as they contain records nowhere else available. Antiquarian covetousness no doubt accounts for the disappearance in some cases, but accident, as well as non-appreciation of their worth, explains others. Thus in our neighbourhood the old Nurstead register, though not lost, is much damaged by being thrown out one wet night into the churchyard by thieves; and it is recorded in the register of Kingsdown Church that the old parish registers were burnt in 1814 by the Parish Clerk, William Phillips, who thought they were only waste paper! (Fielding).

A quaint entry appears in the burial register in 1624:

Parnell Cooke a poore stranger was most Christianlike brought to the earth by ye neighbours of Kemar Street.

From the church registers the late Mr. Lewis compiled a complete list of names of parishioners in different centuries; a few have survived or reappeared in later years; these I extract from his compilation:

Sixteenth Century

Clarke, Cooke, Cooper, Cripps, Crowhurst, Day, Edmeds, Garratt, Master, Skudder, Sparrow, Stevens, Taylor, Turner, Underwood, Whait or Wheit or Weit.

Seventeenth Century

Alard or Aylard, Alchin, Baker, Bennett, Berry, Booker, Budd, Clarke, Clements, Cooke, Cripps, Crowhurst, Dalton, Day, Dirling, Dorman, Edmeds, Everden (? = Evenden), Fowler, Garrett, Godden, Godfrey, Godwin, Goldsmith, Grinwell or Grinnell, Gunning, Hazell, Henfield, Hollman, Hunt, Ifield, Kemslay, King, Lake, Lofte, Lynne, Martin, Master, Norton, Osmer (? Hosmer), Paine, Richardson, Sampson, Seamark, Sexton, Skudder, Smyth, Sparrow, Stephens, Terry, Turner, Tradescant, Underwood, Usher, Warren, Wellard, Wells, Whiffin, Williams.

Eighteenth Century

Allchin, Annanias (!), Ashernden, Baker, Barnett, Bennett, Bird, Brown, Buggs, Chapman, Cherry, Clerk, Clements, Cook, Cronk, Dalton, Day, Doe, Durling, Edmeades, Evenden, Evernden, French, Godfrey, Golding, Goldsmith, Green, Hawley, Hodges, Hooker, Hunt, Ifield, Inpin, Jeal, Johnson, Johnstone, Kellick, Killick, Langford, Loft, Lomas, Markett, Marshall, Martin, Masters, Matthews, Mepham, Miles, Miller, Munday, Mungeam, Oliver, Owen, Paine, Packer, Parsons, Percival, Phillips, Pollard, Richardson, Roots, Russell, Scudder, Seamark, Sergeant, Sexton, Steele, Stevens, Stone, Tatham, Taylor, Terry, Tomlyn, Turner, Vennison, Wade, Walker, Ware, Wells, Wellard, West, Whiffin, Williams, Woodhams, Wright.

In 1905 Mr. (now Sir Thomas) Colyer-Fergusson of Wombwell Hall and Ightham Mote transcribed our registers, and a complete typed copy of them in one volume is in the hands of the Vicar of Meopham; it has therefore made it easy to extract any entry of interest without the labour of deciphering the various specimens of orthography that the originals present.

The most notable names to be found in them are those of the Tradescants, father and son (*v.* Tradescant). The father, on June 18, 1607, married a certain "Elizabeth Daye"; and though not so stated, there can be little doubt the young lady was the youngest daughter of a former Vicar, the Rev. James Day (1576–1593). The first entry of this family is:

Año 1576. Ap. xxii. Jhon Day the s of Jeames Day, Vicar, his Borrowes were Jhon Child, Willm̃ Nordishe and Elizabeth Warren.

Then there follow in due course Daniell, Sara, Dorcas, Matthew, and on August 22, 1586, "Elizabeth, d. of Jeames Day," was baptized. Two years later was another son, "Samuell."

As Elizabeth married Tradescant in 1607, she was just twenty-one at that time. The following year—August 4, 1608—John, the son, was born of this marriage—a man destined to become almost if not quite as eminent as his father (*q.v.*).

Two other entries may be mentioned.

Under date January 31, 1758, is recorded the marriage of John Wade, surgeon, of Meopham. If this means that he practised here, it is an interesting record; for there is no other record of a resident doctor in the village till the arrival of Dr. Matthews, the predecessor of our present and valued surgeon, Dr. Griffiths.

In 1756 there were no marriages, and the scribe who made the following note of the fact was evidently something of a wag. It runs:

O.   Marriages out of fashion.

Against a signature at a wedding on October 12, 1775, is the curiously spelt note, "and I want at the weding"; and under date February 17, 1778, there is the register of the marriage of William Bennett of Luddesdown to Jane Weller of Meopham; and against the gentleman's name is the memo: "Minor, with consent of W. Bennett his father." It looks as though the Rev. Allen Fielding, Curate, who married them, desired to have it quite clear that he was not a party to a runaway marriage. The young lady was, I find by reference to the register of baptisms, twenty-three years of age, so had she inveigled William into marrying her, he not being twenty-one?

Charities. Old Meopham Wills

The custom of leaving by will sums of money for the benefit of the Church and of the poor was more frequent in the past than at present, for the simple reason that provision is made for these cases in a different way nowadays. Sometimes the bequest would be in the form of loaves of good wheaten bread for the poor, to be distributed every Sunday; and though such was never the case here, I can well remember as a boy the new loaves on shelves in the north aisle of Tonbridge Parish Church that used to be placed there for distribution after service in fulfilment of an old bequest.

Mr. Lewis says that he was able to obtain a list of our earliest charities through the courtesy of the Rev. T. S. Frampton of Platt, and I follow the order of his list; the entries under dates 1327 and 1517 I owe to the researches of Mr. A. A. Arnold of Cobham.

Cir. A.D. 950. Byrhtric the Saxon (*q.v.*) left a legacy in these terms:

To Wulfstane 60 mancuses of golde to deale for us and our elders; and other such to Wulfsic to deale and have they with God together, if they it do not.

This is taken to mean a distribution of money to the poor of Meopham.

1327

1st Edw. iii. Grant by Edmund de Mepham . . . of land in Mepham to a chaplain in the Chapel of S. James de la Dene in Mepham (*v.* Chap. XI).*

1460. "Hugo Chiddinstone de Mepehm" stated in his will:

* *Testamenta Cantiana*, published by the Kent Archaeological Society, 1907.

Corpus meum sepeliendum in Cimitio (cemeterio) ecclīe pochialis sancti Johannis Baptiste de Mepehm p̄ dict. Item lego summo altari p̂ d̄ce ecclīe xii d. Item lego summo altari ecclīe de Sundrissh sex solid̄ et octo denar̄. Item lego cuilit [cuilibet] eccliarum p̂ d̄tarum unum torticium p̂ cij [precii] septem solidorum. Item lego Repacionib₃ ecclie de Sundrissh xl. s. Item volo q̃d executores mei inveniant post decessum meum immediat̄ unū capellanū ydoneum p dimidiū anū pro anima mea & animab₃ bn̄factorum meorum diuina in ecclīa poch̄ de Mepehm p̄ dict celebratur̄ et habeat pro suo labore ꝑ idem tempus quinq₃ marcas.

Anglice:

My body to be buried in the churchyard of the parish church of St. John the Baptist at Mepeham, aforesaid. Item I leave to the High Altar of the aforesaid Church 12 pence. Item I leave to the High Altar of Sundrissh Church 6/8 . . . Item I leave to each of the aforesaid churches one torch (candle) of the value of seven shillings. Item I leave for the repairs of the church at Sundrissh 40s. . . . Item I will that my executors find at once after my decease a private chaplain to celebrate Mass, for six months in the aforesaid parish church of Mepeham for [the peace of] my soul and those of my benefactors; and he may have for his labour during that time five marks.

This will shows that the original dedication of our church was to St. John the Baptist (v. Dedication), and besides his gift to the high altar the testator bequeaths a goodly wax candle to be burnt in the church; and his "moneth minde" is to be celebrated for six months. Judging by his legacies he apparently was more of a "Sundrissh" than a "Mepeham" man.

This will was proved February 20, 1460.

1473. Thomas Strawton, citizen and fruiterer of London, in 1473 left 6/8 for the fabric of Meopham Church, i.e. "Church repairs," in these terms: "Itm̄ lego ffabrice ecclīe de Mepehm̄ in dict com̄ Kanc̄ vj s. viii d."

Will proved November 12, 1473.

1483. "Martyn Bloundell a cetezin and ffruterer of London" makes the following bequest: "Item I bequeth to the Chirch werks of Mepehm̅ in the Counte of Kent where my moder and I were borne and cristened iii s. iiij d."

Will proved March 22, 1483.

1517. Thomas Taylor of Rydlegh (Ridley) in his will says: "to be buried in the churchyard of Saynt John Baptiste in Mepham . . . to the reparation of the Church of Mepham xx^d, to the reparation of the Steeple and Belles there xx^d."*

1525. William Sprever of Dartford bequeathed as follows: "Also I bequeth to the most necessary repacioñ and other necessaryes bilonging to the pishe churche of Mephm̅ as the wardeyns and the parishe thinke best to be bestowed upon x s̃. Also to the light of Saint Kateryn in the same Churche xii^d." He leaves also 13/4 for solemn dirge and masses at his burial and as much for his "moneth mynde" at Meopham. Also to the wardens the profits of a "tenement lying at the parish cross within the parish of Meopham" to the value of 6/8 for a "yerely obite" to be kept for him and his friends in Meopham Church, whilst surplus moneys from the rent of this tenement are to be devoted to church repairs.

Regarding this bequest the following extract from Chantry Certificates, Roll 28, 2nd Ed. VI. m. 8 (Public Record Office) is of interest:

Obite rent gyven and bequethed to the parishe Churche of Meopham by the laste will & testm^t of Willm̅ Spreũ for that one yerelye obit shulde be kepte within the said Churche for eũ [ever].

The same rente is by the yere	vi^s	viij d.
Whõf to the pore there	ij^s	vi d.
And so remaineth clere	iiij^s	ij d.

* *Testamenta Cantiana*, published by the Kent Archaeological Society, 1907.

The will further gives to a nephew, Richard Sprever, lands and tenements at "Kenm̂" (i.e. Kenmer) "in the pishe of Mepehm," when he shall be of age in sixteen years; but failing this, or his having no heirs, this property is to be sold for the "best price and value that may be, and when it shall fortune to be put to sale to be openly proclaimed in the pulpitt of the parishe churche of Mepehm̃. And he that will geve most for hit to have hit." He put a reserve price of £8 6s. 8d. upon it, and when sold the purchase money is to be used to find a priest "to syng for my soule and my frend' in the said church of Mepehm̃ during the space of two yeres taking for his labour vj. li. And it to be paid quarterly. . . ." Finally, he gives out of the remainder of this purchase money 40/- "for the most necessary Repacions or other necessaryes bilonging to the parishe Church of Mepehm̃."

The bequests in the first part of this will had effect given to them, no doubt; but these last ones, being contingent upon the sale of the property, which again depended upon the life of a nephew, may never have materialized.

The will was proved July 14, 1525.

It was the abuse of the pulpit, as a good public place for announcing and advertising purely secular affairs, that gave rise to the wording of the Rubric in 1662 that follows the Nicene Creed, where restrictions are placed upon what shall be thus given out. (Ditchfield.)

Though Sprever was a Dartford man, he must have had some close connection with our village; and in "a coppie of yᵉ church assease made by yᵉ Parishioners in 1630" appear the names of Widow Sprever and Robert Sprever (v. Appendix Q).

The "moneth mind" and the "obite" are explained under the Funeral of the Sixteenth-century Vicar (q.v.).

1542. The will of "Richard Adene (a'Dene) of the pyshe of Seynt John Baptist in Meophm̃ gent." . . . "My body to be buryed in the Chapell of our Lady wᵗin the pyshe churche of Seynt John Baptyst in Meopham and for breaking of the ground there I give and bequeth vj s. viii d. Also I give and bequeth for my tythes and oblacions necligently forgotten or w^tholden to the High Altar there in discharging of my consyens iii s. iiii d. sterling. . . . Also I give and bequeth to Syr John Birde vicar of Meophm̅ vj s. viii d. sterling."

Will proved November 18, 1542.

The bequests in this will are only for what one may term post mortem benefits to himself! For on the testator's own confession he had been negligent in his gifts in support of his church, so now quiets his conscience for 3/4; and the legacy to the Vicar of 6/8 seems likely to have been prompted by the same desire. *Requiescat in pace!*

Legacies to the priest for tithes forgotten were not uncommon at this period.

1604. Robert Sprever bequeathed 13/4 to the Meopham poor, payable each Michaelmas for fifty years. Doubtless a descendant of the benefactor of 1525.

1617. Henry Haslen bequeathed £5 to the poor.
1618. Thomas Warren bequeathed £5 to the poor.
1618. Edward Haslen bequeathed £5 to the poor.
1620. Thomas Harman £10 17s. to the poor.
1623. Thomas Grinnell 8/- to the poor for ten years; distribution on St. Thomas's Day.
1629. Henry Audwell 6/8 to the poor.

1662. James Taylor (by his will dated July 7, 1656) left 10/- per annum for ever to the poor of Meopham (5/- at Christmas and 5/- at Easter); the gift to be provided by a small tenement at Wouldham.

1665. Judith Markland devised to the Churchwardens of Meopham, *for ever*, an annuity or yearly rent of £3 derived from certain lands and messuages, to be laid out as follows:

£1 to be paid to the "minister or Parson (of Meopham) for his pains to preach a sermon in the said Parish Church every New Years Day"; and £2 to be distributed "to twenty poor people being inhabitants of the said parish of Meopham in manner following, that is to say, to each of them two shillings, but if there shall not be so many poor people there then to such fewer number of poor people who shall happen to be there and then resident at the discretion of the Churchwardens." The money both to the minister and the poor is to be distributed immediately after the sermon.

If the Churchwardens fail in carrying out these conditions, a penalty of £10 is imposed on them as a fine.

(With the church books is a parchment leaf from a lost Churchwardens' book, containing a certified copy of the Markland will, made in 1666, with a record of the first distribution of the charity; and similar records are added for many years after.)

1843. By the will of Miss Frances Smith of Camer, the interest on a capital sum of £100 was left to be distributed annually to the poor at Christmas for ever.

1890. Mrs. Jane Frances Barnett of Meopham Court left £500 to be invested in 3% Consolidated Bank Annuities, in the names of the Vicar and Churchwardens of Meopham, upon Trust, for ever, to pay the interest thereon for the benefit of the poor in Meopham in such manner as the Trustees shall think best; the only proviso being that the distribution shall be on New Year's Day, or as soon after as convenient.

The last four bequests still hold good, and distribution of the funds still takes place in accordance with the various wishes of the donors.

Two entries dealing with the above charities may here be given:

1617

Memorandum that the daye and yeare above written Henry Haslen of this Parish did paye into the use of the Poore of Meopham and into our hands the some of five pounds which sayd sum was given in and by the last will and testament of Henry Haslen his father deceased and which said money was then distributed amonge the poore accordingly by us.

Thomas Pigott—James Taylor—Robert Bulcher— Thomas Ketteridge.

1623

Memorandum that Thomas Grinnell of this parish buried upon the second daye of February Anno. Dom. 1623 did in his last will and testament give and dispose to be yearly distributed among the Poor of this Parish the sum of 8/ to be paid into the hands of the Church officers always upon St. Thomas' Day by his exors: and this sum to continue by the space of ten years after the decease.

This donor gave his name to "Grinnell's Pond" (q.v.); he was also Churchwarden in 1616.

Similar entries in regard to the charities between 1618 and 1629 are to be found in our earliest Churchwardens' book (the one now missing).

A minute of the Parish Council of March 20, 1895, records the report of a committee the Council had appointed to consider the relationship of the Parish to these various trusts. It pointed out that at present (1895) there was only one of these charities (Smith's) in which the Parish Council had the power of joining in the administration by means of the appointment of an additional trustee. It further added that the "Barnet Charity, £520.16.8, invested in 2¾ % Bank Annuities, will eventually come under the same control, but not till 1930; till then it will be administered by the Vicar and Churchwardens."

There is one other charity—the Clay Cottages Charity—not a bequest, which will be treated of when speaking of the Parish affairs later on (v. Clay Cottages).

In 1853 a resolution was passed by the Easter Vestry that

a board with a list of benefactors to the Parish written upon it should be put up in the church, but nothing came of it. The same subject was again brought up at the Easter Vestry, April 9, 1896, and the same resolution was agreed upon, but the practical result was also the same!

Before leaving the subject of the charities the following from the Churchwardens' books are worth recording as throwing a sidelight on a practice that continued from Elizabeth's time to 1828:

1690	June	9th	Collected upon Bungay Brief 10/6
,,	July	6th	Collected upon Bishops Lavington Brief 5/2¼.
,,	July	30	Collected for Stafford Briefe 4/4¾
,,	Oct.	6	Collected for Southwark Briefe 8/1
,,	Nov.	23	Collected for Morpeth (Brief) 7/6
1691	April	5	Collected for Clopton Brief 6/1½
			Christopher Copland, Vicar.
1692			Two boxes to collect brief money 2/
1777			6 Briefs 1/– each.
1782			10 Briefs.
1799			Procurations, Briefs, etc. £1.0.8.

Cox, in his *How to Write the History of a Parish*, explains that these briefs were "Royal Letters Patent authorizing collections for charitable purposes, within churches, and sometimes from house to house." Their frequency at last becoming quite an abuse, it was ordered in the middle of the eighteenth century that they would only be granted on an application at Quarter Sessions. That they were frequent in this Parish, at any rate at times, is shown by the numerous entries for 1690; and in 1782 there were no less than ten issued. The repair or rebuilding of churches for long after the Reformation was carried on, says Cox, almost entirely by this means.

Our entries also show that these clearly were not only for the needs of our own Parish.

John Evelyn, in his *Diary*, has the following, under date May 29, 1686: "A Brief was read in all Churches for relieving the French Protestants, who came here for protection," etc. Briefs were also issued for the benefit of individuals, as the historic instance of Stow, the sixteenth-century antiquarian and author of the *Survey of London*, shows. A full account of it is given in *Knight's London*.

Although the name has been dropped, and legal authorization is no longer required, the spirit of the brief is not dead in this twentieth century.

CHAPTER VI

THE CHURCH BELLS

THE Meopham peal consisted of five bells till 1910, when the sixth was added. The description of the five bells I quote from Mr. Lewis, with the inscription on each:

Treble. Diam. 31 in. (C♯) I.S.R.W. Antony Bartlett, Michael Darbie made mee 1650.

Second. Diam. 32 in. (B) John and Christopher Hodson maide me 1677. William Swift, Francis Bright, Churchwardens.

Third. Diam. 34½ in. (A♯) John and Christopher Hodson made me 1677.

Fourth (Clock Bell). Diam. 37 in. (G♯) Michael Darbie made me 1651.

Tenor. Diam. 40 in. (F♯) Christopher Hodson made me 1679. William Swift and Francis Bright, Churchwardens.

The letters I.S.R.W. on the first bell clearly are the initials of the Churchwardens at that time, John Skirmer and Robert Whiffin.

From measurements taken in Mr. Lewis's time and forwarded to Messrs. Mears & Stainbank, the successors of Bartlett, in Whitechapel, the weights (approximate) of our bells were calculated to be as follows:

Treble	5½	cwt.
Second	6½	,,
Third	7½	,,
Fourth	9	,,
Tenor	12	,,

The dates on the bells are, of course, those of their casting or final recasting; and the first account of any casting of bells is in the oldest Churchwardens' book under date 1648. The names of the bell founders are not given, nor does it say if *all* the bells were then cast or not; but the fact that "crainding at Gravesend" is charged clearly points to Bartlett & Darbie of Whitechapel having been the founders.

The entry above referred to is as follows:

1648	£	s.	d.
Laid out for casting the new bells and for 100 of "mettle"	20.	10.	0
Paid for hanging the bells	1.	9.	0
Carriage and cost of 18 feet of timber	1.	10.	0
Paid for bread and beer and other charges for the bell founders		11.	0
Paid for wharfage, weighing, crainding and carriage .		13.	0
Paid for charges of the Bell founders and ourselves .		14.	0
Paid for taking down the Bells		5.	0
Paid for fetching and carrying the Bells		10.	0
Paid for carriage of the Bells up and down . . .		16.	0
Paid for carrying the Bells to Gravesend and fetching		10.	0
Paid for weighing of the Bells in and out . . .		13.	0
Paid for wharfage and crainding		6.	0
Paid for charges of them by water up and down, and crainding at Gravesend		14.	0

It might seem as though the bells still bearing Bartlett & Darbie's names were referred to, but this cannot be the case, since three years later the same firm did a further recasting here in Meopham. Mr. Lewis was much puzzled to account for this second casting, and finally adopted the view—and I think his supposition must be correct—that injury was done to our bells just after they were cast in 1648 by General Fairfax's army, which encamped here that year. The accounts show that all the bells were recast except the treble bell—that is, four out of the five; and the treble now bears the date 1650, as though it were first cast, and then on being hung and rung it necessitated the others, in the next year, being altered to harmonize with it. However that may be, it is certain that the other four were recast in 1651, and the record is as follows:

1651–1652			
Paid to Michael Darbie for casting the Second and Tennor	£4.	0.	0
Paid for a hundred and three pounds of Bell Metal for the third and fourth bells	£4.	18.	0
For hanging the bells		7.	6
Bell Ropes		7.	6

Bell Clapper	6.	0
Bell Ropes	7.	0
Hanging the bells.	17.	6
For Coals to dry the moulds for the Bells . . .	10.	0
For the casting of the Bells . . . . . £2.	10.	0
For casting the third and Tenor . . . . £4.	0.	0
For wood to melt the Tenner	10.	0
Three bell ropes	9.	10
do.	12.	10
To Henry Reeve for taking down the Tenor . . .	5.	0
Bell Wheel	10.	0

The local casting of bells was not uncommon, either in the churchyard or some neighbouring field, the moulds being dug in the soil; and Michael Darbie was an itinerant bell founder employed by Bartlett of Whitechapel. Of this casting only one bell remains, our fourth or "clock" bell, bearing the date 1651.

A quarter of a century later three of the bells were again recast; it can scarcely be that the casting at Meopham had been unsatisfactory, for the bells had answered their purpose for so many years. Something must have happened to them—perhaps they cracked; at any rate it was determined to change them, and this time another firm was employed, viz. John and Christopher Hudson, who had a bell foundry at St. Mary Cray. The three bells still bearing their names are, however, differently dated; two are 1677 and one 1670. This apparent discrepancy, in view of what follows, can be easily explained. Owing to the recent loss of our oldest Churchwardens' book, I have had to rely on the copy made of the entries by Mr. Lewis; two of these given by him in full are quoted above; the following, however, are sufficient to explain the different dates on these bells:

1677.   Paid to the Bell founders £15.

This clearly refers to our two bells bearing this date.

1679.   Paid when the bell was taken down 6d.
1679.   Paid for carrying the bell to St. Mary Cray £1.0.0

These refer to the tenor bell bearing the date 1679. Then:

1680. Paid at the casting of the bell at St. Mary Cray 2/2.
  Spent at the Georg. [*sic*] when the bells were taken down 2/-.
1680. Paid the bailiff when I was arrested 5/.
1680. Paid my charges at the suit of Hudson £4.6.0. [This Churchwarden was Mr. Swift of the Court. The other was Francis Bright, and he was mulcted in the same amount.]
1680. Paid Mr. Hudson towards the bells £38.5.2.
1680. Charges at the suit of Hudson £4.0.0.

From the above, which now are rather amusing reading, though hardly so to the parties concerned, it would appear as though two bells were first sent to St. Mary Cray and £15 paid for recasting them, a sum apparently "on account"; then in 1679 the tenor is sent, and though cast at once, as its date shows, some disagreement must have arisen over the payment, which ended in 1680 in the arrest of Mr. Swift, the Church-warden (and presumably of Francis Bright also). The balance due to the founders, £38 5s. 2d., was finally paid, which, with the £15 already paid, brought the total for the three bells to about £53. Judging by the former account for recasting, it looks as though this time one or more of the bells must have been new and not merely recast.

These three bells cast by the Hudsons are all impressed with the patterns of the crown or half-crown of Charles II. One bears the impress of an oval medallion, but it is too obliterated for its meaning to be deciphered.

In 1837, when the church tower was raised 20 feet, the bells had to be taken down, and were not rehung until 1840, their removal and replacement costing £12.

The Sixth Bell

When in 1837 the new bell-chamber was built, an endeavour was made to raise money to add a sixth bell; and though this attempt failed, yet room was left for one to be added at some future time; and the sixth bell became an accomplished fact in 1910.

It was subscribed for by the Parish in memory of King Edward VII, and was hung in October 1910. The inscription on it tells its tale.

MEARS ET STAINBANK . LONDINI . FACERUNT

A . M   D . G

IN   MEMORIAM   EDWARDI   SEPTIMI

OMNIBUS   GENTIBUS   AMANTER   VENERANDI

SEPTEMBER   1910

The bell was hoisted into position directly from the ground, being passed into the bell-chamber through its south window after removal of the wooden louvre.

Having now six bells, and starting with the new one as treble, the village peal is: D♯, C♯, B, A♯, G♯, F♯.

When the new bell was put in, tuning and repairs of the old bells were also undertaken, and the total cost came to £123 12s. 1d.

Up to the early part of the last century the church bells were a distinct feature in the life of the village, for, not confined to the services of the church, they were called into operation on every possible public occasion. This accounts for the repeated entries for new bell ropes, one of which is rather quaint: "1647 Ropps for the Bells 16/-." A slacking off of the practice of bell-ringing is shown under 1835: "May 28. The Parish not to pay any more money for the ringing of the Church Bells on the 5th of Novr and the 29th of May." The following extracts show the varied uses of our peal, and also that Meopham largely rejoiced at being relieved of the presence of James II and the success of William of Orange.

1689

Paid for a form of prayer and proclamation for the Prince of
  Wales 2/

For mending the Belfry door and the church Style [*sic*] 3/9

For the book of prayer on account of the Invasion 1/

For the parator [apparitor] for a form of prayer and thanksgiving for the Prince of Orange's success 1/6

Paid to Barker for altering the prayer concerning the King and
  Queen 1/6

Ringers on Coronation Day 2/6

1691

Ringers upon the King's return from Ireland 5/

Given the Ringers Nov. 5. 3/

Given the Ringers for the battle of the Boyne 2/6

1692

Ringers on Gunpowder Treason 6/

1693

Ringers for the victory at Sea 3/
  for ringing 4 several days 12/
  for King's Birthday 3/
  for Gunpowder Treason 8/
  for Thanksgiving 3/
  for Coronation Day 3/

1694

Paid John Reeve for ye knell of 3 hours ye day ye Queen [i.e.
Queen Mary] was buried 3/

Owing to our having such a good peal of bells, change-
ringing has always been practised in Meopham, and from time
to time the village has had strong teams of ringers. As long
as the bells were rung from the level of the church floor the
sound of the bells high up in the tower did not interfere with
the ringers; but in 1915 the Vicar, Mr. Owen, had a deadening
floor inserted above the present ringing chamber, which is just
below the bell-chamber. The ringing of the peal is peculiarly
English, and dates from the ninth century, when the first peal
in England was rung in Crowland Abbey; and Meopham has
never lost touch with the custom.

The knell or passing bell has till quite late times been observed here regularly. Originally intended to be sounded when a parishioner was on the point of death, that those who heard it might offer a prayer on his behalf, it has now become the means of announcing that a parishioner has died; and on this Mr. Lewis has the following remark: "One of the ancient Canons of the Church prescribes, 'When any is passing out of this life a bell shall be tolled, and the minister shall not then slack to do his duty' . . . The following rules are observed in this parish in tolling the 'passing bell': For a man, three tolls on the Great Bell, three times repeated. For a woman, two tolls on the Great Bell, three times repeated. For a (boy) child, three tolls on Treble Bell, three times repeated. For a (girl) child, two tolls on Treble Bell, three times repeated. This preliminary tolling is followed by tolling the same bell for half an hour. It is no modern system, but is mentioned by a writer on ecclesiastical law in the beginning of the twelfth century, when laying down the rules of the Church in tolling the knell: 'Let this be done twice for a woman, thrice for a man, and at the conclusion a peal on all the bells.'"

CHAPTER VII

BURIALS IN THE CHURCH

BURIALS within the four walls of a church were common till the last century, and the custom is known to be as old as the time of St. Augustine's visit to England at the end of the sixth century.

In the floor of our church at the west end of the nave are a number of inscribed memorial pavement stones representing such interments in old days; and the greater number have been removed from the chancel—where the burials had taken place—at the time that the floor was tiled (1859). Only one of the original stones remains within the altar rails; it will be described later on. The chancel was for centuries the burial-place of the clergy and of the occupants of the Court. The north wall of the church holds the memorial tablets to various generations of the occupants of Camer.

The following list of the memorials—other than windows —in the church was compiled by Mr. Lewis, the Vicar, in 1894:

In the Chancel.

Thirteenth century inscribed slab; name unknown (see below).
Rev. John Folsham—a brass (see below).
Francis Markett 1821 (not buried here).
Sir John Bayley, Bart. 1841, and his wife, Elizabeth, 1837 (see under "Notable People").
Elizabeth Bayley (daughter-in-law) 1838.
Isabella Markett 1851.
Percy Markett (her daughter).

In the Nave: North Wall.

Katherine Masters 1750.
George Masters 1757.
William Masters 1761.
William Smith 1764.

In the Nave: North Wall—continued

Catherine Smith 1777.
Rebecca Smith 1802.
Catherine Smith 1814

George Smith 1834.
Rebecca Smith 1832.
William Smith-Masters, M.P. 1861.

William Smith 1830.
Henry Masters-Smith 1832.
Catherine Smith 1839.

South Wall.

John Baber, M.D. 1894.
Emma (*née* Du Bois) his wife 1875.

On Pavement (of Nave).

(Some have been removed here from the chancel.)

William Mungeam 1818.
Sarah Mungeam 1825.

Thomas Copland 1739.

Joseph Rabenett 1718.
Melchia Rabenett 1724.

Elizabeth Copland 1699.

Martha Bay 1707.
Mrs. Martha Evenden 1725.

Elizabeth Gunning 1745.

Mrs. Margaret Copland 1727.

Robert Scriver 1639.

Henry Stickings 1773.
Mary Stickings 1750.

Henry —— 1618.

Catherine Thesdell 1767.
Samuel Thesdell 1801.

On Pavement (of Nave)—continued

{ Ann Markett 1763.
{ John Markett 1801.

John Markett 1789.

Ann Markett 1775.

Rev. Christopher Copland, Vicar, 1707 (see below).

Besides the memorial mentioned in this list to Elizabeth Gunning, 1736, there are in the churchyard the tombs of six of the same family ranging between 1702 and 1783. The Kentish Gunnings were large landed proprietors in the county in Henry VIII's time; early in the seventeenth century a branch migrated to Ireland, where the celebrated beauties, the Miss Gunnings, were born. These two ladies and their sister— afterwards Lady Lyster—were the sisters of General John Gunning of Roscommon, Ireland, who married a Somerset lady in 1768, well known later as authoress and playwright, whose daughter Elizabeth was also a noted beauty and authoress as well. The above-mentioned beauties, Elizabeth and Maria—who became in 1752 the Duchess of Hamilton and subsequently of Argyll, and Countess of Coventry respectively—were held to be the "handsomest women alive," Maria being the handsomer. The king, George II, took great notice of the Countess, and on account of her being mobbed when she went out in the park, His Majesty offered her military protection, which she accepted! And the next Sunday—in June 1759—she actually walked in the Park with a halberdier each side of her and twenty foot soldiers behind! (*Dictionary of National Biography*).

By the marriage of a Mr. Peter Gunning with Katherine Baker in 1814, and of this lady's brother, Thomas Baker, with Miss Maria Edmeades of "Jeskins" in 1822, the two families of Nurstead, and of the "Owletts," Cobham, became united; and the son, Thomas Henry, of the last-mentioned couple was the late owner of "Owletts," and his widow still (1915) resides there. The present owner and occupier is Sir Herbert Baker, the well-known architect, and this lady's son (1934).

A sister of George Masters of Camer married Robert Gunning of Cobham, and she is buried in our churchyard (1736), as is also her daughter Elizabeth, in 1783. Their tombs are still cared for by members of the family.

We have two very ancient memorials of old chancel burials; one a small brass, the other a stone from which the brass has been torn. There is nothing now to show that our church ever had more than these two brasses, though tradition speaks of several (see below). The brass, an inscription 15 inches by 3 inches and let into a rough piece of stone, from which (by marks upon it) efforts have been made to prize the metal up, lay till March 25, 1905, on the floor of the tower, so its original position is unknown. At that date the late Mr. Tweddell gave permission to the writer to have it and its stone let into the south wall of the chancel within the altar rails, where it still is to be seen. The inscription is in the usual abbreviated Latin, but, expanded, runs as follows:

Hic jacet Dominus Johannes Folsham quondam Vicarius de Meapham qui obiit tredecimo die mensis Junii Anno Domini millesimo CCCC° LV° cujus animae propicietur Deus.   Amen.

Anglice:

Here lies Master John Folsham, formerly Vicar of Meapham, who died on the 13th day of June in the year 1455, on whose soul God have mercy.   Amen.

As Folsham's successor was appointed in 1452, it seems clear that Folsham resigned in that year; and the wording of the inscription, "formerly Vicar of," suggests that he had ceased to be Vicar an appreciable time before his death: he had been Vicar since 1414.

The pavement tombstone from which the brass has been torn was originally on the north of the altar, but was moved in 1859 to the front, just within the rails; it is now covered with a piece of carpet.

The inscription was deeply cut in the stone before the molten brass was poured into it; and in 1769 the well-known archaeologist and writer, John Thorpe, deciphered it as follows:

Credo quod in nov[issimo] di[e] de t[erra] [surr]ecturus sum et in ca[rne] mea vid[ebo] Deum S[alvatorem] m[eum]. Hœ[c] [fi]des reposita est in sinu meo.

Anglice:

I believe that in the last day I shall rise again from the earth and in my flesh shall see God my Saviour. This faith is buried in my bosom.

The inscription is written round the stone in Gothic letters, and the middle is occupied by a floriated cross; the style of the whole belongs to the thirteenth century. There is no name.

This is the oldest tomb record we possess here, and the disappearance of the brass may be due to the presence in the church of some of General Fairfax's army on the night of May 31, 1648. The Parliamentary soldiers were merciful to no monuments, brasses, bells, or stained-glass windows. One other explanation is given by John Thorpe in his *Registrum Roffense*, a work written in the first half of the eighteenth century. He writes: "Mr. Copland of Meopham says that within the memory of several old men now living at Meopham some of the Bells of the Church being to be new cast, and there being an insufficient quantity of metal to do it, some persons (one of which is now living) tore off all the brass inscriptions from the stones in the Church, except that of Follham [*sic*] before mentioned, and threw them into the melted metal, to add to its quantity for casting the bells."

The Rev. Christopher Copland was the Vicar of Meopham from 1670 to 1707; and supposing Thorpe's interview with him took place only just before the Vicar's death, an old man of seventy-five would have been twenty-five years of age at the recasting in 1650 which was done at Meopham. I venture, therefore, to think that the statement about the brasses being used in the bells may be correct, though it seems strange that only one flagstone from which the metal had been torn should now survive. One fact against the brasses being thus used, however, and insisted on by Mr. Lewis, must in honesty be mentioned, and that is that the addition of the brass from "brasses" would be very detrimental to the bells, as this metal contains a fair proportion of lead, and good bell metal is only of copper and tin.

The tombstone of the Rev. C. Copland, just mentioned, bears the following inscription:

Hic depositae sunt Exuviae viri Reverendi Christopheri Copland hujus Ecclesiae Vicarii. Qui Ministerii annis 37 vitae 61 impletis exteriorem hanc Mysteriorum cum visione commutavit.

(Here are buried the bodily remains of the Reverend Christopher Copland, Vicar of this church; who, having completed 37 years of his ministry out of a life of 61 years exchanged this outward dispensation of the Mysteries for the vision of God.)

He died in 1707.

Churchyard and Burials

Leave to enclose and consecrate ground immediately round a church was not obtained, it is said, till the eighth century, by the influence of Archbishop Cuthbert of Canterbury (740–758); and the rich, when not buried *in* the church, would also build sepulchral chambers or chantries attached to the church, and endow them for the support of priests to say masses for their souls' welfare and those of their descendants who should be buried with them afterwards. I will, when speaking of Archbishop Simon de Meopham, discuss the possibility of what is now the vestry having been used as one of these chantries.

Our churchyard—the old and beautiful name for these enclosures was also "God's acre"—is just 1 acre, 2 rods, 10 perches, not counting the 25 perches occupied by the church itself. Except on the west side it is fenced round, and, from frequent entries in the church books of the repair of the fences in old times, it would seem to have been always thus enclosed; but on the west it has a rubble flint wall now, and for long past. It is at present capped with worked stone, some stones being chamfered and channelled, evidently once part of the church walls. The Rev. Mr. Hooper used to say that they once formed a parapet along the tops of the aisle walls.

Access in the seventeenth century was gained by a stile; there is this entry in the books: "1684. Churchyard Style 6/-"; and as in 1652 appears "Thomas Johnson for making a gate for the churchyard," it would seem that one entrance was at any rate a gateway—probably the south one.

It must be owned that there was a time when "God's acre" was not treated—to our present way of thinking—with the reverence due to it; and what I am about to mention applies to churchyards generally, and not ours alone. Thus it is on record that in 1638 an official inquiry was held into church matters generally, and the question was asked if plays, suppers, banquets, church ales, court-leets, musters, dancing, and football were held in the churches or churchyards. It is further on record that in 1640, on certain occasions—one being the Saint's Day or Name Day of the church—faits were held in the churchyard, and tradesmen brought their wares to sell there. It is a matter of common knowledge that the nave of old St. Paul's was the regular place for business people to meet and transact their affairs, and for attorneys to meet their clients.

All this was a relapse from the year 1603 (Queen Elizabeth), when it was ordered that "The churchwardens shall suffer no plays, feasts, suppers, Church-ales . . . to be kept in the Church or Church Yard."

The church ales require a few remarks. They were periodical festive gatherings held in connection with a church. Stubbes, a writer in 1583, in his *Anatomie of Abuses*, says: "Against a Xmas, an Easter or some other day the Churchwardens provide a score or twenty quarters of mault; which mault being made into very strong ale or beere is set to sale either in the Church or in some other place. . . . they repair their churches with it and they buy books for service, cuppes for the celebration of the sacrament, surplesses for Sir John, and such other necessaries" (quoted by Hazlitt). The money for the ale was partly provided out of the money in the hands of the Churchwardens and partly out of contributions made by the parishioners. Doubtless the object was a worthy one, and the suppression of the church ales must have been called for by the abuses sure to follow the imbibition of the "strong ale or beere." The ale, however, does not seem to have been always of this kind; for Peacock (*Architect. Journal*, vol. xl), quoted by Cardinal Gasquet (*Parish Life in Medieval England*), says: "The drink itself was apparently a sweet beverage made with hops or bitter herbs. It was not the same as our modern beer, but was less heavy and hardly an intoxicant."

The modern outdoor summer church bazaar would seem to be the lineal descendant of the church ales.

Writing on the churchyard burials, Mr. Lewis pointed out that there were 359 named (and legible) tombstones or memorials in 1898, and draws attention to the proportion of burials in the different aspects of the burial-ground, the greater number being on the south side (eighty-nine), though closely followed by eighty-seven on the north. Writers on this subject all agree that there is a preference always for the south side, the north side of the church being in some instances invariably chosen for still-born infants and suicides! The reasons for the south of the churchyard being most chosen—and they seem sufficient to explain it—are that it is the bright and sunny side, and also that which is crossed by the path by which in most cases in the country the church is entered, worshippers being thus on every Sunday reminded of their departed relatives. A few years ago it became necessary to enlarge the churchyard, so on March 27, 1919, part of a field opposite the church was duly consecrated for the purpose. A lych-gate, designed by Sir Herbert Baker, and dedicated to the memory of the late Vicar, Rev. A. G. Tait, was erected in 1934.

Our oldest tombstones are those of Richard Masters (1689) and of Nicholas Piggott (1701).

The late Rev. T. S. Cogswell, son of an old and respected former parishioner, drew up a list of all the burials. It will be found in Appendix E.

Though sometimes buried, as said, on the north side of the churchyard, yet generally suicides used to be buried near to but outside the consecrated ground; our books afford these instances:

Robert Cooke was buried without the wall of the Church Yard near the passage to the entrance of the said Church Yard, on the South Side, having murdered himself by hanging in his House at Pitfield Green in Meopham, A.D. 1667.

1697. Anne Withen, who threw herself into a well in "Pitfield Green," was buried near where the former suicide had been, at the south entrance of the churchyard. The well must be that at the Green Farm; it is the only one in Pitfield Green.

Everyone knows—or thinks he does—what a "winding-sheet" is; but no man living, I am confident, ever saw one, for it was that in which the corpse was wrapped when not buried in a coffin. Up to about three hundred years ago burial in the churchyard without a coffin was the custom, except in the case of rich or notable people; and as late as 1638 coffin or non-coffin burial was a matter of choice. For the scale of fees in force in that year in the parish of Birchington ran thus: "Coffined Grave 8d.; no coffin grave 6d."

Coffins, then, are a comparatively recent introduction for the people generally, and we need not consider such a church-yard as ours as over-full because it has been a thousand years in use, for whilst coffins undoubtedly prolong the occupancy of any spot of ground, the places where hundreds of the "rude forefathers of the hamlet sleep" are no longer traceable; their mortal remains, being buried merely in a winding-sheet, soon disappeared, incorporated with the dust from which they sprang.

In our old church books are some curious entries, as: "1755. John Elliots daughter hanged herself. Paid Jury 6/. Coffin 9/. Beer at her Burial 5/. Digging grave 2/. A pound of wool and laying her forth 2/."; "1762. 1 lb. of wool and carding" and "1776 a woolen shroud"; and old registers everywhere show similar entries, such as "buried in Wollen or woolen." From early times wool had been the staple commodity of England, and in order to keep the price up and add to its market, it was enacted by Parliament in 1667 that "no person shall be buried in any shirt or sheet other than should be made of wool"; and in 1678 (30th Charles II) it was enacted that in registering burials an entry was to be made that the Act had been complied with under a penalty of £5. This Act was in force till 1814 (54th of George III), though a dead letter long before that year.

In the register of Trottescliffe Church is the following:

Aug: ye 26th 1719. There was buried in Woollen Ann Helker of ye parish of Mepham. Affidavit was made before Mr. Wright vic: of de Mepham.

In *The Bride of Lammermoor* Scott, in describing old Alice's burial, mentions her being shrouded in woollen.

The 1 lb. of wool just mentioned, under date 1775, is now explained; instead of wrapping the corpse in a woollen shroud or providing a woollen sheet, a pound of wool was put into the coffin and buried with the body in order to comply with the Act and avoid a heavy fine! Dr. F. W. Cock, the well-known Kent antiquarian, stated to the writer: "I remember I was told by an old woman at Battle, in 1884, that as a girl she had helped to card the wool," i.e. comb it out of the fleece into the coffin over the corpse.

Among Mr. Lewis's papers I find the following manuscript, which must be given in full; it is of profound interest, and unique. It gives the estate and funeral expenses of a former Vicar, in Henry VIII's reign, and must refer to either the Rev. William Marshall (1524–1533) or the Rev. John Byrde

(1533–1550); the name, however, is torn from the top of the document. He was buried in the chancel, as one entry shows: "for his gravemaking in the quere [choir]".

The mutilated title should read: "Memorandum of the receipts of —— Vicar of Mepeham. Goods when he died."

TRANSCRIPT FROM MS. SLIP OF PAPER IN THE LIBRARY AT CANTERBURY

M^d of the rese   Mepeh$\overline{\overset{oo}{m}}$
good when he

In hys purse was	iiij^s	iiij^d
Itm̃ on 'Mydsom̃ day for offeryng	v^s	x^d
Itm̃ at the beryeng of ffullars chyld off'		vj^d
Itm̃ for candell to offerre		j^d
Itm̃ at the beryeng of John Myllare		iiij^{d}ob
Itm̃ at the weddyng of Willm̃ Warreyn . . .		xvj^d
Itm̃ reseyued for xxxijth tythe lambys ⎫ viij^d a pece . . . . . ⎭ . . .	xxj^s	iiij^d
Itm̃ reseyued for x. stonne of tythe Woolle ⎫ p̄c' the ston' xviij^d Sm̄ . . . ⎭ . .	xv^s	
Itm̃ reseyued of Rob̃t Mede for tythe cheryes . . .		xij^d
Itm̃ of Edmund Style for tythe cherys		vj^d
Itm̃ for Mortuarys that dyed ij pro-unts ⎫ of the fferme at deenyz . . . . ⎭ . .	iiij^s	
Itm̃ reseyued of Stonyng of Snotlond ⎫ for tythe wode . . . . . ⎭ . .	ij^s	iiij^d
Itm̃ for seche goods as was there at ⎫ Mephm̃ whan he dyed an envetery made ⎪ thereof and preysed by John Overey ⎬ Sm̄a . . xix^s and Willm Coke, smyth ⎭		

Sm̃ . . . iij^{li} xv^s ix^d oƀ

M^d of the payment for the vekery first

at hys beryeng for bred.		xij^d
Itm̃ for on' dusseyn and half of ale	ij^s	vj^d
Itm̃ in beeff'		iiij^d
Itm̃ a pegge p̄c'		iij^d
Itm̃ for chese at the churche		vj^d
Itm̃ for hys gve [grave] makyng in the quere . . .		iiij^d
Itm̃ for hys knylle and for ryngyng		viij^d

Itm̃ for the wast of lyghts abowght the corss . . . . . } . . . .   iiij^d

Itm̃ for the wast of vj torchys . . . . . .   xij^d

Itm̃ to vj powre men that held the torchys . . .   vj^d

Itm̃ to vj prests that sang masse . . . . . . ij^s

Itm̃ to ij clarks that day . . . .   iiij^d

Itm̃ to a prest that Sang masse days byfore . . . } . . . . .   viij^d

Itm̃ to a man that goed to london to my lord . . .   iiij^d

Itm̃ for makyng of iiij tapyrs . . . . . .   ij^d

Itm̃ for Syngyng bred and wyne . . . . .   j^d

Itm̃ at hys moneth mend to ij prests that ware at the masse and diryge } . . . .   xij^d

Itm̃ to v prests more at the masse . . . . .   xx^d

Itm̃ to iij clarks . . . .   vj^d

Itm̃ to vj powre men that heyld torchys . . . .   vj^d

Itm̃ payed for waxe that daye . . . . . .   j^d

Itm̃ to the clarke for the bellys . . . . . .   iij^d

Itm̃ spended v busshells of wheth in bred . . . vj^s iij^d

Itm̃ a quart of malt in Ale . . . . v^s iiij^d

Itm̃ in beeff' . . . .   xiij^d

Itm̃ half a veelle p̃c' . . . .   x^d

Itm̃ ij geesee p̃c' . . . .   viij^d

Itm̃ for a capon p̃c' . . . .   xij^d

Itm̃ for Spycs . . . .   iij^d

Itm̃ for bakyng brewyng and dressyng of mete and for
my besinesse and my wyvys wessyng and wrynggyng

"fferme at deenyz' " = Dene Farm.
"Mortuarys" = payments on death.
"p c" = priced (at).
"Vekery" = Vicar.
"wyvys wessyng and wrynggyng" = women (for) washing and
wringing.

"Moneth mend" (also written "Moneth's mond" and
"moneth mind") was a memorial mass held a month later for
the repose of the deceased's soul. It, and the "obit," which
was a similar service held soon after the burial, were often
provided for by will. Thus the will of Thomas Windsor, who
died in 1479, provides as follows: "Item that there be a
hundred children within the age of 16 years to be at my

moneths minde, to say for my soul. That against my moneths minde the candles bren before the Rude in the Parish Church" (*Gentleman's Magazine*, 1793, lxiii, 1191).

Of the obit, Dr. Gasquet remarks that the "obite rent or obits were for the most part money left quite as much for annual alms to the poor as for the celebration of any anniversary offices." The obits were, when it was so arranged, repeated yearly, and our memorial services, which have been adopted largely in late years, seem to be lineal descendants of these old services.

The funeral feast, as well as that at the moneth's minde, seems to have been on a liberal scale, and the beer was not forgotten.

The use of lights dates from pre-Christian times, but they were retained by Christians to "shew that the departed soules are not quite put out, but having walked here as children of the light are now gone to walk before God in the light of the living" (Gregory 1649, quoted by Hazlitt).

The rest of the document speaks for itself.

The Tombstones

Stones, single or as buildings, have in every part of the world, and before history was, been erected in memory of the dead; and all have more or less meaning, apart from any inscription they may bear.

Our churchyard has a good variety of the forms of grave-stones commonly met with in old burial-grounds. We have the square, box-like form of tomb of upright side stones with a cover or cap stone, the whole generally enclosed with iron railings, which must be surely the lineal descendant of the dolmen of old times, of which Kits Coty House on Blue Bell Hill above Maidstone is a good example, and familiar to most Kentish people.

But it is in the simple gravestone that we find variety.

Hardly ever straight along the top, though sometimes

curved like a Cupid's bow, most of the old ones show forms that have a distinct meaning. In these the top is slowed up towards the middle, where it rises into a more or less rounded head or projection. This is taken to represent the head and shoulders of the deceased, and a face may be seen rudely carved on the flat surface of the top projection. Sometimes it is occupied by a skull and cross-bones—emblems of death—instead.

Some of these stones have double projections at the top, representative of husband and wife; and on careful inspection it can be made out that on one in our churchyard is the face of the man, rudely carved in relief, and on the other the woman; it must be confessed, however, that were it not for a species of cap also carved, the sex could not be distinguished by the features.

This is the case in the oldest tombstone with a legible inscription, to Richard Master and his wife Joan, 1689; and it was in the seventeenth century that tombstones came into use in churchyards. These early ones, of which we have several, were 5 to 6 inches thick, bevelled at the top and curved; the figures or faces at the top of the stone were scratched in a very primitive style, and not sculptured in bas-relief. On the east side of the churchyard are the two tombstones of Thomas Edmeades, *aet.* 34, 1723, and of Sarah his wife, *aet.* 36, 1728, placed side by side; the former has a skull and cross-bones carved in lieu of the man's face, but the wife's face is represented. There is also a curious carving on a more modern stone of a closed hand with the thumb pointing downwards—a sinister meaning, if interpreted classically.

Mr. F. J. Bennett, in his well-known book on Ightham, devotes a chapter to this subject of tombstones, which he made a full study of, and draws attention to the often quaint bas-reliefs carved on headstones above the inscription—and indeed, he uses these as ground for classification of them into four groups. There is a curious instance on the south side of our churchyard near the tower, which shows Father Time reclining on one elbow, with his scythe and a skull beside him. This is of course a familiar emblem, but I mention it, as I have been seriously told by a parishioner—and I gather the belief is common here—that it is the gravestone of a man who lost his life in the hayfield or harvest-field by having his head cut off; witness the scythe, and the head on the ground!

Emblems of Immortality and the Resurrection, such as angels, cherubs, the rising sun—perhaps with an eye, the eye of God, introduced—are often, too, employed on tombs; and in the case of a husband the surviving widow may be seen depicted weeping over a funereal urn.

Edwin Harris, in his local historical publications, has the following paragraph: "Old Sayings: 'Cobham Churchyard's full of Savages,' 'Northfleet Churchyard's full of Badgers,' Meopham Churchyard's full of Buggs.' " The name of Buggs has existed in the parish from the eighteenth century.

A further reference to our churchyard will appear under the account of Simon de Meopham.

The late Mr. Lewis compiled in 1899 a list of all the epitaphs in the church and churchyard; they were for the most part of the old and hackneyed variety. He also gave at the same time the number of tombs in the churchyard with legible inscriptions as 359, and the total burials for the nineteenth century as 1697. The numbers in the eighteenth and seventeenth centuries, owing to imperfections in the registers, he could not state accurately, but estimated them at 1,300 and 1,117 respectively. He found no instance of a centenarian in the Parish, the oldest parishioner buried in our churchyard being James Killick, *aet.* 97, in 1889. There is, however, on the south wall of Milton Church a memorial-stone to Elizabeth Ribbens, who died in 1862 at the age of 105; she was Meopham-born, but lived her life in Gravesend. The epitaphs, etc., were fully set forth in the *Parish Magazine* for 1889.

CHAPTER VIII

INCOME OF THE CHURCH, RECTORS AND VICARS

IT has been mentioned that the widow of King Athelstan presented the Manor of Meopham to the Prior and Monks of Christ Church, Canterbury, and in their possession it remained till Henry VIII's time (1542); but the advowson and patronage of the church had a rather chequered existence.

The income of old churches was and is still often derived from tithes; but at times the larger tithes would be appropriated, much to the impoverishment of the parish, and employed for perhaps the cathedral or monastery; and the incumbent, receiving only the lesser tithes, lost his title of Rector and became Vicar.

All this has happened at Meopham. I here quote from Mr. Lewis:

It seems that before the Norman Conquest all the Manors, Benefices, and lands which belonged to the monastery of Christ Church, Canterbury, were shared by the Archbishop, who was in reality the head of the house and stood in the position of an Abbot. When Lanfranc, in 1070, succeeded to the See he separated the rights of the Archbishop from those of the monks, apportioning to them the manorial rights, rents and revenues, and the tithes* except those of corn, vegetables, and hay, while he retained for himself the advowson and patronage. This arrangement was undisturbed till the time of Archbishop Richard in 1174, who handed over the advowson and patronage, and, of course, the tithes attached to them to the monks.

Archbishop Baldwin, who succeeded him in 1185, resumed the rights alienated by Archbishop Richard, whereupon great litigation ensued, which did not cease with the death of Baldwin in the Third Crusade (1191). The question had been referred to several Popes,

---

* Hasted says on this point that Lanfranc allocated the Manor of Meopham to the monks of Christ Church, Canterbury, for their substance, clothing, etc.: "this manor was *de cibo monachorum*," i.e. to the use of their refectory.

in course of time; and Archbishop Hubert in 1193 continued to maintain the rights of the See, in spite of Papal threats, till, at last, recourse was had to arbitration. Two of the greatest men of the age, Hugh, Bishop of Lincoln, and Samson, Abbot of St. Edmundsbury (1182–1211), were called in to judge between the litigants; and they decided that the Archbishop was to retain the advowson and patronage, as it was before the time of Archbishop Richard. This settled the matter for 180 years, when Archbishop Courtenay (1381–1396) reverted to the policy of Archbishop Richard.

It may be mentioned that Abbot Samson was the celebrated man whom Carlyle has immortalized in his *Past and Present*; one of the most upright men of his time; and besides discharging his duties as a churchman he was, for his great judicial capacity, chosen by the king to be one of his "Justices in Eyre," i.e. Circuit Judges, as we say nowadays.

Courtenay—the Archbishop William of the letter following —appealed for support to King Richard, who on November 17, 1385, wrote the following letter, which ended the dispute, and upheld Archbishop Courtenay's views:

Nov. 17, 1385

Richard, by the Grace of God King of England and France, and Lord of Ireland, to all to whom these present letters shall come, Greeting.

The Venerable Father, William, Archbishop of Canterbury, Primate of all England, has prayed us that whereas the church of Mepham, in the county of Kent, was long since canonically appropriated to the Prior and Convent of Christ Church Canterbury, and thenceforth the same Prior and Convent had quiet possession of that church to their own uses, until one Baldwin, formerly Archbishop of Canterbury, a predecessor of the present Archbishop, unjustly took the advowson and patronage of the said church of Mepham out of the hands and possession of the same Prior and Convent, and of his own will removed and expelled the same Prior and Convent from the advowson and patronage aforesaid, whereby the successors for the time being of the aforesaid Baldwin, Archbishop of Canterbury, held this advowson and patronage in turn until the present time—We may be willing that the royal favour [sought] in the premises be fully granted to the Prior and Convent of the place aforesaid, to the end that they have again the church aforesaid to their own uses, to possess it for themselves and their successors for ever.

We, being favourably inclined to the prayer of the Archbishop in this particular, of our special favour, and at the special request of the said present Archbishop, have granted and given licence for ourselves and our heirs, as far as in us lies, to the same Archbishop that he may deliver back, grant, assign, and give the advowson and patronage of the said church of Mepham to the same Prior and Convent, and also restore the Church itself, to have and to hold to them and their successors for ever. And if it happen that there is no occasion for such restoration, we have [still] given special licence by the tenor of these presents, to the same Prior and Convent that they may receive and have the advowson and patronage aforesaid from the before-named Archbishop, under the form aforesaid, and to appropriate anew the aforesaid church, and hold it so appropriated to their own uses: and [we have granted] to the same Prior and Convent, and to their successors, to make and found for ever certain charities and other charges in accordance with the will and appointment of the said Archbishop in this particular. The statute that lands and tenements are not to be placed in mortmain, or that the said advowson is held of us "in capite" or that the same advowson is part of the temporalities of the Archbishopric of Canterbury, which is in our patronage, notwithstanding; saving nevertheless to ourselves and our heirs the services thereof due and accustomed.

In testimony whereof we have caused these our letters patent to be issued. Witness myself at Westminster, the seventeenth day of November, in the ninth year of our reign.

The references in the letter to the Archbishop's charities, and to the repairing of the church, will be considered when speaking of Courtenay himself among the notable people concerned with Meopham in the past.

The king's ruling held till the dissolution of the monasteries in 1542, when the Dean and Chapter of Canterbury took the place of the Abbot and monks; they retained the temporalities— the Manor and Rectorial tithes—but the advowson they once more resigned to the Archbishop.

In June 1914, by an Order in Council, and with the mutual agreement of exchange of advowsons between the Archbishop of Canterbury and the Bishop of Rochester, the advowson of

Meopham, along with others, was exchanged and handed over to the Dean and Chapter of Rochester by the Archbishop, thus reverting once more to Archbishop Richard's policy in 1174.

In Richard II's time, before the date of the letter just quoted, "the portion paid by this [Meopham] church to the Almonry of the Prior of Christ Church was £61 3s. 4d. per annum; and this church was taxed also at £26 os. 8d. for the half tenth that the clergy had to pay to the king" (Hasted).

A hundred years before, 15th Edw. I (1287), the church was valued at 40 marks per annum (Hasted).

In the "Taxatio Ecclesiastica Angliae et Walliae auctoritate P. Nicholai IV. A.D. 1291" appears:

Decanatus de Shorhm̃

Ecclĩa de Mepehm̃   £26.13.4.

The whole Manor was taxed at £46. The above refers to the grant made in 1288 by Pope Nicholas IV to Edward I of the tenths for six years towards a crusade.

In the "Valor Ecclesiasticus" (*temp.* Henry VIII) an ecclesiastical survey to discover the value of all property belonging to religious bodies was ordered, and the value of the "living" of Meopham with five acres of glebe, the income paid to the priest by the Manor, including the Parsonage (£5 6s. 8d. per annum), tithes, and "oblations," is assessed at £16 3s. 4d. per annum.

In 1650 the Commonwealth ordered a survey of church property, and Meopham is returned as a "vicarage presentative worth £50 per annum"; the survey also states that "a pension of £5.6.8 per annum [i.e. income to the parson] was paid by the Dean and Chapter, who had the impropriation, worth £120 per annum, let on lease to Mr. Henry Haslin" (*v.* also Meopham Court). In 1841–1842 the Rev. J. Thompson, Vicar, received no less than £400 from hop tithes only.

The following list of incumbents at Meopham is mostly

taken from that given by Fielding in his *Records of Rochester Diocese*.

To the time of Richard II the incumbents were Rectors; but the granting of the Rectory and Rectorial tithes to the Priors of Christ Church, as just narrated, made the incumbents vicars.

RECTORS

A.D.		
	940	Wina (Saxon Priest).
	1200	Virgilius
	1296	Alexander de Martin Thorpe
	1305	John de Banquett
	1308	John de Baknel
	1314	Thomas de Stowe
	1318	John de Sandale
	1325	Ade de Baldock
		Gerald: *ob.* 1344 (see below)
	1345	Stephen de Itham
	1348	John de Brigham
	1356	Henry de Ingleby
		John Blod
	1367	John de Kirkebi

Mr. Lewis left some notes taken from Papal registers on some of the above:

1308. 14 Kal. Feb. (Papal letters.)
To John son of John de Baknel. He at the age of 20 and not in full orders became Rector of Mepham in the Diocese of Rochester, and has held it for six months without Papal dispensation.
Dispensation to retain the same.

1344. Provision of the Church of Meypham in the diocese of Rochester void by the death of Gerald, cardinal of S. Sabina.

1345. Stephen de Itham, Rector of Mepham in diocese of Canterbury.

1361. On behalf of John de Kirkeby Priest in the diocese of York, for the Church of Mepham in the diocese of Rochester, touching which John Blod obtained a sentence in his favour against Roger Wy, admitting Kirkeby in succession to Blod, in his right to the same, notwithstanding he expects a benefice which he is willing to resign.

1363. Though John de Kirkeby has the church of Mepham

he asks for the canonry, and prebend of St. Cross in Lincoln, value £10.

1367. Provision of John de Kirkebi of the church of Meffam in the diocese of Rochester void by the death of John Blod.

The above extracts are interesting as showing that Kirkeby was determined to have Meopham, and that he had no objection to being a pluralist!

VICARS

A.D.	1403	William
	1408	John Stapelow
	1410	Walter Stonyng
	1414	John Folsham (*ob.* 1455)
	1452	William Baron
	1458	Richard Maidegood
	1461	John Bromfield
		John Veer
	1477	Richard Smith
	1486	Robert Sedgeford
	1494	Richard Smith (again)
	1501	Hugh Saunders
	1504	William Gydding
	1524	William Marshall
	1553	John Byrde
	1550	Edward Burnell Cranmer (resigned)
	1555	Martin Haggard
	1567	Hugh Gewas
	1569	James Drewe
	1576	James Daye
		George Wreake
	1593	Robert Hemmings
	1594	Martin Fotherby
	1594-5	Ralph Shiers
	1609	Thomas Pigott
	1646	William Gibson
	1670	Christopher Copeland
	1707	Richard Collins
	1711	William Gates
	1713	Laurence Broderick
	1742	Thomas Wright
	1763	Samuel Sandys
	1770	John Tatham

VICARS—*continued*

A.D.	1786	(April) Edward Phillips
	1786	Edward Smedley
	1816	John Thompson
	1854	John Hooper
	1875	Lewis Woodward Lewis
	1900	Arthur Frank Cowley Owen
	1919	George Alfred Tait
	1933	Ernest Cannon

Rev. John Folsham was Vicar of Greenford until 1414; he was then appointed to Meopham, and in 1452 to St. Clement's, Rochester; and dying there in 1455, he was buried at Meopham.

Hugh Saunders, whilst Vicar here, held other livings, viz. St. Werburgh's, Hoo (1500–1502), Mixbury (1501–1513), and Deptford (1502–1503), besides being Principal of St. Alban's Hall, Oxford (1501–1503), Vice-Chancellor of Oxford (1501–1502). He was made Canon of St. Paul's in 1509. Of him Hasted says: "He was called Hugo Saunders, *alias* Shakespear, being a man styled in the (Oxford) University Registers: 'Vir Literis et virtute percelebris.'" He died in 1537, having resigned the Meopham living in 1504.

Ralph Shiers, though Vicar for fourteen years, seems to have put in a Curate to do the work; for an entry in our Churchwardens' book, under date 1595, shows the following after a baptismal entry:

Ralph Shiers, Vicar

Thomas Sympsonus, in Theologia Licentiatus, proco curatus ibi, qui etiam nunc litrum scripsit.

Three years later the same Curate was still in office.

Martin Fotherby was Vicar here for only one year (1594–1595), being appointed to St. Mary-le-bow. He was also a Canon of Canterbury, Chaplain to King James I, and Bishop of Salisbury (1618–1619). He was buried at All-Hallows, London.

Of Thomas Piggott, Hasted remarks "he was then [1649] sequestered by the committee for plundered ministers"; and again, "Mr. Gibbon [Gibson] was in 1650 Vicar, *vice* Piggott, then sequestered." A manuscript in Lambeth Palace Library states: "By the Trustees for maintenance of ministers, Oct. 25, 1650. Whereas the committee for plundered ministers have the 1st August, 1645, granted the yearlie sume of thirty pounds out of the revenues of the Dean and Chapter of Canterbury, for the increase and maintenance of ministers. . . ." Then follows "Meopham. Mr. William Gibson, Minister of the Church of Meopham, the sum of £18, for the half-year 25 March, 1650."

The following entries are from the registers at Canterbury: "On the death of Henry Harvey, late Vicar of Mepeham, a new Vicar to be appointed" (ref. "R," f. 64*b*). The name of Harvey does not appear in the records of Rochester, nor does that of Sir John Birde, who (as Vicar) witnessed the will of John Boghurst of Luddesdown on October 1, 1533.

On 4 Feb. 1555 Martin Huggard admitted to the Vicarage of Meopham on resignation of Edward Burnell, late Vicar—Patrons Philip and Mary ("N," f. 98*a*).

Mention of the Rev. James Day is made under "Tradescant."

Laurence Broderick was Prebendary of Westminster Abbey, July 1710 to September 1711.

Richard Collins whilst at Meopham, 1707–1711, was Vicar of Crayford (1708–1737), of Burham (1700–1708), and Minor Canon of Rochester 1701–1713. He died in 1737. There has lately come to light a sermon preached by the Rev. Richard Collins before the Lord Mayor at St. Paul's Cathedral in 1710. It was afterwards published, and the title-page is as follows:

The Way to make a NATION Happy. Consider'd in a SERMON preach'd at St. PAUL'S, before the Right Honourable the LORD MAYOR, *Court of* ALDERMEN, and Citizens of LONDON. Upon *Wednesday*, the 15*th* of *March*, 1709–10. Being the Day Appointed by Her Majesty's Royal PROCLAMATION for a Day of PUBLIC FASTING and Humiliation. By the Reverend Mr.

COLLINS, M.A., Vicar of *Mepham* in *Kent*, and Chaplain to Her Majesty's Royal Navy in Ordinary at *Chatham*.

LONDON. Printed, and are to be sold by *John Morphew*, near *Stationers-Hall*. 1710.

Mr. Collins had been Vicar of Burham 1700–1708, and was Rector of Crayford 1708–1737, Vicar of Meopham 1707–1711, Chaplain to the Dockyard 1709–1714, and also Minor Canon of Rochester 1701–1713. He died in 1737. From this record it is clear that he was a pluralist—a common enough thing in those days. Also it is unlikely that Meopham saw much of him; Crayford is more likely to have occupied him.

The day of fasting and humiliation appointed by Queen Anne was just at the time of the social upheaval caused by the preaching of Dr. Sacheverell, the condemnation of whose religious and political views was pronounced by the Court on the following day, March 16th.

The sermon is very lengthy, and full of scriptural quotations to support his argument, and the preacher insists strongly (as then was the fashion) on the English nation being the chosen people of God—upon whom, for their sins, the present political and religious upset and the continental war had been visited. The text is the latter part of Jeremiah vii. 23, and the somewhat quaint peroration reads: "Let us conclude all with our hearty Prayers to Almighty God, that he will continue to bless our most gracious Queen in Her Person, in Her renown'd General the most Illustrious Prince and Duke of Marlborough, who has already done such great things for us, and upon whose Head and Heart so very much depends: and prosper Her Counsels at Home, and Her Armies Abroad; make Her Reign exceeding Glorious, and long; that She may be as perfectly easie in Ruling Her Dutiful and Obedient Subjects, as they are Happy in Her. And that Peace and Plenty may make this Nation flourish so long as the Sun and Moon Endure. Amen."

The fulsome dedication of the above sermon to the Earl of Dorset reads: "May your Lordship always be the Beloved of

Heaven, as you are now the Darling of your country, the delight of so many upon Earth . . ." and so forth.

Our late Vicar, Rev. G. A. Tait (1919–1933), was Domestic Chaplain to Dr. Harmer, Bishop of Rochester, from 1907–1930. During the Great War he was Chaplain to various contingents in England 1917–1919, and he then was with the Salonika Field Force and with the army of the Black Sea. He died in 1933.

CHAPTER IX

MEOPHAM COURT

THE proximity of the Court—or, as it used to be called, the Court Lodge—to the church makes it certain that the site of the present building is, to all intents and purposes, that also of the residence of the ancient Saxon chief of the village; for his residence was in the "Demesne," where also the church was situated. The property in Athelstane's time (925–941) was given, as already mentioned, by the king to "his faithful servant Ealdulf"—and as this date corresponds with that attributed to Byrhtric's will, it is possible, since Byrhtric evidently was a great man here, that he inhabited the "Court" of those days. In speaking of Saxon times I have mentioned how the property changed hands; but from the time of Queen Ediva, Athelstane's widow, it remained the property of the monks of Christ Church, Canterbury, till Henry VIII's time. When Edward I returned from the Holy Land he instituted inquiries as to the various manors and tenants of the Crown who, during the previous reign, had become lax in their duties and payments, and taken upon themselves rights that belonged to the king. Meopham Manor was duly examined into by a jury, with the following result (Placita Rolls, Edward I, 1279):

The jurors say that the manor of Mepeham was formerly the king's, and is now in the hands of the Prior of Holy Trinity, Canterbury: and is worth thirty pounds a year: but by what warrant they know not, nor from what time . . . . Also he said master Clifford came to the court of Mepeham and took there seisin for the lord the king, the Prior still living, on the occasion of the election of the Archbishop of Canterbury: and from the said manor unjustly took nine pounds six shillings, and from the tenants of the said manor he unjustly took five marks. And Adam de Mulef burn his serjeant took for his expenses there one seam and a hal- of corn. And the same took and unjustly carried off thirty shillings collected for Rochester Bridge, belonging to the whole of the aforesaid Hundred and Community. And the same Adam unjustly took from John Ash [Johannes de Fraxino] another half mark.*

Again, from the same documents in the sixth year of Edward II (1312):

The jurors present that the manor of Mepham was formerly of ancient demesne of the crown of our lord the king, and that the Prior of Christ Church Canterbury now holds it: they know not by what warrant. And the Prior comes and says that he found his church seised thereof: and that he and his predecessors were in possession of the said manor from time which is before memory, as a right of his church aforesaid. And that he is not bound to answer thèrefore to our lord the king without a writ etc. Therefore information is given to G. de Hertepol, who acts for our lord the king, that he may sue by writ, if he will.†

This further extract, from the same source, shows that the writ was issued:

Concerning liberties they say that the hundred of Toltingtre is a hundred of the Lord Archbishop of Canterbury, and is worth forty shillings a year. And that the Archbishop also claims to have return of writs, and escheats of amercements, and to determine pleas of unlawful distress, in the said hundred. And the Prior of Christ Church Canterbury who holds the manor of Meopham claims to determine pleas of unlawful distress in the same Manor, and to have return of writs of the said Archbishop; also gallows, pillory, tumbrell and amends for breach of assize, of his tenants in the same manor: [but] they know not by what warrant. And because the aforesaid Archbishop [i.e. Archbishop Winchelsey, 1294–1313] is dead, and the archbishopric is in the hand of our lord the king, therefore it rest until etc. And the Sheriff is commanded to cause the said Prior to appear etc. Afterwards come G. de Hertepol, who acts for our lord the king, and states that he sues the said Prior by writ. Therefore nothing further thereof here.

The Prior who thus upheld his convent's rights was Henry de Eastry, who held his post forty-seven years (1285–1331),

* Official reference $\left.\begin{array}{c} \text{m} \\ 2 \\ 30 \end{array}\right\}$ 1. m. 7. 7d. & 8.

† Kent $\left.\begin{array}{c} \text{m} \\ 2 \\ 3 \end{array}\right\}$ 9. m. 14. 14d. 15. 15d.

dying at the age of ninety-two. Hasted speaks most highly of him as a just and upright man, who maintained all his rights fearlessly in the interim between the death of the one Archbishop and the election of his successor, in which there was some delay, the matter of who should be chosen having to be referred to the Pope.

To the Manor of Meopham was especially allotted the duty of supplying the monks' refectory (Hasted); and among the "Customalia" paid "Curiae de Mepham" (in the Steward's Book of the monks*) appear the following, besides some hens and eggs paid by Pettefelde (? Hamlet of Pitfield):

1370.   Tenentes debent pro Culversolelond ii gall:
         (Tenants owe for Culversole two hens)

1370.   Tenentes tenement. de Dodemere xi. gall:
1370.   John Dene pro tenement: Dene xiii. gall:

Phillpot (*Villare Cantiarum* (ed. 1659, p. 235)) says: "Mepeham was given to the monks of Canterbury for their supply of Dyet, by Ediva, mother of the two kings, Edmund and Edred." Also, on a picture of Queen Ediva is a scroll bearing an inscription to the same effect. The date of the gift was 961.

In Mr. Lewis's notes is a reference to a document of Edward I's time, dated 1306†; and from it he quotes: "There is mention of a fence round the Court, called 'Burgh-yard' and also of an 'inclosure round the corn called Swinhey': also of 'sixteen perches and five feet of wall within the Court from the door of the Hall, towards the Court gate.' There is mention also of 'mashing the apples,' which points to cider, and the expense of 'roofing the Grange' is referred to" (*v.* Appendix M).

In 1450 a certain Walter Chypp occupied the Court Lodge or Manor-house (at the time that John Folsham, whose brass we have still, was Vicar of Meopham); he was the tenant of

---

* Harleian MSS. 1006, Brit. Mus.
† In Somner's *History of Gavelkind*, 1728.

the monks of Christ Church, Canterbury, and paid £40 a year for the Manor and Parsonage.

There is still extant, says Mr. Lewis, a bill of Walter Chypp's against the Prior of Christ Church for expenses incurred when the Prior paid a visit to his Meopham property, and put up at the Manor-house; it also includes a charge for putting up a beam in the hall to hang the bacon from (*pro baconibus desuper pendentes*).

In the "Valor Ecclesiasticus" of 26th Henry VIII, for the purpose of determining the values of Church properties, the Manor of Meopham, held by the monks, is thus valued (in 1535):

Manor of Mepham	£	s.	d.
Item, from the Manor Farm with the rectory of the same, per an:	30	13	4
Item from rents (of assize) of the same, per an: .	25	6	2
and from the sale of woods of the same—on an average of years		15	0
From perquisites of the same court (nothing): which the farmer holds under covenant	0	0	0

Total £56. 14s. 6d.

	£	s.	d.
Paid out of the above with offerings per an: . .	3	6	2
Item, to the Vicar of the same for his income per an.	5	6	8
Item in taxes and fees ("in procuratione") to the Deanery of Shoreham		6	8
Item in charitable gifts to the Poor		7	6
Leaving	£47	7	6

	£	s.	d.
And in charity for the infirm brothers on the foundation of Dominus Courtenay, at one time Archbishop of Canterbury	£11	0	0

Deanery of Shoreham
Mepham

The vicarial living itself is valued (including 20/– from the vicarage home farm, and five acres of land: £5.6.8 paid as a certain income (to the Vicar) per the Rector of the same: £2.16.8 in wool and lambs: and £6.10.0 from all other tithes; and oblations to the aforesaid vicarial living averaging £1.12.4) per an: . . . . £16 3s. 4d.

The first extract gives the income of the Manor and the expenditure in regard to the church living and certain charities by the monks. The entry about the Courtenay charity is very interesting; it shows that the four almshouses this Archbishop built near the church were for infirm old men—possibly infirm "brothers" of the religious order.

The last extract is a note on the value of the living for the information of the deanery office, Meopham being then in the deanery of Shoreham.

Until the time of Henry VIII, all the taxes were from 1288 (Edward I) regulated by a "Valor" or "Taxatio Ecclesiastica," taken by the order of Pope Nicholas IV, in order to determine the value of property in England and Wales, that a tenth of the taxes raised might for six years be given to the king towards a Crusade. In this valuation the following appear:

Manor of Mepham with rents from Freningham .	. £46	0 0
Church of Mepham	. £26	13 4

(The church at Wrotham is valued at the same time at £53 6 8)

In 1524 a John Haslyn was the tenant of the Manor; and eighteen years later, at the Dissolution, the Dean and Chapter of Canterbury took the place of the old monks as owners of the Manor, but not, as already stated, of the advowson.

In 1536 a correspondence took place between the Prior of Christchurch and Thomas Cromwell on the subject of "Mepeham Farm"—possibly the home farm of the Court Estate. Mr. Lewis gives a list of the tenants of the Dean and Chapter at the Court to the middle of the last century, as far as he could obtain their names from 1574. I transcribe from him, but I would first quote the title to a deed of the time of Henry III (1240) and referred to under "Melliker," as it seems to show that at that time a certain Godfrey Traunceys was tenant of the monks and held Manor lands. It runs thus:

Carta qua Godefridus Traunceys concedit Priori et Conventui

S. Trinitatis Cantuar. quemdam annuum redditum in manerio de Mepeham.

Test: Will. de Dodemere. Reginald de Mildenakere. Walter de Isebere (*v.* Appendix F).

The deed hands over to the monks certain rents of the Manor of Meopham.

LIST OF OCCUPANTS OF THE COURT

1574. George Gainsford
1595. H. Haslyn
1630. Francis Courthopp
1642. Thomas Swift
1652. William Swift
1685. Captain Swift
1691. Thomas Cox

> Mr. Thomas Cox seems to have been the leading man in the West Borough about 1700, for his property is assessed that year at £145. When Mr. Calverley succeeded him at the Court in 1714 the assessment was £150.

1714. James Calverley
1717. John Markett

In old times part, at any rate, of the Manor property was held by service; but in 1306 (35th Edward I) "Henry, the Prior of the Chapter of Christ Church, commuted certain services the homagers had rendered hitherto for an annual rent" (Hasted). In 1649 the Commonwealth ordered a survey with the view of raising money for the State, and the returns made showed the tithes of "corn and blade" were £120 per annum, and had been let to Francis Courthop and Nicholas Barham in 1630; and the Court Lodge, Demesnes, Parsonage, houses, etc., were let also for £36 per annum, the lessee to do the repairs of the chancel of the church; but at the Restoration the Dean and Chapter resumed their full ownership and occupation.

Before the Restoration, John Hastlelin or Hastling became tenant of the Court and Demesnes of 650 acres, and the Parsonage, at £30 6s. 8d. per annum; but soon after the

Restoration the tenant was one Johnson, followed by Christ-mas, and then Spratt; but in 1724 John Markett became tenant, and his son rebuilt the Court Lodge (note from Hasted).

From the above it would seem that in the interval between 1652 and 1685 no less than four different tenants occupied the Court.

The Markett family of Huguenot origin, the name being Marquette, held the property for over a century. The names of various members of it buried in the church are, with their dates: 1751 Elizabeth Markett; 1763 Ann Markett; 1775 Ann Markett; 1789 John Markett; and in 1801 John Markett. In the churchyard lie the following: Elizabeth Markett 1719; Mary Markett 1724; Thomas Markett 1728; George Markett 1733; John and Ann Markett 1750.

The list now continues:

1802.   Francis Markett
1821.   "Mrs." Markett
1829–1852.   Rev. W. Mansfield

This gentleman was the litigant in the matter of the Carnarvon Door in the south chancel wall; and he married the eldest daughter of Francis Markett, and was the last of the lessees of the Court.

In 1811 (F. Markett) the property consisted of, and was assessed at, the following: Court Lodge £381, Clements Reach £22. In 1818 (F. Markett) it has "Loamer" added, valued at £92; and in 1836 (Isabella Markett) "house and land at Meopham Street" is added, assessed at £2 10s.

In 1852 the property was bought from the Dean and Chapter of Canterbury by Mr. Robert Barnett (*ob.* 1872), and his widow resided there till 1884 with her son, Mr. Joseph Wheelwright.

In 1884 John, the brother of Robert Barnett, succeeded to the property, followed by his brother Herbert in 1887, who sold it two years later (1889) to the Rev. W. Crookes, from whom it was purchased by Mr. Ralph Hart Tweddell in 1890; he died in 1895, and his widow, well known to and valued by all the village, occupied the Court till her regretted decease in 1914.

The purchase carried with it no Manorial rights, only the Rectorial tithes. The Ecclesiastical Commissioners are the present (1934) Lords of the Manor of Meopham in trust for the Dean and Chapter of Canterbury, but the advowson belongs to the Dean and Chapter of Rochester. The property is vested in Mrs. R. Arnold, daughter of the late occupant.

The extent of the property in the past has varied from time to time, more being added and taken from it by various occupants. The estate of the Rev. W. Mansfield was 715 acres, but when bought by Mr. R. Barnett in 1852 the Court Lodge Estate, including Lomer Farm and Clement's Reach, was 910 acres (Lewis). At his decease it was about 1,400 acres. The Rev. W. Crookes, who held it but one year, parted with much of the outlying lands. At the present time the exact extent of the Court Estate is 436 acres, 3 roods, 31 perches.

The ground-plan of the Court and its immediate surroundings are shown in the Parish Map of 1842; extensive outbuildings are indicated, running in zigzag fashion from the house and lying mostly in the field immediately north of the churchyard and facing the Court. They also extended along the road front of the same field. One of these buildings was the old Tithe Barn, where the tithe corn was stored and threshed. It was of immense size, and two loaded wagons could enter it side by side, whilst several threshers could use their flails at the same time. Just before its destruction Mrs. Robert Barnett gave a feast to the village in 1862, on the marriage of the Prince of Wales (King Edward VII). The good old customs were kept up, including the greasy pole, and grinning through the horse collar!

Old Mr. Ashenden, now (1915) ninety years of age, has told me that these buildings by the road, which he remembers well, were the estate workshops and farm buildings, and near them was the saw-pit. No wall then separated the field from the turnpike road, only a hedge; and the pond, which now is behind the wall, was a serious obstruction to traffic, as it swamped the road often after rain, and the road being lower than at present, the water (says Thomas Hawley, another village father, who remembers the circumstances well) was at times knee-deep. Generally, however, foot passengers could pass dry-shod if they kept close to the field on the other or west side of the road, where the ground was higher, and I have little doubt that this is what is referred to in the following from the Parish books: "1754. John Allchin's bill for . . . work done at the *Causeway* by the street" (*v*. Rochester Bridge).

In the field against this causeway, formerly a hop garden, and just below where the post office now is, came first the village pound, which I can just remember. Next to it were the kennels of the Court, swept away with the other old buildings of the Court.

The lower level of the field north of the church, especially as it nears the churchyard and present garden of the Court— from which it is separated by a sunk wall—must have attracted the attention of any passer-by; the explanation was given me by Mr. Ashenden, who told me that when the railway was being built (it was opened here in 1861) Mr. Barnett sold the gravel out of the field for ballast for the line, an immense quantity being removed; so that what is now a field was just then in large part a huge gravel-pit. A large pond is shown in the old map between the present cow-house and the church-yard. On the east side of the Court House there stood, till early in the last century, the "Chapel of the Court Lodge"; and though my aged informant does not remember seeing it, he said that it was situated not many feet from the east window of the present library or morning-room; and in digging where a flower-bed now is, in old days he has come down upon its foundation. It was pulled down rather more than a century ago. It is mentioned in the *Gentleman's Magazine* for 1809 (Vol. I, p. 513) as having the same style of windows as the church—presumably, therefore, Geometric (Early English).

It was in 1862 that Mr. Robert Barnett carried out extensive alterations at the Court. He removed the ancient outbuildings above referred to, and an enumeration of them made when he acquired the property in 1852 says they consisted of "large barns, granary, cart and waggon lodges, stabling for twenty horses, cattle sheds, bullock and cow houses, nag stabling for 7 horses, piggeries, carpenters' and wheelwrights' shops, sawpit, blacksmith's shop, and an abundance of useful out-buildings."

Such a list points to the magnificence of the property in the old and prosperous days of farming!

The real alteration in the house itself by Mr. Barnett consisted in pulling down the south end, and building in its place the present spacious hall, with drawing-room and library, and rooms above, as now exist. He also added a tower with a belvedere on the top, from which a magnificent view was obtainable; but this, becoming unsafe, was removed a few years ago.

The architect who carried out the alterations wrote an account of the "discovery of remains of an ancient building at Meopham Court," from which I extract the following:

Many old inhabitants of Meopham well remember the old house before the alterations were made by the late Mr. Rob.ᵗ Barnett and that the site now occupied by the Hall, Drawing Room and Library was covered with a square Hall, with small sitting room behind and a long, lofty but narrow Drawing room with a bird room behind. The drawing room was a gloomy apartment with walls between 6 and 7 feet thick including the casings and although externally cased with bricks the same as the rest of the house the walls were evidently not solid and often and often loose flints and rubbish were heard to fall between the walls and the wooden internal linings.

When these rooms were being pulled down and the woodwork removed it was discovered that the apartment had originally been 2 storeys in height. The lower one was only about 7 feet high and seemed to have been a sort of store house or granary. The walls were pierced with 4 or 5 stone pointed doors and windows with the door hooks remaining in the stone work. The upper apartment contained 9 or 10 pointed openings, some doors, some windows, and a large and beautiful fireplace. The moldings all beautifully cut and perfect and of 13th-century work. Accurate copies of these were at once taken—fortunately, for in the course of a few days the stonework so long protected from the air began to crumble away. The chimney piece in the Hall of Meopham Court is an exact reproduction of the old one, only half the size (this does not refer to the upper part containing the mirror, which was put up many years afterwards) and the archway leading to the kitchen offices from the Hall and the trefoiled arched recess for umbrellas, coats, etc., are reproductions of the old door and window openings. When the garden walks adjoining this portion of the House were lowered to prevent the new rooms being below the level of ground outside, very extensive remains of the foundations of old buildings were discovered which leaves no doubt that the parts alluded to above were only a small portion of a large group of ancient Buildings.

FRANCIS G. LEE,
Architect,
Upper Clapton, London.
January 18*th*, 1879.

It is also known that there lie under the lawn, and in a direction reaching from in front of the west window of the drawing-room, towards the churchyard, the foundations of an old building; the line of the foundation is indicated in dry weather by the state of the turf covering it. It further suggests a structural connection in old days between the church itself and the Manor-house or "Grange" buildings; and doubtless excavation would reveal evidence of more extensive buildings than now are even thought to have existed. The old ecclesiastics were great builders and knew how to make themselves comfortable; and their Meopham property was one of great importance and value, as they relied, as already mentioned, largely upon its farm produce.

CHAPTER X

THE VICARAGE, THE SMEDLEYS, AND DODEMERE

Vicarage

UNTIL 1386 (Richard II) the living of Meopham was rectorial, but the great tithes being then by royal edict taken away it became vicarial. The last Rector given in the *Record of Rochester* was Henry de Ingleby (1356).

The present Vicarage was built just after Mr. Hooper's appointment in 1854; and during the building he and his family occupied the two houses (Alma Villas) at the top of the hill above the street, a doorway in the partition wall being made to throw the two into one; and, as their name shows, recently erected.

The old building, known as the Parsonage, occupied almost the same site as the present house, but slight differences in the laying-out of the grounds are shown in an old ground-plan of 1790 by Glover Mungeam. The land belonging then to the Vicarage consisted of:

	A.	R.	P.
House and Garden .	–	2	20
Meadows . . .	1	0	31
1st Field . . .	3	–	9
2nd Field . . .	2	–	25
Churchyard . .	1	2	10
Church . . .	–	–	25
	8	3	0

Mr. John Ashenden, our oldest inhabitant now, remembers the Parsonage well; he described it to me as a cottage building of two storeys.

By here introducing an account of the Smedleys, father and son, we shall better picture the old Parsonage and its garden.

The Rev. Edward Smedley was Vicar from 1786 to 1816, and was besides for forty-six years an assistant master in Westminster School. To his connection with Westminster we may trace the reason of our owning the beautiful pulpit already described, and which during his Vicariate found its way from St. Margaret's, Westminster, to Meopham. Though Vicar here, Smedley was also Vicar of Coles Parva in Lincolnshire; he was, therefore, a pluralist. He kept a Curate to work for him here, and spent but little of his time in the village; we have for this statement the evidence of his own son (shortly to be mentioned), and the fact that in our registers the names of various Curates are given against the offices of the church performed during his Vicariate, but very rarely his own, and then almost only during the summer holidays, but occasionally at Christmas or about Easter or Whitsuntide. Thus I find in the marriage register his name appears as follows: 1700 in August, September, December; 1793 August; 1794 June; 1795 and 1796 August; 1798 May; 1801 August; 1802 April and September; and in 1812 September.

Indeed, during the thirty years he was here Meopham seems to have provided its Vicar with the "loaves and 'fishes" and to have received little personal service from him in return. But we must not be hard on him; for do we not owe to him our pulpit! and besides, he presented the village with a gifted son, the author of "*Poems*: by the Rev. Ed. Smedley, 1837."

He was his father's second son, born in 1788; in his book he says his holidays were spent at Meopham, adding: "At this pretty Vicarage my father used to spend his Whitsun and St. Bartholomew tide vacations, and here his children learned to relish the simple and wholesome pleasures of country life."

He (the son) was ordained Deacon in 1811, and, gaining a fellowship at Trinity College, Cambridge, he lived there till his marriage; but he sometimes came to Meopham to help at the church, and it was in the Parish Church that he first did duty after his ordination. In 1812 his father was presented with a living in Devonshire, and as he did not resign Meopham

till 1816, he must for the last four years have been the holder
of no less than three livings! He tried on his retirement to
get the living here for his son, but failed; and the disappoint-
ment was most acutely felt by the son, who makes no secret
of it, in one of his poems entitled "On leaving Meopham in
1816." His biographer, in a preface to his book of poems, says,
"Meopham was the Utopia of his fancy"; and "the most
fervent wish of his heart and ultimatum of his ambition was
to succeed his father as its pastor." The poem is as follows;
and the explanatory notes that I add are either from those
made by the Rev. J. Hooper, a former Vicar—whose daughter
lent me both them and the book of poems—or from the
Rev. E. Smedley's biography:

> Swiftly, though silently, the foot of Time
>   Falls on its path; and ere it treads again
> Some few brief circles more, the happy clime,
>   Our little Empire, and our Childhood's reign,
> May pass unheeded to another's hand   5
> And stranger steps profane our Father's land.
>
> My infant thought, the wish which earliest grew,
>   As if instinctive on my boyish heart,
> The dream my Youth, the hope my Manhood knew,
>   Ah! who from these without a tear can part?   10
> Sadly I turn away my lingering eyes,
> Before the enchanted land for ever flies.
>
> The boughs with golden-sprinkled apples bright,
>   Fairer to us than those which Hesper bore—
> The bashful Clematis, whose virgin white   15
>   Veil'd with its cluster'd hair our eastern door—
> The garden's prickly rampart, and behind,
> The cottage front with honeysuckles twined—
>
> The antique Yew trimm'd into quaint alcove,
>   The churchyard Elm rows' venerable pride—   20
> The Poplar, giant of our humble grove,
>   Sure landmark in our voyagings and guide—
> The gravell'd bank, where still I seem to lie,
> Bedew'd with morning dreams of Poesie—

Oh! were ye mine!—but now another sways   25
  Who little recks your consecrated pale,
Hears not sweet voices of departed days,
  Nor peoples with remember'd joys your vale.
Oh! were ye mine!—but HE who best decides
Spreads all the world before, and only Eden hides.   30

Lines 6 *and* 26 are hardly complimentary to his father's successor, the Rev. John Thompson; they may be condoned as a poet's "licence."

The whole poem bears out his longing and love for Meopham.

Line 16.—The front door of the old Parsonage faced east (as at present), but Mr. Thompson changed its position to the north.

Line 17.—The "prickly" hedge was killed by the shadow of the overhanging trees and grubbed up by Mr. Hooper.

Line 19.—There was formerly a thick yew-hedge bordering the kitchen garden by the road, where now the high brick wall stands; and at its north end stood a yew-arbour, the arched entrance to which still exists; and, referring to it, Mr. Hooper wrote: "I am happy to have preserved this relic."

Line 21.—Mr. Hooper says: "The venerable poplar was standing when I came first to Meopham (1854), but I had to cut it down in my second year, as it was half dead. It stood on the right-hand side of the meadow, and was a landmark for miles round."

Line 23.—The gravel-pit was, says Mr. Hooper, "in the glebe, but now filled in; a walnut-tree was planted on its site." This site is now within the garden enclosure, and the walnut-tree was blown down in a gale this winter (1915–1916). Another gravel-pit was opened in Mr. Lewis's time in the middle of the glebe meadow (now also filled in); and, speaking of the excavations made for gravel in this second pit, Mr. Edward Payne, the present curator of the Rochester Museum, wrote me that there were found by Mr. Lewis in 1895 "pot holes 4 ft. deep, at the bottom burnt matter, pre-Roman potsherds, pieces of stone like 'sarcens' and lumps of clay of curious (dome) shape 1½ in. thick." None of these finds have, however, been preserved, but they are evidences of the occupation of the land by early man.

An entry in the burial register records a tragic event at the old Parsonage. "In the year 1667 Mr. Dalmahoy, a scotchman, quatermaster to my lord Midletone's troop of hors, died in yᵉ Vicaridge hous of Mepā Aug: ye 25 and was buried att Cobam Aug. 29, 1667." This was the year when the Dutch fleet sailed up the Thames as far as Tilbury Fort, burning the ships at Sheerness and Chatham. The "troop of hors" may have been quartered in the village, guarding this part of the country; or the man may have been brought from Gravesend to be taken care of, ill or suffering from wounds; but on this point local history is silent.

Cruden (*Hist. of Gravesend*) says of the above: "Lords Middleton, Douglas and Carlisle, with a force of 6,000 men, assembled at Chatham and in the neighbourhood."

Manor of Dodemere

Dodemere, also written Dudemere in the thirteenth century, and later Deadmore and Deadmer, is a small Manor of less than 50 acres; and the Manor-house stood till 1852 at the corner of the street, next to the old workhouse, and extended up the hill, opposite the George Inn, covering the ground that is now a garden. At that date the Manor was purchased by Mr. W. Masters-Smith, who pulled down the Manor-house, erecting the present small house at the corner in its place out of the materials of the old house. The Manor-house in the last years of its existence was an open butcher's shop facing the high road; just such a one as exists now at Cobham. The manorial character of the property has long lapsed through its Court not having been regularly held. At the time of its purchase the lands of the Manor consisted of about 30 acres.

Mr. Lewis published, in his papers on Meopham, a deed of gift of land in the time of Henry III (1260) (*excerpta e Rotulis Finium*). The original, he says, is among the valuable manuscripts left by Mr. L. Larking, the well-known Kent antiquarian, and is in the Maidstone Library (*Codex de Kent*, Vol. III). Whilst the deed does not say the lands were actually those of the Manor, their acreage, however, would agree with their having been so.

The following is Mr. Larking's translation, the title of the deed running:

Carta qua Radulphus Clericus filius Ricardi de Dudemere concedit Priori et Conventui ecclesiae Christi. Cantuar totam terram suam in villa de Mepeham. Test: Thom. fil. Constantine. Robert fil. Baldwin. Thom. de Westland. et aliis.

Let all men now and in the future know that I, Ralph, Clerk, son of Richard de Dudemere, have given and granted, and by this my present deed have confirmed, in pure and perpetual charity, to the Prior and Convent of Christ Church, Canterbury, the whole of my land in the township of Mepeham, viz. forty-six acres of land with all that belongs to them.

Five acres in the field which they call Lullindene in the southern part, and five acres which lie in a field which is called Ewesfield, and one virgate and three daiwerks and a quarter in Le Hooe in the southern part; and two acres and one virgate and three daiwerks and a quarter in the field which is called Bechwelde in the southern part, and one acre and three virgates of land in the field which is called Godriches croft in the middle of the land of Adam and Emma of Dudemere; and two acres and one virgate, and three daiwerks and a quarter in a field which is called Alwines Land in the northern part; and one acre and one virgate and three daiwerks and a quarter in the middle of the field which is called Turgares land; and six acres and a half and one virgate and three daiwerks and a quarter in the field which is called Donhamme, and one quarter in the field in the west on the side of the King's high way (*cheminus Regalis*) which goes through Dudemere towards the north of the Messuage of Emma de Dudemere; and six acres and a half, and three daiwerks and a quarter in the west in the wood which is called Le Frit, and one acre in the middle of the wood which is called Hegewood; and four acres and a virgate and five daiwerks of pasture over against the gate of Dudemere, and six daiwerks of pasture at Kokel-slane; willing and granting that the aforenamed Prior and Convent should hold and possess happily in peace, freely and without dispute, in its entirety and for ever, the whole of my land before described, with ways, paths, and hedges, in pasture, wood, and arable, with rents, reliefs, homage and escheats, and with all other things that belong to it.

I also give to the Prior and Convent the whole of that I have possessed, or was entitled to possess in the township of Mepham or elsewhere, constituting the same my heirs in respect to all property which by right may come to me; and in order that this gift and grant of mine, and confirmation of this my gift, may hold good and be firmly established for ever, I have sworn with my hand on the Sacred Scriptures that I will never contravene this pact, nor consent to any one who wishes to call this deed in question; and in testimony that I have done this on the Holy Scriptures I have thought well to strengthen with the safeguard of my seal, with these witnesses:—Thomas, son of Constance, Robert, son of Baldwin, Thomas de Westland, Gilbert de Pettefield, Richard de Bosco, Alfred the Carpenter, Hamo de Halifield, Adam de Halifield, Thomas de Halifield, Reginald de Estburgh, Peter de Cherechward, and many others.

This deed is perhaps mainly of interest now from the old names of Meopham lands that it contains, though impossible now to identify with certainty. Of the land measures mentioned, "the Virgate in Norman times was equal to thirty acres, but in Henry III's time clearly is less than one acre; it is considered to stand for 1 rood; the daiwerk was one-tenth of a rood" (Lewis).

In 1259 Fulk de Sharsted and William de Dudemer brought an action against a certain Roger de Sancta Elena, late bailiff of Meopham, on the ground that the defendant had usurped the wardship of the lands and heirs of John de la Dene (whose lands were held in gavelkind), the said Fulk declaring he, on the mother's side, was nearer akin to de la Dene than Roger was.

William de Dudemer also complained that the bailiff had kept back the sum of 2/- to which he was entitled for work done at the Manor of Meopham.

Fulk further complained that Roger and the other bailiffs of the Prior of Holy Trinity, Canterbury, had refused to give up the wardship till he, the plaintiff, had paid a fine of 5 marks.

He also took from him as heriot a horse valued at 40/-. The parties, however, came to terms and the case was dismissed. (Placita de Assis: Juratis et querelis le 43 Hen. iii. mem. 9. Public Record Office.)

In the "fine rolls" (*Rotulae Finium*) of Henry III, 1260, appear the names of William de Dodemere and Cecilia his wife.

In 1279 William de Holbourne (Holborn), poulterer of London, held the Manor of Dudemere, in which year he was summoned for closing a right-of-way through the Manor. (Placita Rolls, *temp*. Edward I.)

In 1290 Sir Peter de Huntingfield was Lord of the Manor of Dudemere, and also Sheriff of Kent. His bailiff, Robert de Wandesley, was accused by him of falsifying the accounts, and he was outlawed and eventually imprisoned. But his dishonesty was eventually disproved, and he was released.

In 1313 Sir Walter de Huntingfield, Sir Peter's son, owned the Manor, which in 1325 (Edward II) became a bone of contention between two members of the family. At least, the property mentioned below apparently formed part of if not all the Manor at that time, though the document from which the following is taken does not call it manorial land.

In the Kent Fines (*Pedes Finium*), *temp*. Edward III, No. 838, is recorded a "fine" (a form of conveyance) at Westminster, between Walter de Huntyngfeld and Laurence his son as plaintiffs and the Rev. Benedict de Huntyngfeld, Parson of Eselyng "deforciant," in respect of land at Meopham, consisting of 1 messuage, 1 carucate of land, 30 acres of pasture, 80 acres of wood, with 40/- rent and also rent of 30 hens and 300 eggs, with appurtenances.

By 1373 Dodemere seems to have passed into other hands, as Richard Idleigh was then Lord of the Manor.

In 1384 a Thomas de Dodemere was parliamentary burgess for Rochester (Smetham). In Henry VIII's day the Manor was held by Thomas Cavendish of the King's Exchequer. Thomas in the next reign parted with it to John Gifford, after whom it was held by Walter Powree; then Henry Collins; and in

1603 by Walter Kipping; then by the Darrell family; by George Lallenden of Frindsbury; and in the middle of the eighteenth century by Thomas Elliot (Hasted).

On April 17, 1861, a court Baron of W. Masters-Smith was holden at the Manor House, being the accustomed place, before George Henry Knight, Steward of the said Court.

Plaints—none.
The Homage: Mr. Albert Dorrington.
Essoigns of Tenants:
  R. W. S. Wilson
  C. Gustavus Whittaker
  E. Coombes
  B. W. Horn
  A. Fletcher
  R. Barnett
  C. Susannah
  — Dawson
  Francis Andrus
  John Usher.

A copy of the Rent Roll on that occasion is of interest, and will be found in Appendix G. This was, I believe, the last Court to be held.

As Dodemere is often confounded with Dode, a hamlet on the eastern borders of the Parish, it may be well to state that there is no connection between the two. Dode is not in our Parish, and all that remains of the hamlet is the small wayside church formerly in ruins, lately, however, "restored" (!) by Mr. Arnold, late Mayor of Gravesend. It ceased to be a parish church in the middle of the fourteenth century, when all the inhabitants died from the plague; the church plate and other belongings were transferred to Paddlesworth—which was often known as Paddlesworth-cum-Dode. I am told the foundations of some of the old cottages—there are none now—still exist just below the surface of the meadow in which the church stands.*

* *The History of Dode Hamlet and its Norman Church* was published in 1905 by George Matthews Arnold, F.S.A., the restorer above referred to. See also *The Records of Rochester Diocese*, by Rev. Henry Fielding, p. 136.

CHAPTER XI

ARCHBISHOPS SIMON AND COURTENAY— THE TRADESCANTS.

AT least five men in the past who have made history have been connected with Meopham, viz. Simon de Meopham, William Courtenay, the two Tradescants, and Sir John Bayley. Each of these must now receive notice; and I will speak of them here, as the two first were intimately connected with our church, and the account of it would be incomplete without their introduction.

The pre-eminently great Meopham man in the past was Simon de Meopham, Archbishop of Canterbury. The date of his birth was about 1272; he was presumably born in the village, but the site of his home is unknown. Tradition places it at Dene, but the sequel will show that this cannot reasonably be correct (v. Dene). He was one of four, having two brothers and one sister. He was educated at Merton College, Oxford, where he matriculated in 1290. In 1297 he was ordained priest, and became Rector of Tunstall in 1310, which cure he held till he became Archbishop. He was also Prebendary at Chichester and a Canon of Llandaff. In 1314 he applied for leave to absent himself from his clerical work for a year for the purpose of devoting himself to study; and licence to do so was granted.

Though not reckoned as one of the greatest of our Archbishops, he was a man of stern and upright character; but being bent always on imposing his own will on others where he considered it his duty to do so, his career as Archbishop was no "bed of roses," and he came into collision with his colleagues, and finally with the Pope himself.

The see of Canterbury becoming vacant in 1327 by the death of Archbishop Walter, the Prior and the Chapter of Christ Church, Canterbury, appointed three of their number—

Robert de Dovaria, Thomas de Greneweye, Richard de Oxenden—to choose seven other monks, and with them to proceed to the selection of a successor. They chose the following, viz. Hugh de Sancta Margarita (Sacristan), Geoffrey Potinel (Almoner), Thomas Stoyl, Nicholas de Ivingha, Hugh de Sancto Ivone, John Everard, Edmund de Adesham; and, forming themselves into an elective body at Christmastide, 1327, they chose Simon de Mepeham, Rector of Tunstall, to fill the vacant see.

This choice was not, however, everywhere acceptable; for Queen Isabella (the widow of Edward II, who had been murdered three months before, on September 21, 1327) favoured the appointment of Henry, Bishop of Lincoln; but the monks of Canterbury, backed by Henry, Earl of Lancaster, carried the day eventually. Edward III wrote to the Pope in Simon's interest in 1327, but the Pope hesitated to confirm the election, and the king wrote again on April 20, 1328, and the Pope gave way, and confirmed Simon's election on May 27th of that year. Simon in the meantime had left for Rome, sailing from England on January 17th, and was duly consecrated at Avignon on June 5, 1328.*

Simon was apparently a poor man; and in order to meet the expenses connected with his travel abroad and his election he had to apply on June 23rd for a faculty that he might contract a loan of £2,000, to be repaid in four years. It almost seems as though the monks of Canterbury were unable to assist their candidate pecuniarily, for it is on record that in October 1327 the Prior and monks begged the Bishop of Rochester that they might appropriate the living of Westerham, as the convent had had so many losses; and amongst these it is mentioned that Meopham had failed to supply that year

---

* The British Museum possesses a sulphur cast of Archbishop Simon's seal, inscribed: MON: DEI.GRA. CANTVRIEN: ARCHIEP. . . . TOCI'. AGLIE. PRIM.

A copy of the seal, in bronze, made by the firm of John Pinches of Lambeth (one of the Churchwardens), was presented by him to the relatives of Meopham men who fell in the Great War.

nine oxen, seven cows, and some sheep!* It seems to have been a bad year with the farmers here.

Simon returned home on September 5, 1328, and before the year was out became embroiled with the Prior of Christ Church; and the monks must soon have found out that in electing a strong man they had also elected a masterful one, who would stand no nonsense when he thought any step to be in the path of duty.

One of his earliest public acts was on February 10, 1329. During the troubled times attending the deposition (January 1327) of the feeble King Edward II, Walter de Stapleton, Bishop of Exeter, who had sided with Queen Isabella against the king her husband, was murdered by a London mob, and the renowned Abbey of Bury St. Edmunds had been plundered and burnt. Simon, on the date mentioned, summoned a number of Bishops, Abbots, and others to a council at St. Paul's, London, and there and then publicly excommunicated the murderers of the Bishop. It was a bold act, and might have brought the same treatment on himself.

A few months later another public act shows Simon in a different light, and must, I think, be taken as a proof of his affection for his native village, as well as of that for the memory of his parents buried in the churchyard at Meopham. He issued an Indulgence on July 23, 1329, which Thorpe gives in his *Registrum Roffense*, prefacing it with this remark: "A true copy of an indulgence lately found in this [Meopham] church, and now in the possession of Mr. Wright, the present incumbent" (1742–1763). It reads thus in English:

To all the sons of Holy Mother Church to whose notice this writing shall come, Symon, by divine permission Archbishop of Canterbury, Primate of all England, Greeting in Him through whom there is remission of sins. In order that we may stir up the minds of the faithful, by the grant of indulgences, to acts which obtain merit from the grace of God and His boundless mercy,

---

* Christ Church letters, published Camden Society, 1877.

trusting moreover in the merits and prayers of His most holy Mother, and the glorious martyr Blessed Thomas, and of all the saints, We remit to all worshippers of Christ throughout our province of Canterbury, wherever they may be, being truly penitent and having made confession of their sins, who shall come to the church of Mepham, which is under our peculiar jurisdiction, for devotional purposes, or on a pilgrimage, and shall walk round the graveyard of the said church, and shall repeat the Lord's Prayer, with the angelic salutation for the good and peaceful state of the kingdom of England and for the souls of our parents whose bodies lie buried there, and for all the faithful departed, or who may have bequeathed anything of the goods given them by God, to the fabric of this church, or in the piety of their mind may have offered lights or other things requisite for divine service in the said church—FORTY DAYS of penances enjoined on them, God willing: confirming nevertheless all indulgences hitherto duly granted on account of this matter and hereafter to be granted.

In witness of which we have caused our seal to be attached hereto.

Given at Mortlake [Mourtelack], X° Cal: of August [23 July] 1329, in the second year of our consecration.

A correspondent of the late Mr. Lewis's, writing on this indulgence, remarks:

"I cannot help thinking that the grant of this Indulgence, which I am told was a thing of *very* rare occurrence in the case of small village churches, marks some great revival of religious life in Meopham."

The reference to those who had bequeathed goods for the fabric of the church clearly has relation to the rebuilding of the Parish Church some four years previously; and perhaps we here may trace Simon's influence on the religious feeling of the Parish whereby he in the past, and before he was Archbishop, not only got the parishioners to give to the fabric as it rose from its foundations, but afterwards to supply the necessaries for its adornment, and for the proper carrying out of its services. There is no more evidence than this deduction as to what actual share he took in the rebuilding of the Parish

Church*; that his personal influence was great in the matter, and even that it was due to his initiative, is exceedingly likely; but that he had money himself to spend on it is very improbable as Rector of Tunstall; but we know he, with his brother, did give up some property for the founding of the chantry chapel of St. James de la Dene in Meopham Church, as I will now narrate.

In 1322, whilst still Rector of Tunstall, Simon and his brother Edmund had leave granted them to "bestow a chantry chapel where they would in the parish of Meopham," in memory of their parents buried at the Parish Church. The reconstruction of the body of our church must have been just commencing at this date, but no part of the body to be newly erected offered itself for the purpose. It possessed no side chapel, nor even a room over the porch which might have answered the purpose; the only possible place left was the Lady Chapel, now the vestry, the date of which, as has been explained, is certainly earlier than the fourteenth century; and since, as I am about to show, the chantry was *in* the church, there can be no reasonable doubt of the chantry having been in the old Lady Chapel.

The *Archæolog. Cant.*, vol. xl, p. 64, quotes from the records of the Consistory Court of Canterbury that a licence was granted to Thomas Nicholas of Meopham, in 1348, for an oratory in his Manor.

On March 2, 1327, two years after the reopening of the church, and the same year in which Simon was nominated for the Archbishopric, an order was issued from Westminster by the king (Edward III) that an "Inquisitio" (i.e. Inquest)† should be held to determine whether permission should be given to "Master Edmund de Mepham, Master Simon de Mepham, and John de la Dene" to alienate certain properties

---

* Dart (*Hist. of the Cath. Ch. of Canterbury*, 1726), speaking of Simon, says that at Meopham "he founded a church for the use of the poor, which was repaired by his successor, Courtney."

† *Inquisitio post mortem* (correctly, *ad quod damnum*), 1 Edw. III (2 nos.), 114.

in mortmain for the support of a chaplain to say daily masses "in the Chapel of St. James de la Dene, in the parish of Mepham, for the soul of John de la Dene and for the souls of the aforesaid Edmund, Simon, and John, and of the fathers and mothers, relations and benefactors of the same Edmund, Simon and John, and all who had departed this life."

On March 20th the inquest was held; the following jury was sworn: John de Peckham, Robert de la Dene, Alexander de Northwood, John de Pettesfield, Robert Vyaund,* John de Cosyngton, John de Iseberghe, John de Rigge, Richard de la Bokland, John de la Bokland, John le Conk de Cobeham, and John Elys. The verdict was that the request might be acceded to without prejudice to the Crown; and it also gives the value of the property to be assigned or alienated in mortmain for the purpose named: 1 messuage, 2 mills, 25 acres of land, 4 acres of meadow, 2 acres of wood, and 25/- in rent from tenants in "Est Malling, Berlyng, Northflet, Mepham and Hoo." Then after giving details of the property above-named, the jury declared that they put the annual value of it at £4 5s. 4d.

(Parenthetically, it may be mentioned that such inquests were held when property changed hands in order to determine whether the king would receive loss or damage thereby; hence such an inquiry was called an *Inquisitio ad quod damnum*. Similar inquiries were held on the death of an owner of property, hence called *Inquisitio post mortem*.)

Within a week—on March 25th—a special licence (*v.* Appendix B) was granted, and the property secured for the endowment of the chantry or chapel for a chaplain in per-petuity.† The actual wording of the document describing the situation of the chapel is "in parochia ecclie de Mepham," showing it was in the Parish Church; and the heading of the commission for its dedication runs: "Commissio ad dedicand: capellam de la Dene in parochia de Mepham et unum altare

---

* Who doubtless gave the name to the small Manor of "Vigaund" in Cobham.   † Chantries were suppressed 1549–1550.

in eadem" (Reynolds, fol. 154a). There would have been no necessity to mention the "one altar" if the chapel were a separate unit of itself; but it was necessary to distinguish it from the high altar of the Parish Church.

Further, in an abbreviated index of the contents of the Patent Rolls in the Public Record Office the above document is referred to thus:* "Pro Cantuaria de Dene in parochiā de Mepham . . ." and the definition of "Cantuaria" in Tomlin's *Law Dictionary* is "a little church, chapel, or particular altar in a church endowed with lands or other revenues . . ."; and the article in the *Dictionary of National Biography* speaking of the "Dene" family adds that they "gave the name to the Chapel of St. James de la Dene in Meopham Church."

The only conclusion from all this evidence as to where this chantry was situated must be that it was *not*, as local tradition has it, near Dene Farm or Manor House, but in the Parish Church; and the most likely and indeed the only place there must have been the present vestry.

There is a record of one other transaction in the de la Dene family which, though not bearing on the subject just dealt with, is of too much interest to Meopham people not to be recorded.

At Westminster, Quinzaine of St. Michael anno 18 Edward II. Between John de la Dene of Mepham, chaplain, *plt*: and Master Simon, son of Simon de la Dene of Mepeham *deft:* of 1 mess: 1 mill: 200 acr: land: 5 acr: meadow: 60 acr: pasture: 18 acr: wood: 66s 8d rent: and rent of 32 hens and 120 eggs, with appurts: in Mepham, Ludesdon', Northflete, Swanescomp', Estmallyng', and Clyne next Higham.

Right of Master Simon, who for the admission, grants to John for his life, by the Service of a rose at the nativity of St. John Baptist. After his death to revert to Master Simon and his heirs, quit of the heirs of John (*Arch. Cant.*, xv. p. 290, Kent Fines).

This transaction took place in 1325, and perhaps Simon de Mepham had stood godfather to the defendant: we know the families were connected by marriage (*v.* Dene Farm).

* Patent Rolls, 1 Edw. III (m. 7).

Simon de Meopham's character as a good man comes out in what he did in 1332; and this, it must be remembered, was at a time when he was in serious conflict with the ecclesiastical authorities, the mental worry of which also is thought to have hastened his death the following year.

On July 17, 1332, he called a council at his palace at Mayfield and promulgated a "Constitution" on the keeping of Sunday. He had been shocked at the practices carried on on that day, and complained in the order issued that "Festivals were not observed in the religious spirit that they should be" and that "the tavern was often frequented more than the Church." He also directed that the Lord's Day or Sunday should be considered as commencing on the evening of the Saturday—the Jewish Sabbath Day. He also added special instructions upon the keeping of Good Friday.

In thus acting he followed in the steps of great predecessors; and on this subject the following remarks may be found of interest; they are from an article in the *Encyclopaedia Britannica*, xxii, p. 650.

The first law on the keeping of Sunday was made by the great Christian Emperor of the West, Constantine, in A.D. 321, who in his *Constitutions* stopped all Sunday work, courts of justice and public entertainments, and ordered all his people to rest. He made an exception for the agricultural labourer; but a hundred years later this exception to the law was withdrawn. [Simon in his rules also made an exception in favour of the agriculturist.] In the 7th century, Ina, King of the West Saxons (A.D. 688), made special enactions, under fines, against Sunday work; and Athelstan added to these the holding of public markets; but he permitted works of necessity to be carried on. In the 14th century an Act of 28 Edward III forbad sale of wool at the 'staple' on the Sunday; but Richard II enjoined archery practice on Sunday; whilst in the 17th century, James I (in 1618) in his *Book of Sports*, permitted dancing, morris dances, May-poles, etc., after afternoon service in the Church: but he forbad bear- and bull-baiting. Before the century was out the Puritans of the Commonwealth had thrown a wet blanket on all recreation and not on that of Sundays only.

The Archbishop also considered it his duty to visit the

various cathedrals and religious communities in his province, and he applied for the power to do so, as is shown by the following "Papal Letter":

1329. 2 Id: July. To Simon, indult to visit his province, first his own Chapter and Diocese, and then those of his Diocese which most need it.

He began his visitations in 1331, and in due course he arrived at Exeter, but on his approach he found he was prevented entering the cathedral or its precincts, which were guarded by armed men, by order of the Bishop of Exeter, who considered that the Archbishop was interfering with his own vested rights; he also appealed to the Pope against Simon. The climax, however, was reached at Canterbury. The Abbot and monks of St. Augustine's, from whom he demanded an explanation and account of the many Kentish rectories they had appropriated, refused the information, claiming that they were out of the Archbishop's jurisdiction, acknowledging that of the Pope only, to whom they appealed for protection, and who in due course issued an injunction against Simon. The Pope sent Letherius de Concreto as Nuncio to try the matter and so make peace; the case was duly tried, the Archbishop was found to have acted wrongly, and a fine of £700 was inflicted. This was in 1332. Of this he took no notice and remained recalcitrant (Holinshed).

On behalf, therefore, of the Court an attempt was made to serve him with a writ when he was lying ill at Slyndon; but his servants—it is said without his knowledge—ill-treated the officials, and for this in 1333 the Pope excommunicated him.

Worried and worn out by troubles that he at least thought were only brought on him in his attempt to do his duty, and suffering severely, says Holinshed, from ague, he died at his palace at Mayfield on October 12, 1333. His body was taken to Canterbury and placed in St. Anselm's Chapel; but the monks had their revenge at last, for being excommunicated he could not receive Christian burial. However, this was eventually arranged; the decree of excommunication was annulled, and Simon de Meopham was laid at rest in Canterbury Cathedral, where his tomb may still be seen, on October 25th, the Bishop of Rochester performing the funeral service.

Thorn (Chronicler) says of Simon that he held the see for five years, four months, and one day, "with small comfort the whole time; he fell sick from the continual vexations and troubles he had been involved in . . ."

Weever (*Funerall Monuments*, 1631), writing of the interior of Canterbury Cathedral, says:

Upon the north side of Saint Anselmes Chappell, in a marble Tombe, lieth Simon Mepham Archbishop of this See, borne in this Countrey, Doctor of Divinitie, and very well learned (as learning went in those dayes) of whom I find little worthy of relation; for all the time hee sate (which was but five yeare and somewhat more) he was ever a wrangling with his Monkes of this Church, and with Jo: Graundison Bishop of Exeter, and getting the worse by both, he fell sicke and died, October 12, 1333.

That Simon was a just, good, and sincere man is certain; but his will was law, and he was most uncompromising in enforcing it; he was clearly no diplomatist, nor wise in his dealings with others. Himself a strong man—not to say obstinate—he perhaps despised, where he should have been lenient towards, the weaknesses of others; and he trod rather roughly on the toes of those whose hands it would have been wiser to have shaken in a conciliatory spirit. He also quite rightly stood upon his dignity, as the *Rolls of Parliament*, vol. ii, p. 67*b*, show. He complained to Parliament, held at York (*temp*. Edward III, 1332), against the carrying of the crozier by the Archbishop of York; but at a meeting of Parliament held in December 1932 the following injunction was issued— the original (in Norman French) runs thus: "The business of the King and of the Kingdom ought not to be delayed by the debate between the Archbishop of Canterbury, and the Archbishop of York, upon the carrying of their croziers. It was forbidden by our Lord the King in full Parliament."

But whatever his shortcomings, we of Meopham must always hold his memory dear to us; for not only was he a Meopham man, but he had buried his parents in our church-yard, and thus was held by chains of affection for the village that he never could break; and whilst the founding of the chantry chapel of St. James here may be by some regarded as only a family matter, his affection for the church is shown not only in the unusual act of his granting an Indulgence to those who did penance in the village churchyard, but by his influence (of which there is little doubt) in bringing about the rebuilding of the body of the old church, and so bequeathing to us the noble building that we are the possessors of at this day.*

One of Simon's executors, L. Falstaff, left a legacy of £50 to the Convent of Christ Church, Canterbury, so that 40/- might be annually employed to celebrate the Archbishop's memory. In the Record of the Consistory Court of Canterbury, during the primacy of John Stratford (1334–1348), is the following (quoted in the *Arch. Cant.*, vol. xl, p. 56):

Fol 12ª Nov. 1340. A fine to be paid by Thomas Waryn to Laurence Fastolf, Canon of St. Paul's London, and to Thomas de Waghope Rector of Smerden, the two Exors: of Archbp: Simon de Mepham, the sum of 51s. 8d.

The Meopham or De Meopham family "seems," says a writer in the *Dictionary of National Biography*, "to have been a numerous one"; but we are rather concerned with Simon's immediate relatives.

He had a sister and two brothers; the sister, Joan, married John de la Dene, and her name is first mentioned in the document granting permission for the founding of the chantry or memorial chapel of St. James (*v. ante*). One brother, Edmund, became Rector of Brasted, as shown by the following "Papal Letter":

* There is in the library of Sion College an MS. Psalter in vellum with beautifully illuminated capitals, which belonged to Simon de Meopham.

1328 2 id: July.

To Master Edmund de Mepham S.T.P. Provision of the canonry of Chichester and prebend of Havaville void by the consecration of Simon, Archbishop of Canterbury, notwithstanding that he has a canonry and prebend: of Llandaff and is rector of Bradstede in the Diocese of Canterbury.

His tomb is thus inscribed: "Edmundus de Mepham Doctor sacrae theologiae quondam Rector hujus ecclesie cujus anime propicietur Deus." There is no date.

An Edmund Meopham was ordained sub-deacon in the title of Rector of Tunstall in 1286; his tomb, without inscription, is still in that church (*Dict. Nat. Biog.*). If this is the same person as the above, he must have been much older than Simon de Meopham and have preceded him at Tunstall. Simon's brother Edmund died 1328.

The other brother, Thomas, became a friar.

In different centuries the names of various de Meophams appear; but what branches of the family of the Archbishop—if any—there is nothing to show. Perhaps some were so called from their connection merely with the monastic property here. Archbishop Peckham (1279–1292) is credited with having ordained no less than five de Meophams.

Geoffrey de Mapeham is mentioned in an old history of the Forty Abbots of St. Albans, who exchanged in the time of Richard I (A.D. 1189–1199) some land with Abbot Richard (Lewis).

Thomas de Mepham was Sacristan to Rochester Cathedral in Henry III's time (1216–1272). He, with Richard de Eastgate, restored and rebuilt the west transept of the cathedral that was in ruins, having been burnt down in 1179. He was Rector of St. Nicholas, Strood, from 1269 to 1273 (*Church Builder*, 1865, p. 18).

William de Mepham was Rector of Cranbrook in 1310.

Richard de Mepham was Archdeacon of Oxford in 1263; became Dean of Oxford in 1273; and then Dean of Lincoln. In 1274 he, with the Archbishop of Canterbury and others, attended a council held at Lyons, on the question of raising funds for the Crusades; and when it was proposed that the Church of England should subscribe one-tenth of the cost, Richard in no measured terms objected to this, and complained of the Papal extortions on the English clergy. He thereby offended the Pope, who passed a sentence of deprivation upon him, thus taking away all his emoluments and appointments in the Church. Finding, however, public opinion against him, Richard eventually withdrew his remarks, and was duly reinstated (Prynne Cod: vol. ii, p. 1000, and vol. iii, p. 144). A certain *Henry de Mepeham* in A.D. 1316 was a legatee under the will of Thomas de Woldenham (Wouldham), Bishop of Rochester. "Item, lego fratri Henrico de Mepeham viginti s. (Thorpe, *Reg. Roff.*).

Richard de Mepham (another) was Rector of Boughton-under-Blean, near Faversham, in the fifteenth century.

Last of all must be mentioned an entry in our baptismal register under date July 28, 1717, of the baptism of a "Mary Meopham"; perhaps it was necessary to find a name for the poor baby!

William Courtenay

Courtenay was Archbishop of Canterbury 1381–1396; and his connection with Meopham is a twofold one. It was he who was the means of restoring to the monks of Canterbury the advowson and patronage of our church (*v.* Advowson); and, according to Lambarde, he in 1386 repaired the aisles of the church and put in their perpendicular windows. Though not expressly mentioned, there is no doubt that the old coloured glass (*q.v.*) was put in at the same time. He also built four almshouses near the church for certain poor brothers.* This charity appears in the "Valor Ecclesiasticus," *temp.* Henry VIII (*vide* under Court). He founded a College of Secular Priests in Maidstone, and commenced in 1395 the building of All Saints' Church in that town; he was quite one of the "building"

* *Vide* also Weever's *Funerall Monuments*, p. 124.

Archbishops, and is spoken of as a high-minded and liberal man. His restoring our church shows he had more than passing associations with it; but we do not know what they were. It was he who cited Wycliffe to appear before a Synod held at the Black Friars, London, to answer for his opinions in 1382. Courtenay died in 1396.

John Tradescant—father and son

The senior Tradescant, naturalist and traveller, was gardener to the Earl of Salisbury* from 1607 to 1612, who held the Manor of Shorne, Kent. On taking up this work Tradescant lived in Meopham; and in 1607 he married Elizabeth Day of this village. It is believed she was the daughter of the Rev. James Day, the first Vicar. He was Vicar from 1576 to 1593, when he and two of his children died of the plague. He had a large family of nine children, born between 1572 and 1588; and our church books show that there were two Elizabeth Days baptized about this time, one in 1573, the other in 1586; but there is nothing to show their parentage, nor which of the two Tradescant married. The elder is not likely to have been the Vicar's daughter, as her baptismal date is three years before his Vicariate; and he is not likely to have been living here before his appointment. That Tradescant, on his marriage, lived at Pitfield is almost certain, on grounds that will be given directly.

A son was born to Tradescant in 1608, and the register shows the following entry: "1608. August the iiii day. John the son of John Tradescant was baptized eodem die"—i.e. the day he was born (v. also Church Registers).

I can only briefly summarize some of the numerous events in the life of the elder Tradescant. In 1617 he paid an agent £25 to collect specimens in Virginia, and next year he sailed from Gravesend for Russia. In 1620 he was a gentleman volunteer against the Algerine pirates, and he took this opportunity of bringing back to England the "Algiers apricot." In 1625 he

* Brother-in-law to Henry Lord Cobham.

was in the service of George Villiers the Duke of Buckingham, and on behalf of the Duke wrote a letter to Edward Nicholas in Virginia to collect rare beasts, birds, stones, etc., as the Duke was interested in rarities. He accompanied the Duke at the Siege of La Rochelle; and on the Duke's death he became gardener to Charles I, or rather his Queen, Henrietta Maria, in 1629.

He now lived in London, in the South Lambeth Road, and here he had his celebrated museum or "Closet of Rarities"; and also a physic garden, i.e. one growing medicinal herbs. He called his house, quite appropriately, "The Ark."

King James I (1603–1625) had been most anxious to try to acclimatize the silkworm, and gave facilities for the experiment by offering seeds of the mulberry to anyone who would sow them (1605); he also had a mulberry garden* planted on the site where Buckingham Palace now stands. It lasted until the Commonwealth. When Tradescant was Queen Henrietta's gardener he had orders to plant the royal park of Kennington with the mulberry, with the same object.

Now Tradescant married E. Day in the early years of James I's reign; and there are four mulberry-trees in this parish, whose size and condition show that they were planted about that time. One is in Camer, one at the Court, and two, planted side by side, are in the writer's garden at Pitfield. Mr. Lewis liked to think, and so do I, not unnaturally, that Tradescant planted them—giving two trees to the principal estates in the village, and planting the other two in the garden of the cottage where he in all probability lived, the one to represent the bridegroom, the other the bride.

Tradescant did not introduce the ordinary mulberry (*Morus nigra*); *that* came to England from Persia via Italy in 1596;† but he did introduce the red mulberry (*Morus rubra*). He also brought us the tulip-tree (*Liriodendron tulipifera*), of which there is one in the Vicarage garden; and though it may claim

---

* Evelyn in his *Diary*, May 10, 1654, refers to it as a place of fashionable resort.   † *Flora Medica.*

to have descended from one planted by Tradescant, it is not, apparently, of an age to claim being his direct botanical child! The pretty creeping plant—the *Aster Tradescanti*—was also introduced by him from Virginia; it grows like a weed under glass, and there is abundance of it at Pitfield; and I remember in the palmy days of the Crystal Palace it clothed the beds in the great hall of that building. In all, we owe to Tradescant the introduction of at least two dozen foreign plants into Britain (*v.* also Appendix O).

John Tradescant, Junior

His son, also John, the Meopham-born man, succeeded his father, who died in 1652, as gardener to King Charles I's Queen, hence the epitaph on their joint memorial tomb in Lambeth Churchyard: "Both gardeners to the Rose and Lily Queen."

In 1637 he made a journey of exploration to Virginia; and four years after his father's death he wrote an account of his father's collection or "Closet of Rarities" under the title of the *Museum Tradescantium*, Elias Ashmole and other friends assisting him. In it are two quaint prints of himself and his father.

He died April 21, 1662, and by his will he left the whole collection to his wife for life, and then to the University of Oxford or of Cambridge, as his wife might decide.

He had, however, apparently forgotten that "at 5.30 p.m. 16 December 1659" (says Ashmole in his "notes") he had already bequeathed by deed the whole collection uncon- ditionally to Ashmole; so two years after Tradescant's death trouble began.

On May 18, 1664, Ashmole sued the widow; the Court upheld the deed of gift, so he gained possession of the "Closet of Rarities" or curiosities. He promptly built a house close to that of Tradescant, and removed the collection to it; and it eventually formed the nucleus of the Ashmolean Museum at Oxford, the first foundation of its kind in England. Like all the earlier museums, it was an *omnium gatherum* of every kind; I only mention one thing, and that is the stuffed specimen of the now extinct Dodo from the Mauritius—a live specimen of which was seen in London in 1538. Only the head and one foot of Tradescant's specimen now survives (Ref. *Dict. Nat. Biog.* and Notes and Queries).

Sir John Bayley

On the north side of the chancel is the sculptured tombstone of the Right Hon. Sir John Bayley, Bart. (1841), and of his wife Elizabeth (1837). It is surmounted by a beautifully executed marble bust of the baronet, and the family escutcheon hangs on the wall above.

Sir John Bayley (1763–1841) was a barrister of renown, serjeant-at-law, and Recorder of Maidstone. In 1808 he was made a Judge of the King's Bench, and then a Baron of the Court of Exchequer. He retired from the Bench in 1834, received his baronetcy, and was made a Privy Councillor. He died *aet.* 78 at Sevenoaks. His connection with Meopham was through his marrying Elizabeth, youngest daughter of John Markett of Meopham Court Lodge, as it was then called. A former holder of the title, the Rev. Sir John Lawrie Emilius Bayley, was his grandson, Rector of St. George's, Bloomsbury, 1856–1867.

He is described as a most upright and just man, and one who took life very happily, finding in his judicial work plenty of amusement. He was not only the author of works on legal subjects, but wrote on the subject of the Prayer Book and on the prophecies that bore upon our Saviour. He is also credited with being the author of the phrase referred to by Cobbett (*Rural Rides*, chap. i): "The blessings of paper money, taxes and the national debt."

On the south side of the chancel is another sculptured memorial stone, of Italian workmanship, to his daughter-in-law Elizabeth.

CHAPTER XII

THE PARISH

ALMOST the only records now available for learning what went on in the Parish in old times are our Churchwardens' and Vestry books (for list *vide* Appendix C), and unfortunately the disappearance of our oldest Churchwardens book (1612–1739) within the last few years makes the historians' work still more difficult. The late Mr. Lewis, however, made numerous pencil extracts from it, and these are now almost our only records of the period that the book covered. Many years ago I photographed part of a page; and this, with one parchment leaf from it containing an extract of Mrs. Markland's will (*q.v.*), 1665–1666, and kept between the leaves of our now oldest Churchwardens' book, will give us a little more information. The missing book was a parchment one, measuring 13 inches by 6 inches, and its loss is irreparable.

The Churchwardens (*v.* Appendix D)

The English parochial system can be traced back to Edgar's reign (970), and the parish was exclusively an ecclesiastical area; and when, as was the case in Meopham, the tithes were taken by a monastery, it was enacted at the end of the fourteenth century—the century of our present church—that the monks were to expend at least one-quarter of this money for the relief of the poor.

A hundred—and more—years ago a Churchwarden's office was no sinecure, as will be seen shortly, for the Vicar, with his Wardens and the Vestry, governed the parish. As our books show, the duties of the Churchwardens as ecclesiastical officers were sharply defined from those of more secular character with which they were concerned at the parochial Vestries.

In the former capacity they dealt with church matters only, meeting at the end of every year at first, but after generally every second year, to consider the assessment of the village in order to raise the church rate; and this varied according to the prospective requirements from 2d. to 1/- in the pound. At the Easter Monday meeting they rendered their accounts; and, as now, the Wardens were then either re-elected or new ones chosen. But sometimes the money matters were not disposed of till much later in the year, as the extracts below show; and they are almost the only ones that now can be made verbatim, the first having been recorded by Mr. Lewis; the last two are the photographed ones.

Aug. 23. 1612.

The accompte given up by the Churchwardens James Taylor and Thomas Skirmer, and all things being made even, there remaineth unto the new Churchwardens £7. 11s. 11d.

HENRY HASLEN
THO: PIGOT. Vicar

June 7. 1618.

Memorandum that the daye and yeare aforesaid Antony Swann, executor of the last will and testament of Thomas Warren late of this pyshe deceased, did paye unto the use of the poore of Meopham and into our hands the some of five pounds which said some was given for and by the last will and testament of the said Thomas Warren deceased, and the money was distributed amonge the poore accorddingely by us.

THOS: PIGOT. Vicar
HENRY HASLEN
HENRY EDMEDE
JAMES TAYLOR

Churchwardens { ROBERT BUTCHER
THOMAS TAYLOR, his marke X

May 9. 1630.

The accompts given up by the Church Wardens Thomas Master and Charles Johnson, and all things being made even there is oweinge to these going off the sum of twelve shillings and tenne pence.

FRA: COURTHOPE

THO: PIGOTT

JAMES TAYLOR
ROBERT BUTCHER
JOHN EDMEDE his marke X
WILLIAM TAYLOR
RICHARD WRIGHT his marke X

THE TRADESCANTS, SENIOR AND JUNIOR
(*vide* p. 165)

THE PARISH COTTAGE ON HOOK GREEN (*vide* p. 192)

THE CAGE DOOR (*vide* p. 199)

An entry almost verbatim with the second of the above also exists of the first distribution of the benefaction left by Henry Audwell in 1629. It is signed by:

THO. PIGOTT
THOMAS MASTER } Churchwardens
CHARLES JOHNSON

The first and the last of these quotations belong to the ordinary routine of the Churchwardens' duties, and the Vicar uses quite a stereotyped form of expression in each. The spelling is free and easy, and the Vicar himself spells his name in two ways.

The second extract deals with an old trust no longer existing (*vide* Charities: Warren Trust); but what trust money the church holds now for the poor is still distributed as formerly, and the distribution is as carefully registered.

Of the signatures given above, there is no doubt that Henry Haslen and J. M. Courthope, both in turn occupiers of the Court Lodge, were Mr. Pigott's own Churchwardens; the two bracketed together as Churchwardens, one of whom could not even sign his name, were the people's, one for each of the boroughs (East and West Meopham). Thus in 1613 the Churchwardens were John Edmeds, William Child, Thomas Skirmer; in 1614 Henry Haslyn, Robert Butcher, and Thomas Ketteridge. For from early days till about 1835 the Parish was divided into two parts, the East and West Boroughs (*q.v.*); and when the Churchwardens made their assessments for the Church rate, and also in their accounts, the two boroughs were kept quite distinct.

This last point may be illustrated by an extract from the Churchwardens' book, which also shows in quite an average way the mode of expenditure:

West Borough. The disbursements of Mr. Jn. Salmon, Church-warden in the parish of Meopham in the County of Kent from the 9th day of May 1773 to the 4th April 1774.

	£	s.	d.
Pᵈ Mr. Buggs 5 Ringing Days and Beer 1 pot . .	1	13	8
Pᵈ Richᵈ Buggs's bill for work @ Church . . .		7	4
Pᵈ for Bread & Wine & washing yᵉ Surplice, at Whitsuntide, Michˢ, Christmas & Easter, 4 times . .	1	17	8
Pᵈ yᵉ Clkˢ 1/2 years Wages due at Michˢ . . .	1	5	0
Pᵈ Do. 1/2 year Wages due at Ladyday . . .	1	5	0
Pᵈ Mr. Sutherden's Bill for Bell ropes and oil . . .	1	9	0
Pᵈ for 24 doz. Sparrows		6	0
Pᵈ for a fox head		1	0
Writing an Assessᵉⁿt 28th Janʸ 74		2	6
Pᵈ my Journey to yᵉ Visitation		5	0
Pᵈ for 3 Hedge hogs		1	0
Pᵈ washing yᵉ Old Surplice		2	6
Pᵈ yᵉ Accᵗˢ Engrossing.		2	6
A shovel & spade for yᵉ Church		7	0
Cleaning the Leads		4	0
Disburs'd in all	£9	9	2
Recᵈ of former Churchwarden	£10	7	9
By assessᵉⁿt 28th Janʸ 74	£15	19	6
Recᵈ in all	£26	7	3
In hand in all	£16	18	1

East Borough. The Disbursements of Mr. Jn: Jewiss, Churchwarden, in the parish of Meopham in the County of Kent from the 9th day of May 1773 to the 4th April 1774

	£	s.	d.
A journey to Sevenoaks yᵉ Visitation		5	0
Pᵈ Rev: Mr. Tatham		5	0
Pᵈ for 6 Badgers' heads		6	0
Pᵈ 3 Hedge hogs . . . . Pᵈ		1	0
Janʸ 28th Spent at making an Assessᵉⁿt . . .		10	0
Pᵈ for 2 dozen Hassocks	2	0	4
A Journey to Gravesend		2	6
Spent at Delivering yᵉ Accᵗˢ up		10	0
Disburs'd in all	£3	19	10
Recᵈ of former Churchwarden	£8	14	3
By Assessᵉⁿt 28th Jan: 74	£8	12	7½
Recᵈ in all	£17	6	10½
In hand 10th April	£13	7	0½

The money for the repairs and upkeep of the church, providing the necessary books and furniture, paying the Clerk, etc., had to be raised by a rate on all the Parish, whatever might be the ratepayers' religious opinions; and in this Parish it was continued until the Easter Vestry of April 18, 1873, when the resolution to run the church "on the voluntary principle" was carried by four votes to three. As early as 1866 a similar resolution had been introduced but was lost on a show of hands. At the Easter Vestry of 1875 the Church-wardens were able to report that the voluntary contributions for the past year amounted to £28 16s. 6d. and the expenditure had been £26 13s. 3½d.—leaving thus a slight balance to the good.

The collection of these contributions was for a long time a personal one—the Churchwardens asked individual parish-ioners; for it was not until late in Mr. Lewis's Vicariate that he gave a rather reluctant consent to a collection in church once a month. Nor was it till the Easter Vestry of 1902 that offertories at each service every Sunday were agreed to.

The compulsory Church rate varied from year to year within wide limits. Thus in 1700 it was 2d. in the pound, producing in the East Borough £4 12s. 3d., in the West Borough £7 10s. In 1739 at 6d. it produced in the two boroughs a total of £42; in 1819 it stood at 9d., and in 1836 at 1/- in the pound. The accounts of this last year show that the high rate was because of extensive building operations in the church tower (*q.v.*), the total expenditure for the year being £128, and all but £2 of this was spent on structural repairs; whilst the Churchwardens' outlay was in 1841 £226 17s. 10d.. with receipts from the rate only £196 3s. 6d.

The constantly recurring entries for bricklayers' work on the church show it must have always been in anything but substantial repair, the roof requiring frequently new "shingles." In 1696 is this entry: "4200 shingles—£8.8.0. 31 foot and ½ of timber for laths—£1.14.1½. 23 days work in sawing laths, hewing best shingles and other work—£2.6.1"; and the very

23 foot of timber for laths £1.4.0." In 1698, "6000 plain tiles £6.17.0: and 20 peg tiles." "For carrying of water to the Chancel: for beere that the workmen had, 16/-. G. West for work at the church windo. 6/-." When in 1859 the nave was re-roofed it must have been, judging by the records, an absolute necessity.

It may be added here that the present generation has been free from large expense in serious repairs, and this must be attributed to the thorough as well as generous way in which Mr. Robert Barnett, working with Mr. Hooper, the Vicar, and the parishioners in 1859, transformed the interior of our church and put the building itself into substantial repair.

The money (£315) required for the re-roofing in 1859 was not, however, obtained without a war of words; for it was strongly objected by the Parish that the money (as proposed) should be raised on the security of the Church rates. However, at the Vestry of February 4, 1859, the agendum was "to settle how much the Parish shall contribute for taking off the nave roof and putting on new. The sum to be borrowed on the credit "of the Church rate @ 5 % and repaid in five years." This was carried by seventy-eight to sixty.

To show how the amount of the Church rate varied, I will give the figures for a number of years taken at random over two centuries.

	£	s.	d.		£	s.	d.
1662 =	9	17	2	1752 =	80	0	0
1664 =	11	3	4	1774 =	105	8	6
1665 =	21	11	4	1819 =	91	18	3
1694 =	24	8	0	1848 =	120	0	0
1702 =	36	17	6	1854 =	54	0	0
1739 =	41	19	6				

The two boroughs did not equally contribute; the West Borough was the more populous, in the proportion varying between 2 to 1 and 3 to 2; besides, it contained the richer parishioners; and its contribution to the rate was generally nearly double that of the East Borough. In 1615 the highest payment was by "Henry Haslyn, Gent." of the Court Lodge, who paid his £4 10s.; and the lowest was the humble 6d. of "Thomas Smithe"; and it may be noted that in the list of payers fifteen years later (1660) appear the names of Nordishe—also spelt Nordash—a name which did not die out of the village till the middle of the nineteenth century; and also that of "Widow Grinnell," relict of one of the donors of our benefactions to the poor, and who gave the name to "Grinnell Sole" (*q.v.*).

The different values of the boroughs appear, for instance, in the Churchwardens' book in 1774, where the West Borough is assessed at £1,416, with a rate of £70 16s.; the East Borough at £692 10s., with a rate of £34 12s. 6d.—the rate being at 1/- in the pound.

Two Overseers were also appointed to each borough, as the following shows. At a Vestry meeting, April 4, 1774, with the Vicar, the Rev. John Tatham, in the chair, the following were chosen Overseers:

John Plummer Thos: Weller	} West Borough
Whiffin Salmon Jos: Mungeam	} East Borough

There was also one Surveyor for each division; and their selection on September 22, 1834, is the last time I find mention of the two boroughs as distinct parts of the Parish in the books.

In the accounts given above in full for 1774 will be noticed that the destruction of "vermin" was paid for out of the Church rate; one would have thought it rather a matter for the parochial Vestry; but perhaps the payments made were regarded in the light of a charity to help the cottagers. In the year 1757 the West Borough paid for 13 hedgehogs at 4d. each, 4/4; 4 badgers' heads (also at times entered as "Greys") at 1/-, 4/-; and the East Borough paid for 6 badgers at 1/-, 6/-; and for 3 "Pollcats" at 4d., 1/-. In 1758, 3 "Foox" heads at 1/-

cost 3/-; and in 1740 "Bager's" heads and 17 "Foox" heads cost 17/-; besides 5/- for 15 hedgehogs, and 8d. for 2 "Pulkats." In 1812 the Churchwardens paid for 189 dozen sparrows' eggs at 6d. the dozen, £4 14s. 6d.! and a second entry the same year adds on to this 102 dozen sparrows' eggs at 3d. the dozen, £1 5s. 8½d.; finally, in 1832 is the entry, "Paid for sparrows' heads and eggs, £12.14.1¾"!

Sometimes the entry states "trapping of Badgers," thus showing how these animals were caught. Though rarely seen nowadays, these beautiful "ground bears" are not extinct in our woods; and a pair of them was caught some fourteen years ago, and kept for a time in the village in captivity. The sparrows were often taken in the "clap-net" at night, and sometimes in "sparrow pots," but these were generally employed in obtaining birds for shooting matches. I have one—the last, I believe, in the village—obtained for me by the late Mr. John Durling; it is a vase-shaped bottle of red earthenware of about a quart capacity, with a wide mouth and only a half bottom. Being hung up against a wall horizontally, the bottom was thus closed; and the sparrows nested in the "pot" as in a "nesting-box." To obtain the young birds, one hand was placed over the mouth and the other was slipped up between the wall and the bottom, and through the open half the fingers extracted the birds.

A resolution was passed on March 31, 1834, "that sparrows and eggs should not be paid for in future by the Church-wardens." This prohibition seems to have been tacitly extended to the other vermin. Whether the "Hunt" ever objected to the destruction of foxes does not appear.

In the fifteenth century, and later, it was common for the parishioners to leave real as well as personal property of all kinds to the Churchwardens, in trust, to devote the proceeds of the same to some church or charitable purpose. It might be for the support of a chantry priest; for candles to burn before the rood, or the figure of some saint; or to defray the cost of the donor's "moneth's minde," i.e. a monthly memorial mass;

or for alms for the poor. The gifts ranged from hives of bees, fowls, oxen, and pigs to land and even houses; and of their discharge of their duties as trustees the Churchwardens had to render strict account. This real property was known as "Church Stock." In the oldest of our Churchwardens' books the following entry appeared for November 12, 1615:

Memorandum that the daye and yeare above says Henry Kennett of this Parish yeoman did receive and take into his hands the sume of £3.10.0 parte of the Church Stocke, which sayd some was lately in the hands of John Warren Sen: in the presence of us and is to paye yearely therefore 5/.

That there is in the hands of Nicholas Sprever of the Church Stocke, 13 sheep for which it is agreed that he shall pay yearly 4/4.

There is in the hands of William Hubbard 3 sheep for which he payeth yearly 12d.

There is in the hands of Thomas Boghurst a cow for which he payeth yearly 2/.

The Churchwarden Sprever is here shown farming out the livestock of the church; this was the customary way of adding to the church's income.

Beside all this, the Churchwardens had duties to perform in the parochial Vestry irrespective of their church duties, mainly dealing with the relief of the poor. This from earliest times has been a most complicated question; and was never more so than after the dissolution of the monasteries, which, whilst they did enormous good by real charity, at the same time supported troops of wastrels and encouraged mendicity, though doubtless unintentionally; hence, when the monks no longer were able to do this the country became flooded with beggars and masterless men, to deal with whom it taxed all the art and resources of a country parish.

The late Mr. Lewis, as an introduction on writing of our village, as governed by the Vestry, prefaced it with a pretty full account of the treatment of the poor under the Poor Laws of various centuries; and from this I propose to give an abstract, so that the difficulty of the question even to recent times may be the better appreciated.

In the reign of Edward I (1289) the Statute of Winchester contained a law against vagrants; and in Richard II's time, in 1389, a Law of Deserving Poor was passed; and whilst the country had never been without its poor, whether "Deserving" or "Vagrant," there is no question that their number enormously increased in the suppression of the religious houses by Henry VIII. Till then there was open door kept for every passer-by, and numbers were daily fed at the monastery gates; besides, the religious bodies were good as a rule to their poor tenants, although by their indiscriminate charity they also kept alive a number of masterless men—the "undesirables" of the present day. When the lands passed into other and often less considerate hands the poor workers suffered, whilst now the community at large suffered from the vagrants whose existence, as long as the monks fed and helped them, it cared little about. As our Manor of Meopham always remained the property of the Church, it is likely that our poor workers were better off than those in many other places; but details of their position at that time must be left to conjecture—we have no records. In the reigns of Henry VIII, Edward VI, Mary, and Elizabeth the laws against the masterless poor were very cruel; branding, mutilating, working as slaves for private people or in chains on the public roads, whipping, and even death, were their lot. Their children could be taken from them, and by Justices' order be brought up as servants and apprentices—a good thing for the children, and showing an appreciation of the social law that the nation's future depends on the children of the present; but if the children broke from their indentures, they were liable to be sold as slaves.

In 1535 (Henry VIII) the aged and infirm poor who could no longer work were to be relieved by the Parson and Churchwardens from money collected in a box, to be duly provided, at the church door after a sermon or address by the Parson had been delivered; and no alms were to be given to the above object except in this manner, under punishment of fine, indiscriminate giving being thus recognized as doing harm rather than good; and as the poor of the village would be known to the parish authorities, vagrants could be excluded.

In 1552 (Edward VI) this received modification. The Parson and Churchwardens were required each Whitsuntide to call the parishioners together after divine service, and to elect two of their number as collectors of alms; and on the following Sunday, having made inquiry in the week, they were to enter in a book what each person would contribute weekly, and to collect these contributions.

An obdurate and stingy parishioner could even be haled before the Bishop, who had power to bind him over to appear at the next Sessions under a fine of £10. The Justices in Session determined how much his "gift" for the poor should amount to; and if he now proved recalcitrant he was sent to prison!

But before the year was out it was enacted that Overseers of the poor should take the responsibility of the poor off the shoulders of the Churchwardens and their collectors; and all parishioners were to be taxed for the support or relief of the deserving poor; but any man who could work but would not, whipping and the stocks were to be his lot.

In 1556 (Mary) Parliament allowed the poor of a parish who could not get sufficient relief at home to take out licences and wear a badge and to beg in other specified parishes.

In 1562 every parish was ordered to provide for its own poor by voluntary effort. Later the necessary money was raised by assessment, which rested with the Justices till 1597, when the duty was transferred to the Churchwardens, in whose hands it remained till recent times.

In 1575 Houses of Correction were established in every county, where the lazy were to be sent with the object, which is explained by the order, that each house shall be provided "with implements for setting to work and punishing"! In 1601 (43 Elizabeth, c. 2) property was to be taxed, forming a fund ("County Fund") for the poor, the contribution to which regularly appears in our books. The tax had to be paid to the county, though the parish had besides to support its own poor; the tax was not made general and inclusive till George III's day.

In 1675 the Churchwardens had the power to remove a newcomer from the parish if he were likely to become a charge upon it, unless he could find a security or occupied a house valued at £10 a year, or could be considered as "settled" by having been born in the parish or apprenticed to someone in it, or by having already been in service for at least six weeks, and in some cases for a twelve-month.

In 1692 every newcomer had to give his name to the Churchwardens on arrival, which was read out in church, and any parishioner might raise an objection to his remaining in the parish.

In 1697 a parish was obliged to keep a newcomer if he had a certificate from his native or legal parish, undertaking to remove him if he became chargeable on the rates. It had also to accommodate poor passers-through for the night; such entries as the following are common in our books: "1700. Several seamen and travellers. 7/."

All this now brings us down to our special subject: the Meopham Workhouse and Government by Vestry.

CHAPTER XIII

GOVERNMENT BY VESTRY

IN 1723 a workhouse was established in every parish under the care of the Churchwardens and Overseers, and the destitute poor were obliged to enter it or get no relief at all, for outdoor relief was not recognized until the year 1796, when also, in consequence of the great poverty then existing, the Justices were empowered to fix a labourer's weekly wage and, if he were unable to earn as much, the parish had to make it up to him.

In 1834, after a Commission appointed two years previously had made its report, the new Poor Law came into force and parish workhouses were abolished, those of the Unions taking their place; and in eight months no less than 2,066 parish workhouses, of which ours was one, became merged into 172 Union workhouses; and so the Meopham House was absorbed into that of the Strood Union or, as at first called, the North Aylesford Union. A conference was held with the Poor Law Commissioners on April 8, 1835, and the minutes of that meeting show a reluctance of some of the Meopham people to the new arrangement, lest the Parish should be called upon for some extraordinary contribution towards the erection of the Strood Union workhouse.

In 1724 the old house still standing at the Street, now Mr. Clark's shop, and formerly the post office, was hired at a rent of £6 per annum as our workhouse; but fifty years later the rent was £8 with £2 2s. land-tax. It was in charge of the Parish Vestry; there were no Guardians appointed till after the local workhouse system ceased; and in 1836 Mr. T. Taylor was the first elected Guardian. The Parish Vestry used to meet at the church to make the assessment for the poor rate; but for regular monthly business the usual meeting-place was the George Inn, where any ratepayer—

who had paid his rates!—might be present, and join in the discussion.

At first, at any rate, the Vestry took care to be thorough in its administration, and to be benevolent also; thus it not only helped the poor but even seemed to take pride in the appearance of these dependants, as the following extracts from the Parish books show:

K.J. to take her clothes out of pawn, and to alter her bonnet!

A curious entry in 1777 shows a mixture of judicial strictness with expensive benevolence; also it seems to suggest marriage under compulsion:

Gave T. Oliver for assisting in taking Jn Higgins .	8/
Charges to Gillingham with do:	3/1½
Do. to Rochester and expenses with do: . . .	8/10
Paid for a licence and marriage fees for do: . .	£1.14.6
Journey to Gillingham for licence	5/
Paid to Mr. Buggs for eating and drinking with do:	£2.16.9
Paid Geo: Bennett for attending and a journey to Rochester with do:	10/6

If we add to this one other item, viz.:

Overseers expenses to Farningham to take Higgins .   £1.1.6

the grand total reaches £7 8s. 2½d. !

The marriage in the same year of Mary Codgate was even more expensive, for it cost the Parish just £9.

When the Vestry acted in its judicial capacity and as *custos morum* of the village, it could set the law in motion against offenders through the Overseers; it could and did send refractory young women to Bridewell, and incorrigible young men were forced to enlist! In those good old days anything was good enough for the Services!

The workhouse was under a Master, at £30 per annum, besides board, the use of two rooms, an allowance for beer (!) and £3 extra for tea and sugar. His wife acted as matron, and when a married couple could not be obtained other arrangements had to be made; as, for instance, in 1793: "To allow Widow Jewiss £7 per year to take care of the poor in the workhouse; and Wm. Mungeam £5.5.0 per year to superintend the House." The previous year he had been elected Acting Overseer of the poor generally. The post of Master presumably had its drawbacks, since in 1801 the Vestry failed to persuade a Mr. Tomlyn to undertake the office.

The number of the inmates seems to have varied very much, though 15 was probably an average. In 1787 it was as high as 36; but perhaps there were many children, for in 1774 there were no less than 15 children inmates. In 1792 there were 4 men, 12 women, and 8 children. How so many were accommodated in so small a building passes comprehension, but perhaps these figures include those who were boarded out.

In 1803 the regulations for the occupants of the workhouse were as follows:

RULES AND ORDERS TO BE OBSERVED BY POOR IN WORKHOUSE

1. Swearing, quarrelling or indecent behaviour to be punished by the loss of the next meal.

2. Attend prayers morning and evening and eat their victuals orderly at the common table in the Dining Room; nor leave till after thanks have been returned on pain of losing the next meal.

3. That none presume to play at Cards, Dice or any other game.

4. Not abuse the Master or Mistress but obey them. If they have any complaint, must make it to the Overseer or at the Monthly meeting. If any one abuse or behave disrespectfully to Master or Mistress he shall have full power to confine such person and to keep him on slender diet until complaint can be made to a magistrate.

5. They are to take their clean linen from their Mistress every Saturday evening and bring their foul linen to her every Sunday morning.

6. Not to go out without leave nor stay beyond the time appointed them on pain of losing their next meal.

7. All to be in bed by nine o'clock in summer and eight in winter, and fires and candles to be put out by that time.

8. Not to smoke in any place but the common room, on pain of punishment.

The House was not, however, entirely dependent, after a time, upon the rates; it earned money for itself. At first it does not seem to have done so; but a resolution was passed in 1798 determining the propriety "of putting the poor of the House to some kind of work as soon as convenient." It had already brewed its own beer, pickled its pork, and made its own bread, etc., but now had a loom for making linen and cloth. It also let out its able-bodied inmates to work for a wage by the day on farms, as this entry shows, when Mr. Hodsoll in 1825 pays the Parish "for Mrs. Johnson's Cherrying 18/6": and Mr. Markett, of the Court Lodge, pays the Parish "for Mrs. Bennet's hopping £2.4.0." In the case of children thus "let out," one-fifth of their earnings was taken toward the income of the House. Children, whether in the House or not, were taught weaving, as were also those of the village poor who cared to come to be taught.

The minutes of the Vestry at this period show that the normal business of the monthly meetings was, besides arranging matters for the House, the granting of sums of money, even up to a guinea, to the outside poor, as well as gifts of clothing, etc.

The following extract may be taken as typical:

Nov. 25th 1794. At a Vestry held this Day the Overseers Disbs for Novr were allow'd, also for Richd Bennett's Wife to have a petticoat, a shift, a pr of Shoes & a pr of Stocking & a Gown for her Child, and for her to have 3/6 per week—also to let the Widw Freeman have some Cloths for her Children—also for Heny Wood to have a pr of Sheets and Clothes for his Children, also to give John Lee a Guinea to buy his Boy Clothes being gone to Service—Also to give Thos Vennison half a Guinea —also to allow the Widw Parker 1/6 per week—also to give John Bright a pr of Shoes. 7/o—and the Widw Martin to have a Cord of Wood.

By Us

GEO: SMITH
THOS CROWHURST } Churchwardens
JOSEPH PARKER: THOMAS SALMON
LEONARD HAWLEY

The Vestry also passed a resolution in 1795 that flour should be bought in bulk and retailed at a cheap rate; and this seems to have been the practice for many years. In 1795 fifty-three families thus purchased flour, whilst in 1821 no less a sum than £150 changed hands in this transaction. Flour, however, had always been one of the grants, when necessary; thus: "1801. Agreed that persons having three children should be allowed 3/ per week in flour."

The Vestry after a time seems to have tried the plan of contracting for the feeding of its paupers, so it appointed an "acting" Overseer—distinct from the Master—to supervise everything in connection with the workhouse poor. He received a salary of £35 per annum and, to quote Mr. Lewis's words, "he seems to have contracted in 1782 to feed the inmates at the rate of 2/6 each per week, exclusive of 'small beer' of which the inmates were allowed 3 gallons a day at the cost of 4d. the gallon. Half a crown does not seem a large sum even for paupers; but meat (mutton) then cost only 4½d. per lb."

An entry for 1793 shows the food bills for one month: Butcher £5 3s. 3d.; Baker £12 14s. 11½d.; Shop (i.e. groceries) £8 11s. 8½d. At this time fifteen people seem on an average to have lived in the workhouse.

A doctor visited the House, and apparently he always came from Wrotham; Mr. Crow of Wrotham was the doctor in 1807; in 1776 it was a Dr. Rowley. The pay was at first four guineas per annum, afterwards increased to five, but there were evidently extras, there being a bill paid to the doctor of £17 for attending a case of broken arm! Severe cases were taken to London, generally to Guy's; one case cost £4 for the journey and hotel expenses at the "Nag's Head," in the Borough.

The Vestry also paid for nursing its poor outside, and in the case of male patients it seems to have employed men rather than "Mrs. Gamp." Thus in 1825 we have:

Two men sitting up with a sick man at Loamer 4/.

Two men sitting up with a sick Irishman at Mrs. Markett's 4/.

Thos: Bennett for board, lodging and nursing a sick man for 5 weeks.

This last was probably at an inn, as there is an entry in another place that Thos. Bennett was paid 15/6 for sixty-two pints of beer for J. Weller! It seems, therefore, as if Bennett were an innkeeper.

Until 1798, when Jenner came to the rescue with vaccination, smallpox, both from its fatal consequences and the hideous disfigurement it often left, was the country's curse; and the Vestry of Meopham gave its poor the advantage of the only preventive treatment then known, viz. inoculation, introduced from Constantinople, c. 1718, by Lady Mary Wortley Montague. (Parenthetically, it may be explained that this treatment consisted in actually inoculating a person from a smallpox pustule, and though the patient contracted the disease, it ran a milder course than when caught "accidentally" and perhaps when he was in a less fit condition to fight the disease, whilst the risk of disfigurement was much reduced.)

1776. Paid Mr. Rowley for inoculating 17 persons, and a mixture for Dame Brown £4.10.9.

Inoculation was prohibited by Act of Parliament in 1840, vaccination as we now know it having become recognized. An epitaph in our church, already quoted, bears witness to this, for in 1761 William Masters, heir to the then owners of Camer, died at the age of twenty-five; the inscription runs: "He died of smallpox unhappily procured by inoculation."

Few people nowadays can imagine the horror with which smallpox was regarded in old times; more's the pity! for once to see a face disfigured by confluent smallpox would be enough to alter the opinions of the most rabid anti-vaccinationist. The lasting pallor and the pitted skin of the face destroyed all good looks. In the "good old days" an unspoilt complexion, from its rarity, more than good features, was a girl's greatest asset; and the frequent references by old writers to the blooming countenances of dairymaids is thus explained; for it must be remembered that it was their freedom from smallpox that first drew Jenner's attention to its prevention by the inoculation of the harmless cowpox. In one account of the celebrated Miss Gunnings (*q.v.*) it is suggested that the admiration expressed for their beauty was as much owing to their complexions not having been spoilt by smallpox as to any other charms these young ladies possessed!

A curious instance of "preventive medicine" is on record in 1790. The entry runs thus: "Medicine for 2 persons in the workhouse *who were in danger of madness* £1.10.0." The practitioner in this instance was a Mrs. C.! Hydrophobia was also apparently "cured." "1794. Four Children of Bennett's family bitten by a mad dog," and "1825. Mrs. Chapman curing T. Gates' children of a bite of a mad dog £2." Fielding, in his *Memoirs of Malling*, says that there is a chalybeate spring at Birling, and that the water from it was the celebrated "remedy."

A "remedy" for hydrophobia, known as the "Birling Cure" or "Birling Drink" from its origin in that village, was famous years ago; perhaps "Mrs. C." was its originator.

The Education of poor children was another of the Vestry's duties, and some £9 per annum seems to have been an average expenditure for the purpose; and in 1752 the schoolmaster's pay was 3/9 a week. The pupils averaged twelve–fifteen in number.

| 1774. A Quarters Schooling at 3/9 per week | £2.8.9. |
| 1775. Teaching poor children to read at 3/9 a week | £2.8.9. |

In connection with education, special reference must be made to Mr. W. Mungeam*—a name long extant in Meopham, though now no more, but surviving in Cobham. From 1792 to 1802 a certain William Mungeam appears as Master of the

* The first Mayor of Rochester, after its incorporation in 1461, was a William Mungeam.

workhouse, and then became Clerk to the Vestry; he was also one of the witnesses to the will of John Markett, of the Court, in 1801; and at the time of the suppression of village workhouses the Rev. Glover Mungeam held a school for boys in the Well House, and the Parish paid him 3d. per head per week for the education of fifteen boys. This gentleman was son to William Mungeam above-mentioned, and was curate of Stanstead from 1834 to 1846, but he lived at South Street House (Leylands), then a small farm-house, and he used to drive to his duties in a small pony chaise. He had two brothers, William and Thomas; the latter left the country, but William was surveyor of the high roads (1837) and farmed the Green Farm, afterwards retiring to Pitfield Cottage on Meopham Green; and what has impressed itself most of all on the memory of one of the "village fathers" is that he saw the coffin—when the old man died in 1846—lowered from one of the windows, the narrow and steep staircase rendering it impossible to remove the body by any other way. His son Glover, so named after his clerical uncle, was the maltster at Camer.

There was also a Glover Mungeam (*ob.* 1791), either the father or elder brother of the schoolmaster, William (*ob.* 1818), and to whom we owe the neatly executed ground-plan of the old Parsonage and its grounds, dated 1790, referred to under the Vicarage.

The poorhouse had from time to time to admit temporarily, till they were able to leave, or were transferred to their own parishes, a certain number of casuals. Some were lodged out, and the entries are many where housing was paid for "Strangers"; but the following extracts from the Vestry book (1792) are peculiar in the name given these people, viz. "Accidentials"; and pathetic, if the word "fell" is to be taken literally, that they succumbed to exhaustion; but perhaps in every instance "on the Parish" should be read in after "fell."

Accidentials fell on the Parish of Meopham in 1792.

Fell at the Fair, Wm. Sandford, Mary his wife, Hannah and Thomas his children, July 12, 1792. Left the Parish the 17th instant —14/.

A Chimney sweeper and his wife fell in Wm. Wheatley Esq's Barn July 12. Left the Parish 16th instant—7/.

Oct. 28. George —— fell at Thos. Buggs's—13/.

There were four other "accidentials" besides in this year— their total expenses to the Parish being four guineas.

The Parish no doubt was always very considerate and liberal to its poor; but it appeared to do more than relieve the necessitous and to stand *in loco parentis* to the young. It not only educated these, as we have seen, but it apprenticed out a number of boys to various trades, but the girls it assisted and fitted out for domestic service; and a number of the old indentures of apprenticeship still are amongst the church archives. It gave also assistance to young women when they desired to get married; and it would almost seem (as Mr. Lewis has suggested) that in the following case the Parish encouraged the marriage to get the girl off their hands. "1783. Pd. Timothy Lynch on marrying Sarah Crowhurst a lame person £2.12.6. Fees 7/9."

Other entries show that in the ballot for the militia, if a young man's number were drawn, and the Parish did not want to lose him, it paid for his substitute, or else paid the fine— the sums of money thus disbursed varying from £10 to £20 in each instance.

The village workhouse system, however—and not in Meopham only—became very expensive; and it became clear to the authorities that centralization would be cheaper and more effectual; so the introduction of the New Poor Law in 1834, already referred to, saved Meopham from probable bankruptcy. Not only was the House too small, though some additions had been made to it, but the cost was inhibitory; and in 1818, to take but one example, the poor rate here rose to 8/- in the pound, the average throughout the country being about 13/3 in the pound at that time.

Being at times cramped for room, the Vestry had to board some paupers and casuals out, as has been mentioned, in cottages, and even in the public-houses, paying as much as 4/4 a day; others were transferred to Coxheath Workhouse at 3/6 a day; and in 1787–1788 "Fowlerstone House" was hired for the same purpose from Mr. Markett at £10 rent and 8/- land-tax. The next year (1789), however, the Vestry determined to build cottages of its own for those who were too poor to pay their rents. This was the resolution passed: "1789. Agreed to proceed immediately in the building of the cottages on the Waste for the reception of such Parishioners as are not able to pay their rents." (In 1845, after the closure of the workhouse, the Parish had to excuse eighty-one poor people from paying their rents.)

The Vestry now borrowed £80, as the following shows: "27 Dec. 1789. Agreed to borrow £80 to pay for the cottages that are built for the poor on Pitfield Green and at Greenel Sole Pond." The resolution to begin the building was on August 30, 1789, so they were evidently constructed within four calendar months.

Though it seems contrary to the spirit of the first resolution, it appears that five years later the Parish actually charged a rent for their cottages. In 1793 one William Higgins had one of the cottages on Meopham Green—called the Loam Houses or Cottages—but he clearly did not pay his rent of 1/- a week, for this resolution was passed in 1794: "Agreed, To strain Wm. Higgins for the rent of the house he occupies of the Parish." The arrest of a William Higgins some time before has been already mentioned; if this were his son, the family seems to have been not altogether desirable!

The two thatched cottages on the Green above referred to, and known also as the Loam Pit Cottages, or Clay Cottages, were built on the south side of the Green, on land now forming the kitchen garden of Pitfield, leave having been given by the Vestry to the late Dr. Baber on November 20, 1862, to purchase them, the purchase money being invested in

£216 13s. 4d. Stock Consols; and this now forms one of the Parish trusts known as the "Clay Cottages Trust." In 1855 the rent of these cottages had been allowed by the Charity Commissioners to be applied to the support of the National Schools, and in 1895 the sum of £5 19s. was so handed over. At the annual Parish Council held April 16, 1895, a report of the Council's Committee on the Parish charities stated that the Clay Cottage Trust "did not come under the Council's jurisdiction, and had been for many years, by the permission of the Charity Commissioners, applied to the support of the National School."

At the same time that the "Loam Cottages" were erected the two at "Greenel Sole Pond" were also built. They stood on the left-hand or north side of the road, on the rising ground opposite the pond, and at right angles to the road at Foxendown Farm. Our oldest inhabitant, Mr. Ashenden, remembers them well in his young days.

The following extracts from the Vestry book will be found interesting:

1789

Paid Mr. Buggs for allowance building the house
  near Greenelsole pond £1.17.8
Thatching the cottage on Pitfield Green . . . £1.13.0
Mr. John Lott, Bricklayer, his bill for work on the
  cottages built for the reception of the poor . £13.8.0
Mr. John French his bill for Carpenters work and
  materials on the cottages on Pitfield Green (i.e.
  the Loam Cottages) and at Mr. Markett's Pond £32.3.2½

Mr. Markett now owned the pond once "Greenel's" (v. Grinnell Sole); and when Mr. Robert Barnett bought the Court Lodge and some of the Manor lands the cottages passed into his hands.

In 1806 the Vestry passed the following resolution: "Mr. W. Mungeam, overseer of the poor, empowered to enlarge the present workhouse according to the proposal of Mr. Griffiths the manager." Evidently the two sets of cottages erected were now not sufficient, hence the enlargement of the House; but whether the manager's suggestion and manner of enlargement proving a failure, or for some other reason which does not appear, certain it is that two years later, in 1808, notice was given Mr. Griffiths "to provide himself in three months"!

For a quarter of a century things went on in the same groove, but on June 21, 1832, we read: "Resolved that it is expedient to take into consideration the building some cottages out of the Parish Funds, in consequence of the great number of the poor who are returning to the Parish without the power of finding Houses."

Thereupon the Vestry applied to the Dean and Chapter of Canterbury, as Lords of the Manor, for a small site on Hoo Green for the erection of two more cottages for the poor; and in due course they were built; and they still stand, though for some time they have been thrown into one. During Mr. Lewis's time the building was employed by Mrs. Lewis as a knitting factory, and socks were made in large quantities by machine; part of the building was also for a time used as a private school for children. Within the last few years it has changed hands and has been bought by Mr. Clark the builder, and it now forms his workshop.

Besides these six cottages the Parish also hired the house at Fowlerstone for the same purpose, as has been mentioned already.

With the disappearance of the workhouse in 1834, and the introduction of the New Poor Law, the story of government by Vestry ceases; but I append a number of extracts from the Churchwardens' and the Vestry books which are interesting as records of the past and as illustrations of many of the foregoing remarks. Some have been given already in various connections; but this list is a consecutive collection in three different centuries.

1689. "For the Book of Prayer upon account of the Invasion
1/." [This refers to the landing of the Prince of Orange.]

1689. "For the Parator for a form of Prayer and thanksgiving for the Prince of Orange's success 1/6."

"Paid to Barkin for altering the Prayer concerning the King and Queen 1/6" [i.e. the substitution of William and Mary for James in the Prayer Book].

"Ringers on Coronation day 2/6."

1690. "Given the ringers for the battle of the Boyne 2/6."

1691. "Ringers for the King's return from Ireland 5/."

1692. "Allowed for expenses when he made several searches by night for idle people 1/7."

["He" is the Borsholder; this functionary is explained under the subject of the "Cage."]

"Paid to Goodman Clipton for set of bell ropes £1.0.10."

1694. "Paid John Reeve for a knell 3 hours, ye day ye Queen was buried."

[The above references are of course to William and Mary.]

1695. "For triming Goody Green's house 15/6."

[The old English titles given to the senior village folk should be noticed.]

1753. "Paid the Reeves Bill for going the bounds of the Parish."

[v. also "Beating the Bounds.")

1754. "Charges on account of a man that hanged himself. Carrying him to Mr. Wellers 1/. Paid the Jury 6/. Paid for coffin 9/. At his burial 5/–. A journey to Gravesend 2/. Digging a grave 1/6.

"Received for the man's coat that hanged himself 2/."

1755. "John Elliot's daughter hanged herself. Paid jury 6/. Coffin 9/, beer for her burial 5/. Digging grave 2/. A pound of wool and laying her forth 2/."

1761. "Paid Hutchings laying forth W. Assetur and wool: and an affidavit 4/."

"Dame Fisher for spinning ½ a dozen pound of flax at 6d. per lb. 3/."

1763. "pd to Widow Rumney on account of her airing her daughter who had the smallpox 6/. For the nurse £1.11.6."

1775. "Teaching 15 poor children to read. 3/9 a week. £2.8.9."

"Paid for Eason the Borsholders bill 2/6."

"Land tax and windows for the Poor House 5/3."

1776. "Clearing the Roads of Snow £8.13.9

1778. "Payment for a substitute for John Buggs. £5.5.0."

1779. "Mr. Buggs for liquor for T. Fielder's wife at the time of lying in 10/11."(!)

1780. "Carrying Ann Burges to Bridewell 8/6. Two journeys to Maidstone: 32 weeks at 2/4 with Ann Burges' child and clearing her from Bridewell £4.0.2."

1781. "A woman in the road with the smallpox 2/6."
"A woman and children with a pass from Gravesend 1/."

1782. "Paid the parish of Swingfield for the maintenance of St: Tricker's family, he being substitute for Richard Allchin [of Meopham] £8.4.8."

1783. "Rent of Workhouse deducting 16/ for land tax £5.4.0."
"Gave Esther Allchin clothes, 10/6. and agreed with Mrs. Love of Gravesend to her servant at rate of £1.0.0 per year; a month's wages, or a month's warning."
"Going to the Hospitable [sic] with Dame Batt £1.8.0."

1786. "Paid £3.18.8 to redeem Robert Crowhurst's goods."
[The next year the Vestry put the poor fellow into the Fowlerstone Cottage.]
"Gave Widow Burgis for taking her child from the parish £1.11.6."

1787. To get Abram Boaker and his family, who belongs to Sundrich, off the hands of Meopham Parish cost over £12 of which £9 10s. 2d. were lawyers costs; Sundrich repaid £3 2s. 5d. of the total.

1788. "Apprenticing G. Hills to a fisherman £6.10.0."
"Carrying John Eversfield to Bethlehem £6.18.0."
"Spent on the jury when Dixon Treadwell's wife fell out of a cherry tree in John Nordish orchard, 7/."

1790. "Expenses attending John Carr a housebreaker £1.16.4½."
"Expenses attending John Car a felon who broke open Edw. Jury's house, 15/."

1791. "Rent of Fowlerstone House £5.9.0."
"Agreed to give John Russell on condition of marrying Eliz: Dunk ten pounds to take a child she has now by John Martin clear of the parish."

1793. "To send the Widow Martin to the house of Correction for her bad behaviour with Richard Bennett; and him to be apprehended by the constable as a fit person to serve his Majesty."
"W. Mungeam to become superintendent of Workhouse at £5.5.0 per annum."
"Paid the officer of Chatham for John Armsbury's family, he being a substitute in the Militia for the parish of

1793. Meopham, 5/ per week." [The Meopham man was William Mullinger, the village bootmaker.]

"Expenses attending the marriage of John Bevan to Mary Edmeades. Licence £1.18.6. Fees 7/9. Ring 5/6. Dinner 9/6."

1794. "To give G. Hawley 1/ per week to take Leonard Hawley his nephew for a year and find him necessaries."

"To continue Fowlerstone for the poor: and to pay a part of Lane's daughter's Doctor's Bill."

"The Widow Martin to have one of the Loam Houses on Pitfield Green at Michaelmas, if she cannot suit herself with a room."

1796. "Raising Volunteers for the Navy £23.15.0."

1801. "Loom (for workhouse) £9.1.5."

The superintendent of the workhouse is "to see that they are employed either in spinning and manufacturing linen or woollen cloth, or any other articles or out of doors, in any way the churchwardens or overseers may direct."

1801–2. W. Mungeam ceased to be superintendent of the work-house (Geo. Blackman and then Samuel Callis taking his place); and accepted post of Vestry Clerk at £4.4.0 per annum.

1803. "Weaving of 70 yards of cloth at 7d. per yard spun in the Poor house, £2.0.10."

"Paid for three substitutes in the Militia, Ph. Buggs, John Parker, John Dutton, £10 each."

"James Bennetts wife and family to have half a guinea a week, he having been drawn for the Militia, and joined his regiment."

1806. "Mr. Lawrie engages to supply what small beer may be required for the use of the workhouse, amounting to about 3 gallons a day, at 4d. a gallon. The Master's family to be allowed a pint and a half of strong beer a day; this to continue for one month."

1807. "Mr. Crow, surgeon at Wrotham, engaged to attend the poor for £6.6.0 per annum."

1810. Mr. W. Mungeam is again appointed to superintend the Parish poor resident and non-resident, for £20 a year, with 5/– travelling each time he has to attend a sitting of the magistrates.

"Widow Bennett to continue in the Parish House on Pitfield

1810.   Green [i.e. Loam Cottage] on condition of George Bennett marrying her, till they can find themselves a house."

1818. "Money at the Fair for children of the Poor House July 10th, 8/3."

"July 16. Rev. G. Mungeam for a quarter's schooling for 12 poor children £2.8.9."

1829. "Thomas Bennett for Psalm Singers Feast £1."

CHAPTER XIV

BEATING THE BOUNDS AND THE CAGE

THERE can be but few parishes in which the old, and once necessary, custom of beating the parish bounds is kept up with regularity; for every parish has now its proper map that answers the purpose better. The ceremony, usually on Ascension Day—for it was a religious one in origin*— kept the memory green of the exact limitations of the parish; and with the view of perpetuating this knowledge, a number of schoolboys were always taken, armed with white willow wands, with which to smite the various objects—trees or posts or stones—that marked the parish limits; and, that their memories might be impressed, they themselves came in for a share of the same treatment, whilst adults, with the same object, might find themselves bumped against the boundary marks.

In our earliest Vestry book, under date 1788—amongst several—are complete itineraries for the beating of the bounds, with every mark duly described; for the most part these are trees, and the number of oaks and beeches is remarkable, but yews and whitethorns also figure largely. In the above year the boundary marks mentioned are 139; but they are increased to 208 in 1850.

In towns the boundaries are marked with cast-iron shields or plates fastened on various buildings, and these were the special objects the boys had to hit; where the parish boundary passed through a house, as was the writer's lot in London, the boys claimed right of entry and duly thrashed the tablets; and he remembers being interrupted in a lecture at Guy's Hospital for the same purpose, as the theatre was built over the border-line of two parishes. A difficulty arises where the

---

* Some trace this religious ceremony, which was at Rogationtide, to the Ambarvalia of ancient Rome.

middle of a river is the boundary, as in St. Olave's Parish at London Bridge; but this was also, he recollects, surmounted by taking the boys to the middle of London Bridge, and dropping one of their number at the end of a rope into a boat awaiting him beneath.

Beating the bounds was always a festive occasion, and two entries from our Parish books will confirm this:

1788. Expense of walking the bounds paid by Mr. Smedley (the Vicar), John Markett Esq., and the parishioners equally £1.5.0 each. May 15. Beef 14/7½. Puddings etc. 11/6. Beer and tobacco 4/6. Punch £1.0.0. at the "White Horse" 7/. May 16 (2nd day) Beer and tobacco 4/4½. Punch 13/. Total £3.15.0.

During the Vicariate of the Rev. E. Lewis the beating of the bounds was combined with a short "Rogation Service" on the land of the various farms passed through.

In 1812 the ceremony cost in all £4 0s. 9½d.; the bill was for: Beef £1 13s. Puddings 15/8½. Beer and tobacco 5/4. Punch £1. "White Horse" 8/5. Longfield 2/8.

This old ceremony has been revived in Meopham in May 1914, all the "ages of man," from eleven to seventy-nine years, being represented. The "father" of the procession was Mr. Oliver, whose recollection of everything in the Parish in years past is most keen and accurate, and he had first beaten the bounds when a schoolboy sixty-one years ago. He, with some much younger, footed it well on this last occasion all the way—a walk of nearly twenty miles; though by the close of the day the numbers of the "beaters" had thinned perceptibly. The feast was held at the "White Horse" Harvel, but an interim call had been made at the "Vigo"! The Vicar (Rev. A. F. C. Owen) joined the party for some time, and had his memory duly impressed by being "bumped" on a boundary mark—the alternative to the application of the willow wand!

A full account of this occasion may be read in the *Kent Messenger* for May 20, 1914.

The Borsholder and the Cage

The term Borsholder frequently occurs in our Parish books; and in an old document of the time of Henry III mention is made of "Thoᵐ de la Wesseland, Borghweshold̃,"i.e. Thomas of the Westland (the borough of West Meopham), Borsholder. The following information from Furley's *History of the Weald of Kent* explains the origin of the word. The "Borough" in Kent and "tithing" in other counties was one and the same thing. It was composed of ten freemen or heads of families who were mutually "burgh" or sureties for each other. The head or chief was called the burgh-ealder, head-borough, or borsholder, denominated in other counties the tithing man; ten of these boroughs or tithings constituted originally the "hundred."

In our Parish records the Borsholder largely appears as the recipient of payments for such duties as keeping order at the annual fair, and for arresting bad characters; he was, in fact, the police-sergeant of the day; under him was generally a constable. This bill copied from our books gives an insight into his duties:

1831. Attending at Meopham Fair 10/
Attending the Beer Shops and Vitulars 1 year and half 15/
Paid for a pair of handcuffs 9/
Paid Mr. Tunstall for painting a Staffe . . . 10/
John French for turning a Staffe 1/

H. LANGFORD

The Borsholder or Constable, having arrested the vagrant or drunkard, had to imprison him in the village cage till he could be taken before the magistrate. The Cage was in old days common on every village green; ours was a square brick building some 6 feet square, and stood on the forge green immediately below the pond, in front of the forge cottage and half-way toward the main road. It was closed by a stout oaken prison door studded with iron, and with a strong lock, and two padlocks which fastened the ends of the hinges, 3 feet

9 inches long, into hasps. In it was a peep-hole a foot square and closed with iron bars; but three of them were arranged as a hinged wicket, also padlocked, through which food could be handed to the prisoner; and the late Mr. Durling told me he, as a lad, well remembered handing in beer to a victim inside! The cage ceased to be of use in the 'sixties of the last century, and on November 5, 1875, Ed. Loft, Ted Long, R. Bishop, and J. Long set fire to it by thrusting lighted straw through the "wicket." The Churchwardens then had the building demolished; the bricks went up for use at Culverstone School, then building, and the woodwork that was left went to Broomfield Farm, then occupied by Mr. Bliss, one of the Churchwardens. The old door lay about in the farm-yard for twenty years; it was rescued in 1897 and, after a much-needed cleansing, became the front door of Pitfield, then in building. The old lock, hinges, and other iron fittings remain intact. Mr. James Smith, one of the fathers of the village, gave me the following recollections. He was himself for two years Constable, together with John Bennett, who kept the Turnpike; and, he said, there was not much to do beyond interfering in rows in public-houses or arresting vagrants and drunken people in the road. If it were daytime, they were at once (in his day) taken before Mr. W. Masters-Smith, M.P., of Camer; but if it were night, the delinquents were locked up in the cage till the next day. Three meals were allowed in the twenty-four hours (at a cost of 2/6), and these were supplied from the Cricketers' Inn, whose landlord kept the key of the padlock that closed the wicket. The landlord, at that time and for years after, was Mr. James Buggs, a highly respected parishioner, and still remembered by many, and spoken of by Smith familiarly and affectionately as "old Jim Buggs." Once in Smith's time a prisoner escaped and bolted through the hedge at the corner near where the oast-house of the Green Farm stands, and so escaped into the woods on Cadley Hill; but, added he, "The constables didn't trouble much about him." The old constables ceased to exist

here in 1862, when the first policeman was Greenfield, who two years later was followed by an Irishman, familiarly known as "Old Dodd." "Wednesday, July 10, 1822, at Meopham Fair, when Meopham played cricket against Gillingham, Jerry Tolhurst put in the cage for abusing Mr. Brenchley" (*Diary of Robert Pocock*, by G. Arnold, ed. 1883, p. 142).

By 1870 the cage was falling into ruin, so its destruction five years later was a sentimental rather than a real loss to the village. In the Parish books are occasional entries about the cage, such as:

		s.	d.
1823.	Haprehending of Sammevell J.	5/	
1824.	Apprehending vagrant	3	6
	Two nights' expense of cage	5	0
		8	6

RICHARD CASHFIELD,
Borsholder.

1841. Three new locks [padlocks] for cage.

Mishaps occurred sometimes; we have no record of one, but Fielding (*Record of Rochester*) quotes the following from West Malling: "1784 Jany 22. A stranger woman, name unknown, found dead in the cage"! The problem of "drunk or dying" seems to have been as difficult of solution then as it is sometimes now.

The expenses in the following entry were doubtless, in part, for the cage:

1827, August. David Days bill for taking into Custody the men that robbed Noakes' House (Owl's Castle) £2 10 3½

The Stocks

Punishment could be locally administered in various ways, e.g. whipping and the stocks.

Our stocks stood under the old pollard elms at the Street,

and still known as the stock trees, and no doubt the whipping-post was there too; in some cases one of the posts at the end of the stocks was adapted as a whipping-post, suitable rings being attached for holding the offender's wrists. In some villages the stocks were in the churchyard.

For almost any offence the stocks could be used; and by an Act of Queen Elizabeth, attending bull-baitings or sports on Sunday put a man into them, as did also "profane swearing" in the time of William and Mary; but if the culprit were under sixteen, he was to be whipped instead. Our records show the following amongst others:

1667. New whipping post and mending the stocks 3/ and 3/.
1754. John Allchins bill for a new pair of stocks, and work
       at the causeway by the Street.
1829. A new whip.

There is no mention of the cucking- or ducking-stool—for scolds—in our books. Scolds there must have been! But there was always a deficiency of deep ponds at Meopham; and perhaps there is another reason! Till recent years water was the one scarce commodity in the summer, and the poor had often to use for drinking what they could get from the wayside ponds; and, as I recollect very well, a dog in a pond was held as an injury to the villagers—and rightly too; how much more, therefore, an old "scold"!

The Pound

Whilst "stray" human beings found harbourage in the cage, stray beasts were taken to the pound, which was under the care of the Borsholder, till they could be reclaimed. Our pound stood just below the court cottages at the Causeway opposite the Court pond, but it has been gone over forty years. It was, as was usual, an enclosure made of stout bars, with a suitable entrance; occasionally they were brick-walled enclosures, as may be still seen on Hampstead Heath.

Hearth and Window Tax

From the fifteenth year of Charles II's time until 1688 a very disagreeable duty belonged to the Borsholder. He had, once every year, with two substantial ratepayers or a specially appointed officer, to intrude himself into every room of every house to count the hearths for the tax of 2/- on every fireplace. This visitation was a sore trial to the people, and when the Act was repealed in 1689 it is expressly termed "a great oppression," "a badge of slavery," and as "exposing every man's house to be entered into, and searched at pleasure by persons unknown to him."

The relief from payment was, however, short, as six years later every house was taxed 3/- (except cottages), and every window was taxed, if the number was above nine. Hence the bricked-up window openings that still remain in almost every village. The Borsholder, however, had a less objectionable duty; he had now to count the windows from the outside, and might only enter a house to pass through it, if necessary, to count those in the back.

There is one entry in our books, I find, of a sum of money being paid for windows in the workhouse, which presumably refers to this; the Act was not repealed till 1851. A copy of the Hearth tax roll of 1673 will be found in Appendix I.

Meopham Market and Fair

In the year 1456 King Henry VI granted a fair and market to the Prior and Convent of Christ Church, Canterbury, to be held in the village of Meopham, they being the Lords of the Manor. The original document, from the Charter Rolls 25 and 26 Hen. VI in the Public Record Office, runs thus:

"—— et aliud m̂catum apud Mepeham tenend' ibidem die Sabbi singulis septimanis p̃ annū et similit' vnam feriam ibidem p̃ quatuor dies duratur' tenend' ibidem singulis annis in vigilia et in festo Aplor' Petri et Pauli et duab3 dieb3 festum illud immediate sequentib3."

Anglice:

And another market at Mepeham to be held there on Saturday of every week throughout the year and likewise one Fair there, which shall last four days to be held there every year on the Vigil and on the Festival of the Apostles Peter and Paul and on the two days immediately following that Festival.

This festival used to be on June 29th, but the introduction of the "New Style" made this date become July 11th, on which day the fair, such as it is, is still held; but the market has long ceased to exist. Why this particular saint's day was chosen, and not that of St. John the Baptist, to whom our church is dedicated, is unknown; it was very usual to hold them on the patron saint's day; and indeed the gathering of people for the Feast of the Dedication of their church has been thought to be the origin of fairs, which sacred function was thus combined with festivity and business.

Hazlitt, indeed, defines fairs as a greater kind of market, as they induced a greater influx of strangers than the local weekly market; and the granting of both to a village was a great boon both to local trade as well as to the Lord of the Manor, who benefited by tolls to which he was entitled. Our former Vicar, Mr. Hooper, suggested that perhaps Meopham was singled out for this honour as it was one of the Kentish villages that declined to send men to join Jack Cade's insurrection in 1450. The attraction of outsiders to a fair cannot nowadays be better illustrated than by the instance of the Nijni-Novgorod fair in Russia, which is simply international.

Fairs being held on Church festivals, and thus endowed with a semi-religious character, perhaps was the cause of their even being held in churchyards; but as early as 1285 (Edward I) the Statute of Winchester declares: "And the King commandeth and forbiddeth that from henceforth neither fairs nor markets be kept in Churchyards for the honor of the Church."

Within a year of granting Meopham its fair, the king (Statutes of the Realm, 27 Henry VI, c. 5) had to interfere on account of the abuses attending these gatherings. I here copy a transcript of the original document, which was, I believe, furnished Mr. Lewis by the Rev. T. S. Frampton, then Vicar of Platt.

Item, considering the abominable Injuries and Offences done to Almighty God and to his Saints, always Aiders and singular Assisters in our Necessities, because of Fairs and Markets upon their high and principal Feasts, as on the Feast of the Ascension of our Lord, on the day of Corpus Christi, on the Day of Whitsunday, on Trinity Sunday, with other Sundays, and also on the high Feast of the Assumption of our Blessed Lady, the Day of All Saints, and on Good Friday, accustomably and miserably holden and used in the Realm of England; on which principal and festival Days for great earthly Covertise, the People is more willingly vexed and in bodily labour foiled than on other ferial Days, as in fastening and making their Booths and Stalls, bearing and carrying, lifting and placing, their Wares, outward and homeward, as though they did nothing remember the horrible Defiling of their Souls in buying and selling, with many deceitful Lyes and false Perjury with Drunkenness and Strifes, and so specially withdrawing themselves and their servants from divine Service; the foresaid Lord the King by the Advice and Assent of the Lords Spiritual and Temporal and the Commons of the Realm of England being in the said Parliament, and by Authority of the same Parliament hath ordained, That all Manner of Fairs and Markets in the said principal Feasts, and Sundays, and Good Friday, shall clearly cease from all shewing of any Goods or Merchandises, necessary victuals only except, upon Pain of Forfeiture, of all the Goods aforesaid, so shewed, to the Lord of the Franchise or Liberty where such Goods contrary to this Ordinance be or shall be shewed, the Four Sundays in Harvest except.

It is not often an Act of Parliament is a sermon as well; this one certainly is, and contains many points for reflection. Further reference to the desecration of the churchyard by markets, etc., has been given under "Churchyard."

The Meopham market has long ceased to be, nor is it certain where it was held; it seems likely, however, to have been at the Street, which was the busy centre; and the very fact of the stocks being there renders this the more probable, both as the markets would furnish occupants for them, and as the derision of the multitude was part of the punishment, the place where the stocks stood is likely to have been the one where men did "mostly congregate."

The chartered fair still exists, but all its business character is gone, and it retains but the humbler festive side. Even the day of the sideshows—the fat lady, the hairless horse, and the like—is past; and cockshies, Aunt Sallies, roundabouts, and mechanical music—and steam-worked at that!—are all that remain of its former glories.

One, however, of its "shows" will not be regretted, and that was the roulette-table! It was in 1868 or 1869 that I witnessed the following scene on the green in front of Wellington Cottages. There sat a stout old lady behind a rather flimsy round table with the roulette upon it. Enter Mr. Robert Barnett of the Court, mounted on his stout cob; he quietly rode up to the table and reined in, watching the miniature "Monaco" for a short time; then, wheeling his horse round, he backed it bodily into the table, which he upset; what was on it the presiding lady swept into her ample apron in an instant, herself only just escaping a spill, and made off as fast as her legs could carry her.

The fair has always been on Pitfield Green; further reference to it will be found under the "Dedication of the Church."

CHAPTER XV

THE VILLAGE GREENS

MEOPHAM can boast of having in its parish no less than seven Greens. They are: Pitfield Green, Hoo Green, Culverstone Green, Harvel Green, Priesthood Green, Melliker Green, and Norwood Green, but this last one exists no more. The Greens are the property of the Lords of the Manor of Meopham (the Dean and Chapter of Canterbury), and formerly were intended primarily for the pasture of animals, as well as being open spaces of public resort. On Pitfield Green a right of removal of turf—for which it has always been renowned —was claimed; but the privilege of turfage and the use of the Greens was only for the quit-rent payers or homagers of the Manor; and the Lords of the Manor appointed a Green-keeper, whose duty it was to keep order, as well as to see that no damage was done to the turf, the rights of the homagers not interfered with, and so on. Mr. William Coombes, of Green Farm, was the last of these officials. Long, however, before 1875 the Greens had ceased to be properly cared for, the gipsies constantly encamped upon them, and much injury was done to the turf; and homagers' rights were disregarded, for might had become right in the matter of making use of the Greens.

It is most important that every villager should know his rights in regard to them, and, appreciating their value, take care to ward off all encroachment on or abuse of them; the story, therefore, of the Greens in recent times must be given in some detail.

Up to 1892 it often fell to the writer's lot, when visiting the village, to be asked to use personal influence to stop disturbances caused by strangers and "house-cart" people on the Green, and to persuade the latter to "move on"; but in spite of all "moral suasion" abuses still continued, so on August 25,

1892, the villagers called a public meeting, with the Rev. L. W. Lewis, Vicar, in the chair, and it was agreed to lodge a formal complaint with Messrs. Kingsford, of Canterbury, the solicitors to the Lords of the Manor, and ask what redress could be afforded to the "homagers" of the Manor in this matter. The reply, however, only threw the responsibility of guarding the rights of the Greens on the villagers, it being to the effect that the Commons Act, 39 and 40 Vict., ch. 56, 1875, gave any aggrieved parishioner power to take steps at law on his own account. Thereupon it was resolved to form a "Greens Protection Committee," with R. Tweddell, Esq., chairman of a dozen parishioners, each Green being represented by at least one living near it.

The first step was to visit the various Greens; and their boundaries were found generally not to have been encroached upon for many years. The next year, however, a dispute arose regarding the ownership of the side land on the west of the main road, adjacent to the chapel on Pitfield Green, the boundary between it and Mrs. Church's property adjoining not being clear. The matter was amicably settled, however, and a wire boundary fence was erected, marking off about half an acre of pasture as belonging to the Parish. Since then, however, the boundary has been moved farther north, thus cutting through the old pit that is on the land (now a pond), whereby also the Parish has lost the row of old elms, which now stand in the adjacent garden. But to return to the official visit of the Committee. It reported that at Harvel the pond had been enclosed, and that Culverstone Green had been also taken in by a fence erected by Sir Sidney Waterlow, nearly up to the roadway. The Committee brought this to Sir Sidney's notice, and he moved back the fence to its present position, retaining, however, the thicket or hedge which had always been regarded till then as public property.

The Committee had soon to exercise its legal authority, and in August 1893 to prosecute some "house-cart" people who, in spite of due notice and warning, insisted upon erecting a steam roundabout on Pitfield Green. A conviction was obtained, and a 5/- fine with costs inflicted, on the grounds that the turf had been injured, and the enjoyment and use of the Green by those entitled to it had been interfered with.

The Greens Protection Committee lasted just two years; for, the New Parish Council coming into being on September 27, 1894, it, at its second meeting in February 1895, appointed a Greens Committee, whose members were to be appointed annually. In May 1895 the owners of the steam roundabout and coco-nut shy applied to be allowed to come on to Pitfield Green at the annual dinner of the Kentish Friends' Lodge (Oddfellows). This was allowed, conditionally to all damage being made good; all litter and mess cleared away; performances to cease by 11 p.m.; and the horses were not to be allowed to wander about the Green; also, that leave would have to be obtained annually.

The Parish Council in October 1894, before it had time to create its Greens Committee, had to prosecute another steam roundabout owner, and also obtained a conviction; and seeing how determined the Parish was to protect its Greens has made all strangers careful to obtain the Committee's leave before trespassing upon them.

In June 1897, however, the "house-cart" people encamped, in spite of notice-boards, on Harvel Green; and the Council, having sent them a warning "not to do it again," authorized the Chairman of the Greens Committee to "take immediate proceedings" at the expense of the Parish Council against "any person illegally occupying or damaging any of the Village Greens." To the present time (1934) no legal action has required to be taken under this instruction.

The by-laws regulating the use of the Village Greens are duly exhibited on notice-boards; and though the Parish Council drew up its by-laws in 1895 and submitted them for confirmation to the Local Government Board, it was not until 1898 that they received the required sanction after undergoing slight modification.

The regulations may be thus summarized.

No wheeled vehicle of any kind shall be taken on the turf; nor any fire lighted thereon; nor any damage done to any tree or shrub growing there; nor shall the turf be removed or injured in any way.

Then follow several regulations about games and sports, having regard to the annoyance of people on the Green for other purposes, and to the mutual interference of players with one another where more than one game or sport is carried on at the same time.

Infringement of any by-law renders the offender liable to a 40/- fine; and any officer of the Parish Council, or police constable, is to be the person to put the law in motion.

The Kent County Council also issues by-laws common to all the County Greens, which in general terms cover all the above-named regulations for the Meopham Greens.

It will be noticed how much attention is given to preserving the Greens for public recreation; for it is recognized that, whilst the desire for sport has universally increased of late years, the call for pasture on the part of those living round the Greens has decreased, and for many years past the principal animals that have pastured on Meopham Green have been geese. There used to be always a flock of them, and they added a picturesque feature to the neighbourhood. In a note by Mr. Lewis in 1894, he quotes Horace Smith's remark on the peculiarities of geese, that "they are uncommonly common on Commons"!

In spite, however, of all recent legislation, the "homagers" of the Manor have still rights of pasturage if they choose to exercise them, provided they guard their animals from doing any damage, or from straying on to the public roads or private property adjoining.

The individual Greens will now receive notice.

(1) PITFIELD GREEN (THE Green—Meopham Green) is one of the best in Kent, and thanks to the Cricket Club it is, over its greatest area, kept in admirable condition; and during the

season practices are held almost every evening, and matches weekly, or nearly so. The Meopham Club is one of great excellence, and between it and visiting clubs really good and sound cricket may be witnessed. It is the only one of our Greens large enough, or in sufficiently good condition, for the game.

Football (although by a resolution of the Parish Council in 1899 it is allowed on the Green when matches with other clubs are played) is not, as a matter of fact, ever played there, the parishioners wisely refraining from injuring its surface.

Quoits, for the same reason, are not played, except in the rougher parts; and indeed in April 1898 the Local Government Board, at the request of the Parish Council, issued a special by-law that if the Council notified any particular spot where the game might be played, it must be there and nowhere else.

Bowls have been revived in recent years; and as this game does no injury, the level part reserved for cricket is employed for the purpose when possible; however, even there the ground is not true enough to render the game one less of chance than of accuracy. In years gone by this game was very popular, and the forefathers of the village were great bowls players, and bowling alleys were not only to be found on Greens, but were appendages very often to rural public-houses. That there was one on our Green in 1694 is shown by this entry in one of our Parish books: "Paid Councillor Gifford for advice concerning ye Elmes on ye Bowling Green 10s." These bowling alleys were maintained at the expense of the Parish. The site of ours is unknown; but as the only elm-trees existing on the Green are those on the West Side land, before mentioned, and now enclosed in a garden, it is very likely that it was situated somewhere there.

Pitfield Green was more "private" in old days than at present, for the high road which now cuts off the West Side land just mentioned did not exist before 1825—only a farm track; the high road then, on reaching Lomer from the north, turned to the west, ran behind the gardens that now lie on the west side of the Green, and emerged just above the mill, and then, as Leading Street, continued its course towards Wrotham (*v.* Appendix N).

There can be no doubt that many of the cottages around the Green stand on what was once "waste" land belonging to the Parish; the site of the Clay Cottages, built on the waste, now forms part of the garden of Pitfield, as already explained; and it is traditional that the walnut-trees in front of the Green Farm were once on public land. With the taking in of some "waste" on the west side, as already mentioned, in recent years, encroachments have ceased; and the Parish is not likely to allow any more.

Another thing that some years ago disfigured and destroyed the side lands was the opening of pits for loam; and that this existed long ago is shown by the alternative name the cottages just mentioned also bear in the Parish books, viz. Loam Pit Cottages. In recent years the pits, by the exertions of the parishioners, have been filled in, and the general level of the surface of the side lands restored.

The fact of there being a deep subsoil of loam or brick earth accounts for the high reputation that the Green always had for its turf, which also used to be removed, and found a ready market. The present groundsman of the Cricket Club, Mr. C. Coombes, tells me that it is astonishing in how short a time turf—and I mean turf, not merely grass—will make itself there.

Archery.—Had not our oldest Parish books been stolen, we should no doubt have found some references to the archery butts, such as Hazlitt quotes from St. Giles's Parish: "1566. Itm. for carrying of turfs for the buttes xvi d."—but we can show no such entries.

The erection of archery butts and the practice of archery in every village on holidays was rendered compulsory in the reign of Edward IV. The butts were high mounds of earth, turf-covered, and as everyone knows were, like the rifle-butts of to-day, erected as protections behind the targets. Ours stood on the Green itself, alongside the road passing in front of the Green Farm; one was opposite the farm, the other was some 80 yards away, and about opposite the lodge to Pitfield. Old parishioners can remember the lower of the two, at any rate, it being high enough even then to form a steep slide down which as boys they tobogganned, but without the toboggan! having first rendered it slippery by throwing water on it from the adjacent pond! Mr. George Seager, the gardener at Pitfield, well recollects sharing in this sport; and though the Parish eventually levelled the butts (in 1865), sufficient unevenness of surface remained to show where they had been not twenty years ago.

However, archery still survives as a sport; but Meopham Green must have been an ideal place for its practice in the days when 6 feet of yew formed the "rifle" of the soldier.

The destructive "sport" of a bonfire on Guy Fawkes' Day has never been omitted until 1914, when the Great War put such frivolities aside; and seeing that the function has now everywhere lost its meaning, and here has only degenerated into burning tar-barrels to the great destruction of turf on one of the most prominent parts of the Green, it is to be hoped the Parish Council will set its face against its revival in the future.

The Chartered Fair (q.v.) in July claims its pitch on the Green as a right at law, but every care is taken that as little harm as possible shall be done; and now that the horses that draw the vans are no longer allowed to wander on the Green, what was a great nuisance, and even danger, in the past is removed.

The Diamond Jubilee of Queen Victoria (1897) was the cause of the planting of limes and planes on the Green in commemoration of this event, a row being planted on the south side, and two clumps of trees at the north end; due ceremony was observed on the occasion, Miss Tweddell (Mrs. R. Arnold) planting the first tree.

Three "Sarsen" stones, similar to those at the church (q.v.), which long lay on a side land, have recently been placed at the north corner of the Green by the Parish Council, on either side of the memorial cross erected there in memory of villagers who fell in the Great War; and close by is the drinking-fountain erected to commemorate the coronation of Their Majesties King Edward VII and Queen Alexandra on August 9, 1902. It was erected by the Metropolitan Drinking Fountain Association, whose money grant, together with local subscriptions, defrayed the expense of its erection.

(2) HOOK GREEN (Hoke in 1370, and Hooke in Elizabeth's time, 1597), at the north end of the Parish, is both too small and too much on the slope for purposes of serious sport, so it lends itself to the pasturing of local animals. It has been well cared for by the Parish Council. Trees, in commemoration of Queen Victoria's Diamond Jubilee, have also been planted on it, and a rough farm road that ran across it from the high road has been obliterated. At its south end are the two old Parish cottages already mentioned, now the place of business of Mr. Clarke, carpenter (1919).

(3) NORWOOD GREEN must have been somewhere up Norwood (locally known as Nor'ard) Lane, but its site is unknown; apparently it is absorbed in some of the adjacent property. In 1241 (Henry III) a certain Adam de Northwude was outlawed for the murder of a woman at Meopham; and in Edward II's time a Northewoode lived in the Parish. In 1377, and again in 1523, the name of Alfred Norwode appears in the Steward's book of the monks. Whether the Green took its name from a Northwood, or vice versa, or because there was originally a wood at the north end of the Parish, must be left to conjecture.

In 1624 one William Middleton, weaver, of Meopham, undertakes to relieve the Parish of Bartholomew Carrier, and to let him reside in his house at Norwood Green, and thereby "keep harmless from all cost and charges, this parish and parishioners," etc.

(4) MELLIKER GREEN.—The triangular patch of turf at the

"three-went-way" opposite Melliker Farm is officially recognized by the Local Government Board as one of our Greens, and is under the protection of its by-laws. Its attraction consists in the magnificent yew-tree that stands upon it, its nearest rivals in antiquity and size being probably the well-known ones in Kingsdown churchyard, though Nurstead churchyard contains one of much the same age, if judged by its size.

Some time when the Markett family occupied the Court, they had Melliker Green fenced round, doubtless with the intention of protecting the old tree; but the Parish considered their action to be an infringement of public rights, and so, on appeal to the Lords of the Manor, the fence was taken down (Lewis). In recent years the question of saving this ancient relic of bygone days from injury, which it is annually and increasingly suffering, has been before the Parish authorities, but the expense of an iron fencing they have not yet seen their way to rise to! (It is now, however, railed in (1934).)

Opposite the Green is the picturesque old Melliker Farm, known to be built on the foundations of a still older house. The name has always been a puzzle, but Mr. Lewis has pointed out that it probably is that of an old Meopham family, the name of Reginald de Mildenacre appearing as witness to an old deed of 1240 (Henry III), his co-witnesses being William de Dudemere and Walter de Isebere. Henry de Mildenacre appears in documents of 1306, and in 1377 John Mildenacre appears as the owner of "Merryhaw"—? "Merry Hearth"— the name of a field close by the schools (*q.v.*) (*v.* Appendix F). His name also appears in an extract from the Court Roll of the Manor of Ambree, Rochester, July A.D. 1348, and quoted in the *Archæologia Cantiana*, vol. xxix, p. 132: "Johannes Mildenacre venit et vadit relevium suum pro una acra terrae juxta crucem St[i] Willelmi . . ."—"This land belonged in Henry VIII's time to Cobham College, and may have belonged to it centuries before: John de Mildenacre may have given it" (A. A. Arnold). "Merryweather" is mentioned in a deed of sale of 1714, situated at Culverstone. Cherries were in old times called "merries" in Hampshire.

A local tradition gives the site of the old house as that of the home of the "Meophams," and indeed it may be so; for, as already narrated, the Archbishop's home was certainly *not* at Dene, and after the Court no older site in the village is known than that of Melliker.

The farm at present is part of the Camer estate.

The other Greens, at Culversole, Harvel, Priesthood, will be referred to under their respective hamlets.

CHAPTER XVI

THE AREA OF THE PARISH

THE Parish of Meopham has an area of 4,713 acres thus made up, according to the ordnance survey of 1864:

Land	4,635·271 acres
Public Roads	61·316 acres
Railways	16·358 acres
Water	0·253 acres
Total	4,713·198 acres

Its measurement, as the crow flies, is nearly 4½ miles north to south and 2½ east to west, and the village, with its hamlets, occupies two hogs' backs and two valleys. It lies high on the North Downs, higher above sea-level than many imagine, as the following ordnance survey figures show:

The Station Bridge, 283 feet.
The Mill, 470 feet.
South St. (turning to Ridley), 532 feet.
Hodsole St. turning, 612 feet, and just outside the Parish's southern limit opposite the "Vigo," 688 feet.
The hog's back on which Harvel is situated is slightly higher than Pitfield Green.

East and West Boroughs

It may be owing to the straggling nature of the Parish and its irregular surface—especially, too, when communication was rendered more difficult by the state of the roads, which were only fit for foot or horse traffic, not for wheeled—that it came to be divided into two boroughs, the East and West Boroughs or, as it is sometimes termed, the East and West Lands. As early as the reign of Henry III in 1265 the signatories to an old deed of gift have amongst their number "Thom. de Westland. Godefr' de Westld:" and the name of Reginald de Estb'ge (i.e. East Borough) appears in another document of the same period (Lewis). In the Steward's book of the monks in 1370 the two boroughs appear as Eastlonde and Westlonde; La Wesseland also appears.

The East Borough included part of Camer, Priesthood, Harefield (in seventeenth century: ? Harvel). The West Borough, which was both the more populous and the richer, was made up of Hoo Green, part of Camer, David Street, Meopham Street (i.e. the village proper), Pitfield Green, Leading Street, and South Street.

Each borough, as has been said, had its own Churchwarden as far back, at any rate, as the seventeenth century, and probably much earlier.

The population at the last Census was 1,450, but now (1934) about 1,700; in the fourteenth century (Richard II) it was about 300. A Subsidy Roll of that period shows 58 householders, and allowing five individuals on an average to each household, would give 290; but the peasants must be added in. By the same method of reckoning the population in 1523 (Henry VIII) would be 315; and the Hearth Tax Roll of 1673 gives 42 householders to the East Borough and 68 to the West, yielding a total figure of 550. In 1801 the population was 748; in 1821, 833; in 1848, 790; in 1851, 1,000; in 1881, 1,250; and 1891, 1,200. So on the whole the increase has been a steady one; but here in Meopham, as in many other places, the absence of dwelling-houses of all classes limits mainly the addition of new families (*v.* Appendices H and I).

The Village and its Hamlets

The Parish is made up of the village of Meopham, which from Saxon times centred round the church and the principal manorial buildings adjoining, and of six hamlets which, beginning at the north end, are: Hoo (or Hook), Camer, Pitfield, Priesthood, Harvel, Culversole (Culverstone), and if, following Hasted, we add Melliker (though now consisting of but one farm-house), there will be seven in all.

By studying each of these in detail with their connecting

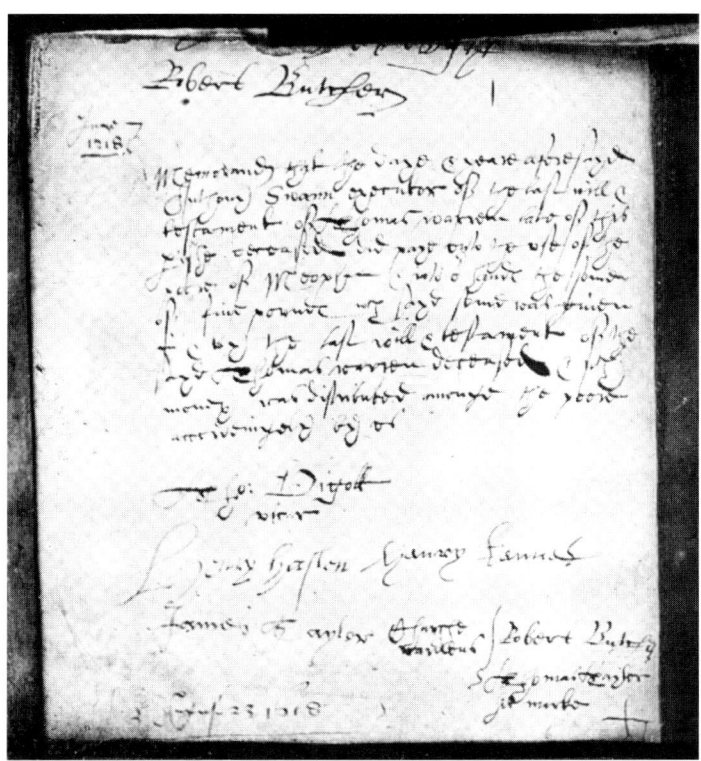

A SUBSIDY ROLL DATED MARCH 30, 1741

COPY OF A PAGE OF THE CHURCHWARDEN'S AND VESTRY BOOK
(1612-1739)

THE TUDOR ROSE (*vide* p. 241)

DOE'S COTTAGE IN 1886 (*vide* p. 235)

roads we shall not miss anything that has a history to record. The various Greens, however, have been separately described.

The village of Meopham—generally now spoken of as the Street—ranked high in the hundred in old times, though Hasted describes it as "a bye out of the way place, lying among the hills, and no well frequented thoroughfare through it . . . the roads are stony, narrow and bad but the air . . . is very healthy." This account of the roads does not hold good now, but its salubrity is to this day universally acknowledged.

The open space in front of the "George"—a "three-went-way"—there can be no doubt, was where the old market was held in days gone by (*q.v.*).

The George Inn at the Street is of very old date, there being a record that in 1668 its landlord was Thomas Boghurst; and another record states that it was held by Richard Buggs in 1789—an old and fortunately still existing and highly respected Meopham name. This inn was where the Vestry used to meet to transact its workhouse business once a month, and an entry in our books under 1810 reads: "Easter Monday: to allow this day and next Easter 40/ for dinner and £3 for liquor for such persons as pay rates who choose to come to the George and partake of the same."

The shop at the Street is a very old building and, in the eighteenth century, was hired as the workhouse (*q.v.*); since then it has been a shop, and at one time also the Post Office. Fifty years ago it was occupied by a butcher named Neville, where a very limited amount of meat could be obtained on three days in the week. On the opposite side of the road and at right angles to it is a typical Kentish cottage, at present occupied by Mr. Oliver, one of our oldest inhabitants, to whom I am indebted for many recollections. The room facing the street was, in the middle of the last century, a saddler's shop kept by Alban Dorrington, and the now bricked-up shop window can still be traced in the wall facing the roadway. The garden in the rear is a long narrow slip of ground, and a rope-walk extended along by the side of the hedge of the road, where Dorrington worked, making anything from cart-ropes to whipcord. From this house to that now occupied by Mr. Scudder was the old toll-bar (*v.* Toll-gate). Adjoining this is the Well House, and it owes its name to the fact that it is built over a deep well; and as a well was often found in a market-place, as being the busiest and most inhabited part of a village, it seems likely that the well was there long before the house, and only in comparatively recent times has the well been built over. It is far from probable that the only permanent source of water for the village itself was at the first in the basement of a house, and in the possession of a private person. In Henry III's time (1241) a certain Alic de Puteo (*Anglice*, Alice of the well = Attwell) of Mepham was prosecuted for receiving stolen property. If the well existed then, she may have lived at the Street; but another explanation offered is that she lived at Pitfield Green near the loam-pits, the "de Puteo" answering for these also, though a well of water is more likely. In the rates list for 1774 the "House at the Well," a literal translation of "de Puteo," appears assessed at £2 10s. For a long time before the National Schools were built (1841) the Well House served as a Parish school (*v.* Parish). The large upper room was panelled throughout with oak; this was removed and put up in the Hall at Camer many years ago.

A little way down the Luddesdown Road is a deep pond on the right, and a farm—Foxendown. This is Grinnell's Sole —i.e. Grinnell's Pond (*v.* Culversole)—and gave the name to the two Parish cottages (*q.v.*) which stood opposite to it. An instance of how names get corrupted and lost is seen in a Vestry minute of April 23, 1858, where the name is written "Green Hill Sole"! Thomas Grinnell was a benefactor of the poor here in 1623 (*v.* Charities), and was Churchwarden in 1616. The name also is spelt Greenel Sole Pond in 1839 (*v.* also Parish Cottages).

The most picturesque objects at the Street are the two very ancient pollard elms, the "stock trees" (*v.* Stocks); and a bench has recently been fixed between them for weary travellers. Three similar trees, and of apparently the same age, are at Pitfield.

The remaining buildings, etc., of interest at the Street, as the Church, Court, etc., are described under their proper headings; but on passing northwards down the main road there are still to be seen the two old "Sarsen stones" at the avenue to the Court, which our oldest inhabitant, Mr. Ashenden, tells me he remembers being brought all the way from the valley below Birling Hill. They are of the usual firm sandstone, belonging to the "tertiary" geological formation that once covered our chalk hills; and the name "Sarsen"—universally given them in the country—is an abbreviation of "Saracen," an old and quaint belief being that they were petrified Saracens! Similar stones are freely strewn now in the village of Cobham, and doubtless gave rise to the story in *Pickwick* of the stone engraved "Bill Stumps, his mark"; these "Sarsens" came from a "Druidical Circle" that existed in old times on the outskirts of Cobham between Battle Street and St. Thomas's Well, which was demolished, the late Mr. Baker of Owletts told me, by either his father or grandfather.* But for Ashdown's positive statement, one would have thought ours near the church to have come from the same source (*v.* also Pitfield Green).

Passing still further north, over the Causeway (*q.v.*), one comes past the schools to the Lances. This modern house derives its name from that of the land on which it is built, known formerly as the Lances, and at one time in the possession of T. Allchin. The short steep hill on which the house stands is Skinner's Hill.

The National Schools were built in 1841, and took the place of the private school at the Well House. The land was given by the Dean and Chapter in 1840, and is described

---

* A reference to this "circle" is to be found in the *Journal of the Brit. Archaeolog. Association* (1854), vol. ix, p. 427, where it appears that Lord Darnley in 1842 removed many stones to form a rock garden at Cobham Hall.

in the deed of gift as being the north-east corner of a field called "Merry Hearth," and bounded on the south by "little Merry Hearth" and on the west by "Mill Field." Under "Melliker" mention is made of a field called "Merry Hay"— probably the same as that mentioned above. For the building of the National Schools £149 9s. was at once raised by subscription, and substantial annual support was at the same time promised (*v.* Appendix K).

Hoo (Hook) Hamlet

In the Parish maps of 1842 the only houses marked in this part of the Parish are the Fox and Hounds Inn and adjacent forge, with its picturesque thatched cottages, where also is an old well; the old farm (now refronted) on the Green itself, occupied by Mr. R. French, and the old low-built cottages on the north side; then the cottages at Waterditch (Water dyche in 1370)—and they were the last in that part of the Parish at that time.

On the Green itself still stand the old Parish cottages, now thrown into one (*v.* Workhouse).

Camer Hamlet

What is now known as Camer Street—a collection of picturesque old cottages in the park—was formerly on the high road, and with the house constituted the hamlet of Camer. When Mr. William Masters-Smith held the property in 1837, the high road separated the house from the park in front, running in a fairly straight line from lodge to lodge, starting at the corner where the west lodge now stands, and in old times known as Money Hole Corner. The remains of a magnificent avenue of elms enable us now to trace the old road that ran directly before the front door of the house and through Camer Village, and the grand old cedar-tree must at one time have been very familiar as a wayside object to travellers. The road by which Sole Street is now reached is the new one that was made in 1837 to the north of the home farm buildings. There was once also a village green in the hamlet (Lewis); and, as mentioned under "Crouches," a wayside cross known as "Kemmer's Crouche."

Of the old Georgian house of Camer, Hasted, writing in 1797, says: "There is there a good modern house built by Mr. George Master; his son George Master followed him; died unmarried and left his sister Catherine his heir, married to Mr. Smith, of Croydon. Her son now resides there." The back part of the house is much older than the front, and early in the seventeenth century (1620) was occupied by Mr. George Master; but the front Georgian portion was built in 1716, at which time, without doubt, the old cedar-tree by the front door was planted. It is apparently to this partial building that Hasted refers.

The earliest history of Camer it is not now possible to trace; but in the thirteenth century it was occupied by one John le Maistre, and in 1293 Gilbert, the son of John le Maistre, was convicted of being an accomplice in a murder (v. Chapter XIX). And in a Subsidy Roll (1524), Henry VIII, Robert Master appears with lands assessed at 40/-, his subsidy being 2/-. In 1620, as just stated, George Master owned the property; in 1783 the name of George Smith appears; he, like all his predecessors and successors, was one of the Churchwardens, and held that office for forty-seven years. In 1787 George Masters of Camer presented the silver communion flagon to the church; and ten years later the following entry is on our books: "1797. Mr. Smith requested to give the Parish information respecting the sum of money expended on the improving of the House at Camer." Mr. Smith, therefore, was the occupant then.

In 1831 Mr. W. Masters-Smith held Camer; it was he who presented the first organ to the church (v. Organ); and was the only M.P. that Meopham can boast of having produced. The Rev. Allan Smith-Masters (nephew) followed in 1861 (ob. 1875), his son, the present occupant, succeeding him.

Old documents show the name Camer to have been formerly

written Kemmer. In Sprever's will (1525) (*q.v.*) it is written "Kenmer," and in a Meopham Subsidy Roll, 1377, appears the name of Johannes Kemmerd: did his forbears give the name to the property? In the Steward's book of the monks in 1348 the name John Kemmer occurs, and some land is also described as "Kemeresfeld"; possibly the present park (Lewis).

In our burial register (1624) the inhabitants of Kemar are spoken of: the nearest approach to the present name of Camer. John Kemmer may have given the name to the hamlet; but the following abstract from the *Archæologia Cantiana*, vol. xxiv, p. 51, offers another explanation. I give it in Mr. A. A. Arnold's own words—to whom I am indebted for the reference; "In Henley wood there is a rampart, square in form, enclosing a large acreage. On asking a woodcutter, an intelligent man, if he knew anything about it, he replied, 'Do you mean the cam?' On inquiring what that was, he said, 'The bank in the wood.' I remembered that Halliwell, in his *Archaic Dictionary*, gives the meaning of 'Cam' as 'an old earthen mound'; and as Henley wood forms a portion of and joins the Camer Estate, it seems to me that we have here a probable explanation of the name of the Smith-Masters' property."

The park has often been lent for the purpose of public functions; but probably the Jubilee of Queen Victoria in 1887 eclipsed all others. No less than £60 was subscribed for the celebration of the event, part of which was spent in a festivity in Camer Park, with refreshments both solid and liquid, sports, the time-honoured "greasy pole," and the roasting of a sheep whole—at least, this was attempted, but want of practice in such wholesale cookery was doubtless the cause of its being found, on dismemberment, very underdone! In the evening fireworks on the Green brought the festivities to a close.

There was a time—the good old days when land was worth holding—that a kennel of hounds was kept at Camer—in fact, the only place in the Parish where hounds were ever kept, and then only for thirty years. Mr. Allan Smith-Masters has kindly furnished me with the following particulars, which he extracted from the old account-book of the hunt, which is still preserved:

Extracts from the account book at Camer dated from 1760 to 1790, from which it appears that a small pack of foxhounds were kept there by William Smith, and afterwards by his son George Smith, the expenses being shared between them and some neighbours: Messrs. Wm. Pemble of Cobham; N. Gilber of Denton Court; H. Edmeades of Nursted; — Bligh of Cobham; W. Comport of Dabbs Place; — Tilden of Ifield Court; and — Harman of Wombwell Park.

The first entry is as follows: "Agreed with Mr. Wm. Pemble to keep fifteen couple of hounds, build a kennel, and find a Huntsman for the hunting season, he to pay me fifteen guineas a year and to take home ½ the dogs at the end of the season and to keep 'em till we begin hunting again. Agreed with John Patridge for four pounds to look after, and hunt the Hounds from Michs to Lady Day and do such other work as I shall set him about."

The other members of the Syndicate seem to have joined at a later date; and the huntsman's name then was Henry Beven. He wore a plush coat and waistcoat which cost £3 7s. 6d. "Dog"-horses seem to have varied in price from 2/6 to 6/-. "A Fox £1.1.0" is an occasional entry! "A Couple of Hounds 10/6": and a "Hurdle of Hounds (? 2 couple) £1.1.0" does not seem an extravagant price.

A pair of breeches, a pair of boots and a cap cost £1 1s. od. each.

An ordinary labourer's wages were then 1/6 a day, and H. Beven was paid 10/6 a week.

The expenses averaged about £140 a year; and it appears from an old notice of the meets that they hunted three days a week and met at 7 a.m.

The meet card for one week in 1786 reads:

C.H.	Hour	House nearest	Farm or Wood	Village nearest
Monday, Feb. 14	7	Mr. Comport	Wells Wood	Cobham
Wednesday	7	Mr. Edmeades	Downs Farm	Nursted
Friday	7	Mr. Smith	Meopham Green	Meopham

C.H. stands for Camer Hunt; and it may be added that the kennels there gave the name to an orchard—Dog-kennel Orchard. Comport was the name of the family at Cooling Court at this time.

Meets are still from time to time held on the lawn in front of the house; and a prettier picture can hardly be imagined than this, having for its setting the old Georgian house on the one hand, overshadowed with its noble cedar, and on the other the expanse of the park with its ancient trees.

Hamlet of Pitfield

The index to the Parish map of 1864 calls this the *small* hamlet of Pitfield; but it is now the largest and most important of them all. Its centre is the Green, and through it the main road runs. There can be no doubt that the Pettesfeld mentioned in a document of 1306 (*v*. Appendix M) is the modern Pitfield. Mr. Lewis concluded (and I quite agree) that Pitfield owed its name to the pits that at one time—on the side lands at least—existed for the removal of loam. The name Loam Pit Cottages seems to confirm this; whilst the deep hollow—now a pond—in the West Side land is clearly the remains of one of them; and as late as in the 'seventies there existed an excavation close against the wall of the outbuildings of the Green Farm, but now filled up. The present state of Greenstreet Green, on the Dartford Road, indicates to what an extent the public land was robbed of its subsoil when of value. In old documents "the wells" are mentioned, as also a Wilhelmus de Welles, who lived at Meopham, and also a certain Alic de Puteo, already mentioned; and both of these, it is suggested, may have lived at or got their names from the pits or wells on the Green. The Latin word "Puteus," though primarily meaning a water well, was used in a secondary sense for a pit (*v*. Well House).

Pitfield Cottage, which stood from 1801 to 1897 at the south-east corner of the Green, was a small farm-house with some sixty acres of land in the valley below. Mr. W. Mungeam, who is mentioned as an important figure in the workhouse records, as Clerk, etc., retired to it when past work, and died there.

In 1862 the property passed into the hands—from Mr.

Evenden—of the late Dr. Baber, who parted with the cottage and garden to Mr. Golding-Bird in 1884. The farm, at Dr. Baber's death in 1894, was sold "in parcels"; and in 1897 the present house (Pitfield) was built on the exact site of the old barn. When the cottage was pulled down an almost perfect pike-head, with a 9-inch blade, was found in the earth beneath it; just such a one as is often pictured in illustrations of the Stuart times. And in the kitchen garden—formerly side land of the Green, as stated in Chapter VIII—have been dug up a silver coin of Henry VIII (? a groat); a copper counter of the same reign, inscribed "Ave Maria Gratia"; a copper farthing of Charles II, date 1672; and a "long cross" silver penny of Henry III, minted at Bury St. Edmunds. A silver groat, 1400–1450, inscribed "Villa Calisiae" (i.e. minted in Calais), was dug up near Hook Green. (The old mulberry-trees have been mentioned under Tradescant) (*v.* also under Steele's *infra*).

The brick-fronted cottages on the south of the Green were altered to their present state by their owner, the late Mr. J. Buggs, in the middle of the last century, when landlord of the "Cricketers." They may be of the same date as an old wooden cottage that stood in the same row till lately, on the site of Mr. Russell's draper's shop. I was shown a plank of wood from the interior which had the date 1667 carved upon it.

The King's Arms Inn, the last house on the south side, may be of about the above date; it is mentioned now and then in our old Parish books; and in 1759 a certain Thomas Howes held it. About sixty years ago it was held by one Nordwich (*alias* Nordish and Nordash), who had also a small butcher's shop there. This name figures for some three hundred years in our records; the above-named parishioner was the last of the family here.

On the opposite side of the main road, on the west of the Green, is the Cricketers' Inn, our most important house of call for travellers. Next to this stands a very old house, now much altered, till lately under a spreading walnut-tree. A photograph

taken in the 'eighties shows it to have been a picturesque
building, whilst the walnut-tree formed the most perfect
hemisphere it was possible to see; but a storm destroyed it
a few years ago. In the seventeenth century the house was
an ale-house, with the sign of the "Leather Bottle." In a deed
dated October 1779 the property is described as a "messuage
or tenement with a garden, orchard, stable and outhouses, and
one acre of hop ground, called or known by the name or sign
of the 'Cricketers,' " and in October 1827 it is leased by the
owner Robert Hills to "John Figgess, of Meopham, Grocer,"
and is described as "*formerly* called or known by the name or
sign of the 'Cricketers.' " Evidently, therefore, between these
two dates it had ceased to be a public-house, its business and
sign being transferred to the present inn; this change most
likely took place in or about 1825, when the new high road
was made (*v.* Appendix N).

The Mill

The windmill was built in 1801; and though now the only
one for miles round that remains "on duty," there is evidence
of at least two others having been in the Parish in the past.
The Mill Field, south of the schools, clearly perpetuates the
memory and site of one; the other was on the eastern ridge
of the Parish between Harvel and David's Street. To the south
of Herring Hill Lane, which connects South Street with
Harvel, a mound on a shaw—Mill-Sole Shaw—marks its site,
and a pond in the field close by still is known as Mill-Sole
Pond. These names alone suffice to prove the past existence
of a mill (cf. Culversole, *q.v.*). Mr. Lewis has stated, but I
cannot indentify his authority, that mills also existed at Camer,
Dene, and somewhere in the south of the Parish.

The chapel in the West Side land of Pitfield Green was fifty
years ago a thatched store-house; and belonging to it, and
behind it, stood an oast-house, removed at a still earlier time.

Adjacent to it was a farm, of which the old barn still remains;
the farm-house, now adapted for the purpose of a butcher's

business, but retaining its old-time characteristics, is occupied by Mr. Leonard Russell. The barn is specially a grand old relic of the past when, the winter through, the first thing to be heard in the morning was the rhythmic beating of the flails thrashing the corn on the old oak floor. In those days the backing of the wagon, loaded with sheaves, into the barn from the road caused no inconvenience, but it is hard to picture it as possible in these times of mechanical, rapid, and continuous traffic.

The forge on the lower or north end of the Green represents the oldest of mechanical trades; the worker in iron must have been in Meopham, and probably on the same site, for untold generations. Closed now (1934) through lack of trade.

The present Green Farm on the east side is a modern building—now a private dwelling-house. The old building—a picturesque old farm-house—was burnt down in the 'eighties, one windy and boisterous night, and with such rapidity that Mr. William Coombes, the occupant, had hardly time to save anything. The one well in Pitfield Hamlet is close to the house, and said to be some 400 feet deep; it does not reach, however, below the chalk into the green-sand. The writer remembers it in full use in 1868, but it took a horse exactly ten minutes to bring a tub of water to the surface. So hard was the water that, if heated in a spoon, a scum of chalk quickly formed upon it. The site of it is now quite hidden, but the well is still there, a few yards from the north-east corner of the house.

Until the introduction in recent years of the "Company's water," the village was almost entirely dependent upon rain for its supply, the wells, by their depth, being impracticable. The cottages generally had the usual large cask just under a spout from the roof; and if the latter were of slate all the water could be caught, but if tiled, as many were, much was lost at first by being absorbed by the spongy tiles. Thatched roofs, of course, gave no water. When their limited storage was exhausted, the wayside ponds were the only source of supply.

Middle-aged people of Meopham can recall many a dry summer when all water has had to be carted up from Wrotham and Gravesend for the barest necessities of life. Animals and vegetation suffered extremely.

The better class of houses were provided with underground tanks, some of large dimensions; but even these, unless the owners' roofage were very large, failed in dry seasons. The chalk subsoil lends itself to the making of these tanks, which the local builders were—and are—extremely clever in constructing; one never heard of the sides of these tanks falling in, and rarely do they crack and leak, owing to the good backing that the cemented brick lining has in the chalk. The storage of rain-water in the village deserved to be ranked as one of the fine arts of the neighbourhood.

There are, however, several wells in the Parish—some eighteen in all—besides those already mentioned; but inasmuch as all—except perhaps that near the "Fox and Hounds" at Hoo Green—are in private property, they were not accessible for the people generally; and indeed the owners themselves for a very long time past have not used them, both on account of the extreme hardness of the water and of the great difficulty in drawing the water by hand, or even horse-power, from the great depths to which they are sunk. Rain-water collected in tubs or tanks gave an easier and better supply. Gradually the sites of the old wells are being forgotten: a list of them is worth recording. There is one at each farm mentioned, and an average depth is about 400 feet: Well House, Broomfield Farm, Green Farm, The Court, Fox and Hounds Inn, Plumrush, David Street, Wood Hill, Ham House, Melliker, West Down, Camer, Camer Village, Norwood Lane, Hook Green Farm, Dene Farm.

A short distance down the old Birling road, passing Pitfield, is a cottage known as Steele's. In old documents it appears as Le Styghele or the Stile; and in 1350 there was a certain place in the Parish called Alcolyn-atte-Stile, held by a man named Wolford; and Mr. Lewis has concluded that this may have been "Steele's," this modern name being but a corruption of Styghele or Stile.

Some old deeds have lately come to hand which throw further light on Pitfield and on Steele's. The earliest is the will of Henry Nordish, dated January 7, 1780, and shows that at his decease in 1800 he was the owner of two properties in the Parish: one, Pitfield Green Farm, of some 50 acres, and the other of 5½ acres, which can be identified as what is now known as Steele's.

Pitfield Green Farm must not be confounded with what is now known as the Green Farm; for the boundaries of the property given in the deeds show that the land was that which was attached to Pitfield or, to use the old name, Pitfield Cottage. Between 1780 and October 1858 when John Evenden bought both properties, they passed through many hands, sometimes separately, sometimes together, and were often mortgaged, but their individualities can always be traced. Perhaps the most interest attaches to "Steele's." In 1790 this property was sold to John French, yeoman; it is described as "that messuage or tenement formerly called Hopwood, with the gardens, orchards, barns, outbuildings and several parcels of land belonging thereto, in all about five acres, now in the occupation of Thomas Steele and Margaret Munn."

That there was at least as late as 1847, a complete farm at Steele's the various deeds make clear; and a map attached to one of them shows the present old cottage—clearly the old farm-house—with several buildings around it as well as on the opposite side of the roadway, where is now a cattle-yard. This and the newer brick cottage attached to the old house were both put up in Dr. Baber's occupancy, there being no other building remaining save the farm-house when he acquired the property in 1862. A deed of 1847 specifically mentions an oast-house also, and to this day tithe is charged on a part of the adjacent field (Brownfield) as hop land.

Unfortunately the recovery of the old deeds destroys the picturesque origin of the name "Steele's" favoured by a former Vicar, Mr. Lewis, as previously mentioned; for, as shown above, Hopwood was its original name, Steele's being clearly taken from that of a former holder of the property. Old Meopham names, as Buggs, French, Munn, Mungeam, and others, figure as tenants or owners from time to time.

Pitfield Green Farm does not seem to have been altogether a paying concern, judging by the number of times it and Steele's changed hands; and John Scudder, to whom Margaret Munn sold Pitfield in 1790, seems to have been very unfortunate. For a time things apparently went smoothly, when he raised a mortgage on it for £400, a mortgage later transferred to Thomas Taylor. In 1815 he obtained a further mortgage from "George Smith of Camer in the parish of Meopham, Esquire, and William Smith of Barking in the county of Essex, Gentleman." Taylor having died, John Scudder in 1820 obtained further advances from the executors, and again in 1821 and 1825, till in 1827 he sold the property to John and William Rushton, corn merchants of London, who parted with it to G. Evered in 1839.

Leading Street. Angel Croft

This is the old name of the highway running south from the mill; the somewhat curious name, however, seems to be explained by remembering that at this point the main road gained its original course after its detour commencing at Lomer, and already described (v. Pitfield Green). Most of the buildings in Leading Street are modern; but of one of these it must be recorded that the large business of the "Meopham Stores," now owned by Mr. Parsons, commenced in one of the "Wellington Cottages" on the Green in the 'sixties by a relative of Mr. James Buggs; and it is to his business acumen and hard work that the village owes both the present building and valuable business.

The site of the Stores and the land extending up the road as far as "Greenfields" is marked in an assessment map of 1840 as Nos. 479 and 480 under the name of Angle Croft, though it appears in the Dudemere Manor Roll (*v.* Appendix G) as Angel Croft. An old deed, relating to Kent Terrace and dated October 5, 1860, reads: "William Philip Snell Esq., to Benjamin W. Horne Esq.: conveyance of a close of land called Angel Croft 1^{ac}. 3^r. 20^p. and two cottages and gardens on Meopham Green 0. 1. 14." Where the Stores are there were two old cottages, partly incorporated in the new building, in one of which, some seventy years ago, the postman—an old man named Tyler—passed his day cobbling boots; but he lived in Gravesend, whence he walked out and back again in the evening every day.

Close by is the Baptist Chapel (1836). Its origin here was not without trouble to the founders, as the following from a pamphlet published in 1866 show:

1814. The West Kent Union of Baptist Independents began preaching at Harvel, in a thatcher's cottage.
1816. They hired a house in Luddesdown and also preached on Harvel Green, when the Constable arrested them; handcuffed the brethren together and took them before the magistrate at Rochester, who at once released them; and only an abject apology saved the constable from prosecution for unlawful imprisonment. For 3 years the preachers preached on Meopham Green on Sunday afternoon.
1827. They started a Sunday School in a cottage hired as a chapel on Meopham Green.
1828. Built and opened a chapel at Meopham.
1832. The Meopham contingent desired to form a "separate church," and this they did on July 27, and in
1836 this chapel, duly enlarged, became their permanent place of worship.

Cherry Hay and "The Coffin"

On the left hand some half-mile along Leading Street stands Cherry Hay, a modern house, nearly opposite "South Street House." It derives its name from there having been (and there still is) a cherry orchard there, "Hay" being the old Anglo-Saxon Haga, a hedge, or land enclosed by a hedge. It was built about seventy years ago as a public-house, the sign being the "Prince of Wales," and Mr. Oliver, one of our now oldest inhabitants, was its landlord; but it was bought and made a private residence by Dr. Baber in 1887, and renamed Cherry Hay. The "Prince of Wales" took the place of a much older inn, which stood further back from the road than the present house, in the meadow that lies to the south of it; the open space then in front of it had a sign-post on it bearing the effigy of a coffin, some 2 feet in length, and its sign was the "Coffin." It was a low-pitched thatched building, and it was a step or two down into it to enter. At the time of its "dissolution" a Mr. Goodwin was its landlord. He for a time also kept the newly built "Prince of Wales," being followed by Oliver. The "Coffin" figures in our Parish books now and then; thus:

1732. Two ringing days at the Coffin 13/4.
1776. The charge of Strangers lying at the Coffin £1.11.6.
1803. Beer at the Coffin £1.1.6.

The first entry refers to the entertainment of the church bell-ringers; the second to the boarding-out of "strangers" by the Parish; the last is left to the reader's imagination.

The only incident I have been able to gather from an old eye-witness is that on one occasion there was a great drunken row in front of the "Coffin," and the constables had to make an arrest; and no doubt the offenders were haled to the cage. This was very shortly before the "Coffin" was pulled down.

Leylands, or South Street House

Nearly opposite Cherry Hay is the private residence with extensive grounds now known as Leylands.

Its original name was South Street House—South Street here succeeding to Leading Street—and in 1842 it was in the occupation of the Rev. Glover Mungeam. At that time it was a cottage farm-house, and the barn belonging to it stood in front against the main road. It was subsequently purchased by Mr. Evenden (the former owner of Pitfield Cottage on the

Green), and he in turn parted with it to Captain Jackson, who changed its name to "The Deodars." Evenden had somewhat enlarged the house, but its present condition is due to Dr. Baber, who purchased it in the 'eighties from Captain Jackson, and added the two wings and built the stables. At his death (1894) Mr. Mackenzie Bradley became the owner, giving it its present name of Leylands. He built the extensive cow-houses for prize Jersey cattle and the up-to-date dairy. It next came into the hands of the late Mr. Biggs of Rochester, who by certain internal changes made the entrance-hall into a large billiard-room. The amount of land attached to it has varied with the different holders, but in the Rev. Glover Mungeam's time land known as Choles Wood, Great Choles, and Little Choles belonged to it; and Mr. Lewis suggests that "Choles" may be the same as "Scholleswode," mentioned in old documents. Since Mr. Biggs's time the property has been, and still is, in the hands of Mr. Tolhurst (1934).

Doe's Cottage

Until 1892 there stood on the right hand of the main road, about eighty yards north of the Ridley turning, a picturesque and half-ruinous thatched cottage known as "Old Doe's"; and on the opposite side of the main road was a barn belonging to it. This Doe, from the traditions about him, seems to have been quite a character. Ostensibly a farmer in a small way, and owning the barn belonging to his cottage on the opposite side of the road, he was, however, a smuggler; and, from the recollections of some of our oldest inhabitants, smuggling was some sixty years ago and earlier carried on extensively in the village, the smuggled goods— kegs of brandy were the staple commodity—being brought up from the Thames or over the hills from the Medway. Doe, however, seems to have been too clever to be caught, though he sailed very close to the wind at times. Tradition says that the excise officers visited him once, and with their iron rods prodded into a heap of barley in his barn, but failed (by good luck for him) to light upon his brandy kegs that were hidden beneath. George Seagar, as a young man, was employed to help with a Harvel man to demolish the ruinous cottage; a cupboard door, locked, was noticed, but it being late in the day the two agreed to open it the next morning; however, when George Seagar arrived next day, the door had been opened and his fellow-workman did not put in an appearance, but is said to have been drunk in Harvel for six weeks afterwards—it is presumed, upon what he found in the cupboard!

Lomer

North of Pitfield Green, and a little off the high road, is the farm of Lomer, which prior to 1852 belonged to the Rev. W. Mansfield, of the Court, but was then purchased by Mr. Robert Barnett with the other lands of that estate; subsequently it was purchased by Sir Sidney Waterlow. The name is a very old one, but its origin is uncertain. In a deed of gift of land early in the fourteenth century the name of one Ricardus de Lomere is mentioned, and Simon the Archbishop is one of the witnesses (*v.* Crouches); and in a Nona Roll, date 1340 (*v.* Chapter XIX), appears the name of Henry Lomere as a parishioner. Lomer possesses the largest and deepest pond in the Parish; and if ever the ducking-stool for scolds were employed in Meopham, it must surely have been here—no other was deep enough; and the further fact that the old high road passed near it lends colour to the suggestion.

The Village Hall

Built in 1912, the Village Hall was opened in January 1913, The building, as suitable in its architecture as in its internal arrangements, was the gift of Edward Moon, Esq., of the Green Farm, and erected at a cost of nearly £2,000. It supplies a want long felt, and has already more than justified its existence. The manifold uses to which it is put are the best tribute the village can pay to the generosity of the donor. A Club-room adjoining has recently been added.

Standing now near the Lomer turning and looking south towards the Green, it is quite possible to conjure up in the mind the appearance of Pitfield Hamlet, say, a hundred years ago. To the left would have been a shaw, now occupied by the nursery grounds, and to the right the main road making its detour behind fields and side lands of the Green as far as the mill. There were no houses there then except the old farm—now the butcher's shop—and its barn and buildings; and beyond it the old house under the walnut-tree, and then the inn and mill—the latter just built. The road that now is the main road was nothing but a lane or track that ran along the west side of the Green, like that that still runs along the east side.

On the left, again, would only be seen the forge, with the village cage in front and near the road; and beyond it the old Green farm and buildings. Pitfield Cottage, with its barn, both now gone, would occupy the farthest corner, and between it and the mill would be the Clay Cottages on the south side land, and then a row of old cottages as far as and including the King's Arms Inn.

CHAPTER XVII

HAMLET OF CULVERSOLE

Culversole Hamlet. The "Soles"

THE name, now corrupted into Culverstone, was originally Culversole, i.e. Culvers Pond; and a pond existed till lately where the roads divide opposite the school church. An entry in the church register for 1776 has the name written Culvertsole—a scribe's manifest error. This is but one of the many "soles" in the Parish (*v.* Grinnellsole). In 1842 "South Sole" appears, apparently meaning the present South Street, or its pond, which still exists. "Brimstone Bottom," in the eastern valley of the Parish, is, according to Mr. Lewis, a corruption of Brimpsole or Brimsole. Just outside our Parish limits is Hodsole Street, written in 1370 "Hoddesole"; but as a man's name Hodsoll often appears in old documents, it may be a corruption of this.*

I am unable to add any old-time associations with Culverstone, the one very old timbered building in it being an old farm, known as Owls Castle, nearly opposite the school church; but the only tradition attaching to it is that it was once broken into by burglars! Just before reaching Owls Castle there stands on the west side of the main road, and at right angles to it, an old farm-house with a large barn behind; it does not seem to possess a name. Originally a farm, but now (1934) it is occupied by Mrs. Fortescue, whose memory goes back over fourscore years. She relates that her father, James Loft, bought the property in 1839 and converted it into a beer-shop (a partly licensed house), and named it the "Two Brewers"; the signboard hung from a tree on the

---

* "Brim" is defined in Wright's *Dialect Dictionary* as a bank covered with rough undergrowth, whilst "Sole" is the old word for pond, and "Culver" for dove or pigeon.

opposite side of the road and bore a rhyme of Mr. Loft's composition:

> Good malt makes good beer;
> Walk in my friends, you'll find it here.

It was largely patronized by travellers on foot, and in the hopping season by the hoppers. The present sitting-room near the road was the bar, the door to it being then at the end of the room facing the road, where there is now a window.

An old parishioner, Mr. James Smith, had one story about this hamlet. He told of a certain William Lane who lived at the White House, Culverstone, when Mr. Thompson was Vicar of Meopham (1816–1854), and with whom the said W. Lane "fell out," and registered a vow that Mr. Thompson should never see any more of his money. Soon afterwards Mrs. Lane died, and as she could not be buried in the church-yard without the payment of the customary dues to the Vicar, the husband buried her himself in the south-west corner of his garden under a yew-bush still existing. In process of time the husband died also—when Mr. Hooper was Vicar—so the body of the wife was exhumed, Mr. Smith assisting in the act, and, her coffin being placed in a wagon with that of her husband, they were both finally interred in Meopham Church-yard. Opposite Lacknut Cottages is a strip of grassland with a small pond and brushwood—Culverstone Green. An attempt was made some years ago to enclose it, but at the instance of the Parish the fencing was removed, but not put back to quite its original position, so that the pond and a little land were lost to the public.

Behind this boundary-line of fencing is a large meadow, which about forty-five years ago was the Meopham Race-Course; at its north end it is separated from a field by a hedge in which two gaps are still to be seen. Through these the race was run, the horses turning in the field, and on back to the actual race-course. The races were of local character, and were started by a "bookie" named Meadows, who occupied a picturesque wooden house where the present "shooting-box" stands. Meadows had been a jockey in France, and came here with a couple of race-horses, Belphoebe and Flying Ben, and these he was always ready to match against all comers. On one occasion he won £100 from Mr. Walls, who kept the grocer's shop at Wrotham, and who entered his own horse against Belphoebe. The races were not "flat," but the usual artificial jumps were arranged about the course. The grandstand and flagstaff were against the road just south of the Green.

The life of the race-course was a short one—only five years. The occupant of the "shooting-box" prior to Meadows, and until 1878, was Mrs. Sevier; it is now (1934) owned by Mrs. Bolster. Water in those days was very scarce, as already mentioned, and one of the village fathers—Mr. David Day—has narrated how he made good profit on the race-course by fetching water from Nepicar and retailing it at 4d. a pint!

The School Church

The School Church is a recent erection. Some dates and facts in regard to it are, however, worth recording here.

1872. School Church built at Culverstone, on land given by Mr. Amos Fletcher (of Holywell Park); the building cost about £800, raised by subscription. (This was collected by the Vicar, Mr. Hooper.)

1873. Feb. 14. Licence issued to Mr. Hooper to hold divine service in Culverstone School Church and to administer the Sacraments.

1873. Bishop Claughton opens it with a service.

1873. Silver sacramental vessels given by Major Edwards.

Camer Hamlet, v. Camer

Hamlet of Priesthood

To account for this somewhat peculiar name it has been suggested that it was the property given by Simon de Meopham to endow the chantry at the Parish Church; and its proximity to Dene renders this possible. Within, however, twenty-five years of that gift the hamlet is named (1348) Priestwode in the Steward's book of the monks, and in 1377 appears the name of one Thomas Prestwode. (Wode = wood; so Woodhill in 1377 is written Wodehelle.) It is therefore quite as likely that it may have been named after some previous landowner; and the name of Prestwode appears in a document of 1279, before Simon de Meopham's time.

The hamlet on the eastern ridge, in East Meopham, contains several old cottages; and one of these, next the small village Green, deserves special mention. It used to be popularly known as "Artichoke Hall"—a thatched building of great age. By the side of the wide fireplace in the kitchen or back room is a carved oak escutcheon 27 inches high, presenting the Royal Rose surmounted by a crown; it is this that has given the cottage the name of "Artichoke Hall"! I am informed that similar carvings exist in what still remains of the old Eltham Palace.

In the front room the upright beams have crowns carved on them in relief.

The property, now owned by Mr. Langridge, till lately belonged to Eltham Parish, a fact that offers a possible explanation of the carvings just mentioned. The following extract from the Report of the Commissioners to inquire into the Education and Charities of England and Wales, vol. xv, p. 460, explains how Eltham owned property in our Parish:

T. SAMPSON'S CHARITY

By an Inquisition, under a commission of charitable uses, taken 20th July, 1626, it was found that Thomasin Sampson died seized of a messuage or tenement, barn, orchard and garden, and six pieces of land containing 28 acres in the Parish of Meopham at Priesthood Green, of the value of £8 a year; and that by her will, bearing date 23rd March 1624, she gave to the poor of Eltham (to every one 12d.) the £8 a year which was due to her for her life, to be employed after her decease to the use of her son, and after his decease to remain to the parish of Eltham and to their use for ever . . .

*   *   *   *

The property belonging to this charity consists of a small dwelling-house, an old barn and stable, and several closes, containing as appears by a map made in 1804, 27 ac. 3 r. 4 p. let to Benjamin Johnson as yearly tenant at a fair rent of £16.

*   *   *   *

In 1903 the gross income was £20, and was employed partly as money gifts to the poor and partly for apprenticing boys out to trades. Judging by figures given by the Rev. Elphinstone Rivers, in his account of Eltham, the money seems to have allowed one boy on an average to have been annually apprenticed.

The following considerations help to fix the date of the cottage, and explain its peculiar fittings.

In the last years of Henry VIII's reign (1546–1547) Eltham Palace and Chapel were in a ruinous state (Evelyn), and what was left was finally disposed of by Parliament during the Commonwealth, and the park was destroyed. These facts suggest that the cottage at Priesthood was built about 1550, carved beams from the wreck of Eltham being employed, whilst the carved escutcheon was put up as a decoration.

It is not known who had the property before Dame Thomasin Sampson; but seeing that she died in 1626, only about seventy years after the ruin of the Palace at Eltham, her husband might even have been the builder of the cottage at Priesthood, if it were erected some thirty years later than the date suggested above (1550); at any rate, her father might well have done it; and her leaving it to Eltham implies a close connection between her family and that parish, so she or her parents could, on this assumption, have obtained the building material from the wreck of the Eltham Palace.

David Street

Though not classed as one of our hamlets, David Street would seem to have as much claim to the title as Melliker; it consists of a farm and some cottages to the west of

Priesthood, and only separated from it by a field. The name is certainly a corruption of Davy's Street, or Davy Street, as it appears in old documents; and in 1532 one Philip Davy lived there.

In 1523 an inn of some sort seems to have been here, for, under the heading of "Davystrete," in that year, in the Steward's book of the monks, appears the name of "Agn. (? Agnes) atte Rose"; and according to Mr. Hooper, our former Vicar, there was known to have been a Rose Inn in the Parish in early days, but he had been unable to locate it.

Hamlet of Harvel

About a mile to the south of Priesthood lies the hamlet of Harvel, at the southern extremity of the East Borough of Meopham; but whether this is the same as Harefield, already mentioned as one of the divisions of the East Borough, is uncertain but most likely. "There is," says Mr. Lewis, "one name which is very common in the old documents, and that is Halifield (Holy Field), also spelt Alyfead and Halifel. It is possible that it was a big place in that part of Meopham, and that it gradually imparted its name to the locality, and came to be called Harvel. . . . There is one other possibility. In one of the ancient Saxon charters connected with the Manor of Meopham there occurs the name of Heorot Field (or Hartfield) not far from Hludesbeorgh, i.e. Luddesdown."

Harvel Green ranks next in size to Pitfield Green. It attained its present size in 1833, when at the request of the Parish the Dean and Chapter of Canterbury, as Lords of the Manor, added to it some waste land on all its sides, amounting in all to about 24 perches. At present the surface is so uneven, and so deeply cut up in all directions by farm traffic, as to render it useless for anything except pasturage. Within the last few years the Parish Council considered the question of levelling it so as to fit it for a recreation-ground for the inhabitants around, but the estimated cost rendered a proposed scheme impossible to be carried out. The same by-laws, however, that apply to Pitfield Green apply to this one also—as indeed, to all the Greens, big and little.

To the south end of Harvel Green, across a meadow, though formerly ploughland, is a shaw in a deep hollow— Cock Adam Shaw. In it are a number of megaliths or large Sarsen stones, lying in confusion and partly hidden by brushwood. Bennett, in his work on Ightham (1907), gives a plan of them, and represents them as twenty-eight in number; but since then several have been carted away to adorn private property. They doubtless represent a fallen dolmen (or dolmens); and those who know the megaliths at Coldrum in the valley below—beyond Trottescliffe—where one dolmen still remains *in situ*, will be struck with the resemblance in the general arrangement to that at Harvel. In each situation the great stones are in a hollow with a steep descent from the level field above; but at Coldrum there is still a "circle" in the field of smaller Sarsens. Such, too, certainly was once the case at Harvel; and Mr. Robert Goodwin of Meopham has told me that as a young man he helped to throw down from the field above into the hollow of Cock Adam Shaw several smaller Sarsens which, owing to their being almost buried under the surface, constantly broke the ploughshares—the field being then ploughland. He added his opinion that, were the pasture broken up, the same trouble would be met with, for all the stones were not dislodged. Presumably these buried stones were at one time part of a circle of stones.

It seems clear, therefore, that, as at Coldrum, a "Druidical Circle" at one time existed in this field, the large megalithic chamber being below. An amusing coincidence connected with Coldrum is given by the Rev. C. H. Fielding in his *Memoirs of Malling*: "Some years ago two young gentlemen found under the cromlech at Coldrum a skeleton, which was removed, and buried in the churchyard at Meopham by the Vicar of that parish. Upon this the Rector of Trottescliffe, in which parish Coldrum stands, wrote to ask the Vicar of Meopham what he meant by stealing his oldest parishioner!"

There is one other interesting fact to be noticed in this part of the Parish. There is, running from Harvel Green, an old road or lane—Dene Lane—at the bottom of a valley, which leads eventually to Dene Farm. On the side of this valley, and practically parallel with the road, at the edge of a shaw (Dean Mead Wood) on Mr. Edwards's property, is a row of fine yew-trees, perhaps a quarter of a mile long, and close to them a pathway is marked on the ordnance maps. Standing on this path one can see in the distance, still parallel with the road, a broken line of yew-trees, so regularly arranged that there can be no doubt of their having been purposely thus planted; and also no doubt that the line of trees was at one time quite unbroken. The local tradition is that they were planted along the footpath as a guide to Luddesdown Church; and, whilst they may have answered this purpose, it is also probable that they or their forbears were along what was in early times a branch pilgrim footway; it being a usual thing thus to indicate the way for pilgrims. A similar line of yews can be seen if one stands in the lane that leaves the main road south of Pitfield, and opposite the Ridley turning. Following the line of the lane it is seen to ascend Herring (Heron) Hill on the opposite side of the valley, and to be bordered with a regular row of old yew-trees; and where this ascent is crossed by the old Birling road—now a mere cart-track—that runs along the valley from the Green to Holly Hill and Birling, a similar line of yews indicating the route will also be noticed.

That yews were cultivated of old for making bows is well known; but for this purpose there would be no need to have planted them in single file along a roadside, nor indeed does this reason explain their frequency in churchyards so satisfactorily as the one that in days of yore yew-twigs were carried in lieu of palms on Palm Sunday by the faithful.

The quaintest thing in this hamlet is perhaps the sign of the old cottage beer-shop, the "Amazon and Tiger," now transferred to a newly and not unpicturesquely designed public-house.

On the north side of the road, through the woods uniting Culverstone and Harvel, are some old farm buildings. The first is Sparrow Haw—probably named after someone called Sparrow—not an uncommon name in the past. Then comes Plumrush, a farm also, and then "Wellard's." This old house has lately been pulled down, but as G. Wellard figures in the Hearth Tax Roll of 1673, the farm probably obtained its name from him. It is the one place in these parts that has a well. The last house is Harvel Lodge. On the same road, about half a mile from Culverstone, stood the old Fowlerstone House, mentioned as hired by the Parish for the use of the poor. Recently built gamekeepers' cottages now occupy the site.

In 1912, through the efforts and pecuniary support of Mr. Edwards of Harvel and by the aid of public subscription, a small village hall was opened at Easter on land given by Mr. Cripps Day of Holly Hill. It has proved of the greatest value to the villagers as a club-room and place of amusement, and on Sundays services are held in it once or twice, there being no place of public worship in the hamlet. Tribute must here be paid to the memory of Mr. Harpley, who died lately at an advanced age and who was the proprietor of the general shop at Harvel. Of him it may be said, "He did what he could" for the spiritual life of his fellow-villagers; for he held on his own private premises every Sunday afternoon, for over thirty years, a religious service for all who would attend; he also worked hard in the establishing of the Harvel Village Hall.

CHAPTER XVIII

DENE MANOR

Dene Farm (Dene Court, and formerly Dene Manor)

DENE, an old Manor-house lying in the easternmost valley of our Parish, is closely connected with the family of Archbishop Simon. The interior, when being modernized in 1930, showed its old timbered structure, and especially a very fine oak "king-post" in the roof.

Denes are frequently mentioned in Domesday, and there the expression "Dena Silvae" means a wooded hollow or valley. John de la Dene is simply, therefore, John of the Valley, and in a document of 1377 the expression "John atte Dene" occurs. Spilman says: "A dene does not contain a fixed measurement of land, but sometimes 500 acres or more, sometimes less than half, whence comes that expression in Domesday of small and large denes."

The term is not found in Domesday Book in the sister county of Sussex, and only once in Surrey. In Kent it is found far more often in the Weald than anywhere else, but occasionally on the higher land, e.g. at "Hagelei" in Achestan (Axton) Hundred, where the survey gives "una dena silue de v porc." At "Redlege [Ridley] una dena silue quā ten' Ricard' de Tonebrigge," and at "Eisse [Ash] Rex ht inde 11ᵃˢ denas" (from Furley's *Weald of Kent*, quoted by Lewis).

The valley in which Ightham Mote is situated is Dinas Dene.

Local tradition names Dene as the home of the De Meophams, but that is disproved by the facts that the owners of the Manor in Simon's time were the de Twythams; and that, as Simon's sister married John de la Dene, it is highly improbable that both families occupied the same house! The late Mr. Lewis, however, always spoke of Dene as the de Meophams' home; and it was this belief, in my opinion, that made him adhere to the further fallacy that the chantry of

St. James de la Dene was on the family property at Dene; though he expressed surprise at no trace of it being left.

In the time of Richard I (1189–1199) the Manor of Dene was granted to Alen de Twythin, who was present with the king at the Siege of Acre, and, says Hasted, it remained in the hands of that family till 1381. In 1259 a John de la Dene's name is mentioned in connection with a "fine" (v. Dodemere); so he, as well as the later John de la Dene that Simon's sister married, may have been of the same family; for "de la Dene" does not of necessity express the family name.

That the Twythams were still in the Parish in the Archbishop's day is further shown by the following from the Cal. of Patent Rolls, Edward III, 1329, October 4th:

Licence for the alienation in Mortmain by Bertram de Twytham of land in Meopham and other places to the Prior and Convent of Christ Church [Canterbury] for the maintenance of chaplains to celebrate Divine Service daily in the chapel of St. Thomas the Martry, for the souls of the said Bertram, his ancestors and others. (Quoted by Lewis.)

After the Twythams' time, Dene passed by marriage to Simon Septvans (de Septem Vannis), in whose family it was till Charles I's reign, when the owner conveyed it, with the adjacent estate of Ham, to Francis Twisden of East Peckham. Early in the eighteenth century Sir Thomas Twysden alienated both estates (Dene and Ham) to Samuel Attwood, Clerk, who willed them in 1735 to Elizabeth Hodsoll, whose niece succeeded to the properties; her son, Richard Gee, inherited them in 1791, who presently assumed the name of Carew (Hasted). The parish map of 1842 shows "much land in the east was owned by Sir B. Carew with Ham Farm and Dene" (Lewis); but that since this date "the Carew Lands with Dene Farm passed to the Westminster Hospital, then to Mr. J. Johnson, and afterwards were purchased by Mr. Raphael" (Lewis).

Of the Twisden family Mr. Lewis has noted that a member of it was one of the judges who tried the regicides of Charles I, and that the name of Francis Twisden, the first holder of the Dene–Ham properties, appears in our Parish accounts for the East Borough under date 1649, together with that of one Edward Deane. This last name no doubt was originally Dene or de la Dene, though by now he had nothing to do with the property. From 1649 the name of Twisden appears in our Churchwardens' books:

Francis Twisden	1649 (Commonwealth)
Francis Twisden	1662 (Charles II)
Sir Thomas Twisden	1678 ,,
Sir Roger Twisden	1683 ,,
The Lady Twisden	1690 (William and Mary)
Sir Roger Twisden	1691 ,, ,,
Thomas Twisden	1702 (William III)
Sir Thomas Twisden, Bart.	1703 (Anne)
Sir Thomas Twisden, Bart.	1727 (George I)

The name then ceases to appear (*v.* also Chapel of St. James de la Dene).*

Hope Valley

The beautiful valley, Hope Valley, or, more popularly, the Happy Valley, that separates East and West Meopham, and through which the old Birling road runs, as already mentioned, has one or two associations with old times. A foot track that crosses "Bullock's Foot" field in the bottom mounts towards David Street up a very steep bank in a shaw; some roughly made steps surmount this difficulty, and bear the name of Wouldham's Steps. The name is a very old one, for in a rate list of 1648 is that of Thomas Wouldham in the East Borough, so probably he or his ancestors made and gave the name to the steps, which they still retain. A Robert Wouldham witnessed a deed of sale of land in Culversole in 1691.

Farther south a narrow path, once a road, mounts the hill

---

* A full account of the occupants of Dene Manor is given by Phillpot in his *Villare Cantiarum*, ed. 1659, p. 234.

to Harvel, the Herring Hill Road. This hill has been referred to as having once possessed a windmill; and the origin of the name may be a twofold one. In a document of 1377 the name of John Heryng appears, and hence perhaps the name of the hill; it is also possible that it may have once been the site of a heronry.

On the opposite or west side of the valley is Hope Hill and Hope Hill Wood; and where in old documents Le Hope is mentioned, Mr. Lewis has suggested that this hill is meant. A "Hope," as Dean Hoare in his *English Roots* points out, has the same origin and meaning as "open," and by transference means an open place; and Mr. Lewis has illustrated it by the quotation:

> He has guided them o'er moss and muir,
> O'er hill and hope and many a down.

In the north-east of England "hope" as part of a place-name is common, as Greenhope, Hopetown; the word Hope (syn. Hoppe and Houp) here meaning a small enclosed valley (*New English Dictionary*). I leave the reader to choose between these various meanings of the word.

There is one other land-name in this and other parts of the Parish which much exercised Mr. Lewis, and is variously written as Purfield, Pirifield, Pirfield, and Purvil in the fourteenth century. His conclusion regarding it is undoubtedly correct, and that is that it means a pear orchard; and he adds: "On the Camer Lands there is a purvil of 16 acres, and on those of Sir B. Carew at Dene a purvil of 30 acres; and on the Meopham Manor lands one of 14 acres; and at Harvel another purvil of some acres." He further concludes from this that perry as well as cider must have been a favourite beverage here in old times.

The Turnpike Road and Toll-gates

Though Hasted (as already mentioned) described Meopham in the sixteenth century as isolated by the badness of its roads, they were probably not worse than many others in Kent. There were few roads in Tudor times fit for anything but horse traffic, wheel traffic for travelling being very limited.

From 1662 until about 1871-1872 our roads were under the care of the Parish, and the money for their upkeep, such as it was, was raised by tolls on all but foot passengers who passed through the "Turnpikes," "Bars" or "Toll-Gates" that were erected at intervals along the highways. The Meopham "Pike" was at the corner of the field next against the schools, thus commanding the traffic of the main road and of that to Longfield. The toll-keeper's house, when the toll-gate was abolished, was transferred to the other corner of the field, and is now the lodge of the Lances. A "Bar" where tolls were also collected once stood across the Harvel Road opposite the old timbered house now occupied by Mr. Scudder.

These gates were farmed out to the highest bidder, and anything over and above the sum that he was thus bound to pay over to the Parish annually was his own to live upon. There was enormous variety in their values; thus, Smetham gives the value of the Strood gate in 1868 at £920 per annum, and that of the Chatham gate as £27 (v. Appendix N).

The Bar at the Street was looked after at the time of its removal by the ostler at the "George," and the year 1851 is well remembered by Mr. Oliver as a lucrative one for the renters of the "bars" and toll-gates. It was the year of the great exhibition, and the traffic all down our turnpike road was phenomenal, people travelling from the Wrotham valley to get the train or a boat to London from Gravesend.

Older Meopham people can well remember the state of the roads in wet weather, and the mode of repair in days happily gone by, when stones—and not small ones—were distributed in the winter to be rolled in by nothing less than the wheels of passing vehicles, and then as certainly picked out again by the horses' hoofs, whilst the ruts formed by traffic and storms were dangers to be avoided! The following extracts from our books bear on this matter:

1776. £8.13.9 paid for clearing the roads of snow in the Frost.
Unrutting from lower side Pitfield Green to near Jos.
Munns 225 Rods at 1½ per rod.

So for some three-quarters of a mile from the Green the road
must have been in a very bad condition. A hundred years ago,
too, the roads were not too safe after dark; and Smetham, in
his *History of Strood*, quotes from the parish books the instance
of a journeyman blacksmith, returning home from Meopham
at 7 p.m. December 6, 1813, being shot at the top of Strood
Hill, and so wounded that his hand had to be amputated. It
does not seem that his assailants were ever caught. The
conversion of the old high road into an arterial one in 1930
has changed its whole aspect.

Roadside Ponds

Old plans show not only many roadside ponds to collect
surface water, but many too in private grounds, for water was
always scarce in Meopham. These wayside ponds have now
nearly all disappeared; but when it was the custom to move
cattle and sheep along the roads, a frequent water-supply for
them was absolutely necessary.

These ponds in many places added to the difficulties of
traffic by inundating the roads in wet weather, as, for instance,
till quite recently at Waterditch, and formerly also opposite
the Court, at the Causeway (*v.* Court).

The necessity of using hard water even for domestic
purposes has been already alluded to.

Wayside Crosses or "Crouches"

In pre-Reformation times wayside crosses were erected from
religious motives, as well as probably to serve as points of
direction; anyhow, they subserved this purpose. The name
Crouch is only an old form of Cross, from the Latin *Crux*,
and several were at one time in our Parish; but by ordinance
of Parliament, August 28, 1643, all "monuments of superstition
and idolatry, etc., to be destroyed both in churches and *out of*

doors before 1 November, 1643." This iconoclastic work was laid upon the Churchwardens, under penalty for disobedience to the order.

The Parish Crouch is mentioned in Sprever's will (1525), *q.v.*; and in the thirteenth and fourteenth centuries appear "Kemmer's Crouche," "Lomery's Crouche," "Giles Crouche," "Galony's Crouche." The sites of the "Parish Crouch" and of "Giles Crouche" are unknown; the "Kemmer's Crouche" stood almost certainly in the hamlet of Camer; "Lomery's," where the old high road turned west opposite Lomer. Galony's Crouche, if not identical with the Camer one, seems likely to have been somewhere on the Camer estate, since in 1370, in a list in the Steward's book of the monks, under the heading of "Kemmer," appears Galony's Crouche. In 1348 a certain John Galon lived in that part of the Parish; it is likely he gave the name to the wayside cross.

"At the cross-roads" may not only mean what it appears to mean, but may originally have referred to the spot where the cross stood; the Kentish "three- (or four) went-way" is a fine non-committal expression.

Crosses were also erected as memorials, as the following account, much abridged from Smetham, but of local interest to us, shows. In the days of the Templars one of their houses stood on the banks of the Medway between Cuxton and Strood. Nothing of the old building remains save its vaults, over which rises the Tudor erection known as Temple Manor.

One night one of their brethren, Sir Reginald Braybrooke, returning home from Cuxton in the dark, was shot by an arrow and killed in the road. The brethren erected *in memoriam* a triangular monument at the spot where he fell, with a cross or crouche or crucifix on each side, "fronting the three roads that united at the place" of the murder.

No trace of the monument remains, but its memory is perpetuated by the "Three Crouches," the sign of the inn on the road from Cobham to Strood. The inn is a very old establishment, and was at one time known as the "Bear and Ragged Staff."

Rochester Bridge

In days gone by Meopham had to help in the upkeep and repair of Rochester Bridge. This may seem to have been hard on a village so far away; but it would not then have been so regarded, as it was held to be a sacred duty* to build or endow or help to support a bridge. Yet there is evidence that the contributions for the upkeep of the bridge—which must have been frequent, as the bridge was a wooden one—pressed heavily on the villages; for when in Richard II's time the promoters of the proposed stone bridge petitioned the king, an argument in their favour adduced was thus expressed, "Les ditʒ s'upliantʒ ayant pitié et consideration de les importableʒ charges . . ."; the "unbearable charges" being the levies above referred to. Bridges were largely in the hands of the monks, who extracted tolls from travellers.

A wooden bridge existed over the Medway between Strood and Rochester from earliest times; and in the deed already referred to, of Athelstane's time, A.D. 939, where land in Meopham is being given away, there is a proviso for the upkeep of the bridge and the building of the castle, or military defence works, both presumably at Rochester (*v.* Appendix A). On the occasion of the consecration of the Cathedral on May 11, 1130, King Henry I, with Queen Maud, paid a visit to Rochester, but, the bridge needing repair, a contribution of 3/4 had to be made towards the expense; and, says Mr. Lewis, the effigies of these two sovereigns "sculptured on either side of the West Door of the Nave are the earliest sculptured effigies of English sovereigns we possess." The wooden bridge had frequently to be rebuilt, as, for instance, after its being burnt by Simon de Montfort in 1264; and the first stone one was not erected till 1392; but it lasted to 1857. Stow, in his *Survey of London* (1598), speaks of a "row of houses and alley gate called after the Shaft, Shaft Alley," being in the possession of Rochester Bridge.

* In *Piers Plowman* it is mentioned as an act of Christian charity,
    "To build the broken bridge, and mend the bad road."

Two ancient documents quoted by Lambarde show how the old bridges were repaired, and how it came about that villages far away had to assist.

The first document (Memorandum de Ponte Roffensi) from Christ Church, Canterbury, gives an account of the ownership of each of the nine piers of the old bridge. Of the ninth pier, i.e. the first on the western or Strood side, it says:

The ninth pier belongs to the Archbishop [of Canterbury] and he is responsible for three beams and has to plank four yards. And this responsibility is to be shared between Northfleet, Clive, Higham, Denton, Milton, Luddesdown, Meopham, Snodland, Birling, Paddlesworth and all the men in that valley.

The other document is the Textus Roffensis of Ernulf, Bishop of Rochester (A.D. 1115). It is in Anglo-Saxon and Latin. Lambarde thus translates verbatim from the Anglo-Saxon:

Then is the nynthe peere the Archbishop's, that is the land peere at the West ende: to Fleete: and to his cliffe: and to Higham: and to Denton: and to Mylton: and to Ludsdowne: and to Mepham: and to Snodland: and to Berling, and to Paddesworth: and to all that valley men: and foure yardes to plancke and three plates to laye.

The Latin version is to the same effect, but adds a general note which applies to the whole bridge, and which runs in English:

And be it known that all the beams which are placed on this bridge must be of such dimensions as to be able to safely support the entire heavy weight of the superimposed planks and of everything else that shall go over them.

In our Churchwardens' accounts for 1668 a fine of 10/- is noted as having been paid in default of a representative of Meopham attending a meeting of the bridge wardens.

1648. Laid out for the choosing of the Wardens of the Bridge, 1/.
1648. Paid to Henry Master for going to the Bridge 1/.
1666. For chusing the wardens of Rochester Bridge 1/6.

The above entries are explained by the fact that the various manors—for it was not the parishes, but the manors and lands in them that originally contributed—sent annually, even to recent times, a representative to vote at the election of the Wardens of the Bridge, the ceremony taking place at Easter in the gardens of Rochester Castle. This custom was continued long after a money contribution ceased to be paid. When the first stone bridge was erected (1387–1392), Sir Robert Knolles endowed it with land—the present Bridge Estate—for its support. In the Hundred Rolls, *temp.* Edward I, that of Kent (1274) has the following: "The King's Escheator was guilty of exaction, in the Manor of Mepeham. This officer also took 30/- of the collection of the Pontage of Rochester" (Furley's *Weald of Kent*, vol. ii, p. 143).

Two curious entries in our books regarding bridges are hard to explain. One, 1647, "John Edmeds repairing of the bridge," can hardly refer to Rochester; it may refer to the Causeway in Meopham (*q.v.*); and Edmeds was the name of the village carpenter at that time. The other, 1647, "Paid for Pharly Bridge 8/"—Pharly must be phonetic for Farleigh, but our Parish never had pecuniary relations with it, as far as is now known, beyond what the above extract shows. Also, 1851, "Repairing Dartford Bridge, 4/10."*

To complete the reference to Rochester Bridge, and to show how intimately bridges were connected with religious feeling, it may be added that at the end of the twelfth century Gilbert de Glanville, Bishop of Rochester, built a chapel at the Strood end of the bridge dedicated to St. Mary; and in 1395 John Lord Cobham did the same at the Rochester end, dedicating the building to the Holy Trinity; and it was served by three chaplains, for the use of travellers (*v.* also under the Court).

* Similar payments by rate for "roads and bridges" out of the Parish are to be found in the Cobham Churchwardens' accounts.

CHAPTER XIX

VILLAGE LIFE IN THIRTEENTH AND FOURTEENTH CENTURIES

I WILL endeavour to convey in this chapter some idea of what life in Meopham was like in the thirteenth and fourteenth centuries. Without written records it is impossible to give an account of the actual goings on in any particular place in the days of old; and unfortunately we possess next to none for the purpose dealing with Meopham. What life generally in an English village was like some hundreds of years ago can, however, be gathered from the numerous popular books on the subject that are within the reach of everybody, as, for example, the writings of Dr.—now Cardinal —Gasquet, and the Rev. P. H. Ditchfield; but I must confine myself to the few records that remain to us, and they are unfortunately records almost entirely of felonious acts from Courts of Law. I say "unfortunately," for it must not be inferred that Meopham people were worse in those days than others; but by "reading between the lines" of what follows, a picture of events is presented to the eye that shows human nature the same then as it is now.

The many reconstructions of old village life show an excuse for much crime that in those times was committed; indeed, it is astonishing there was not more. Between landlords and peasants there was no one who could help the latter, and their condition was almost one of cruel servitude. Their dwellings were mud huts of one room, with straw for beds, and with surroundings altogether such as cattle would not be exposed to nowadays. One quotation will suffice to confirm what I say. Dr. Jessopp, in his *Coming of the Friars* (p. 100), after pointing out that the savagery of the "gentry" six hundred years ago set an example which naturally the poor imitated, adds: "It was only natural that they [the peasantry] should be only too ready to break and defy the law. In a single year in 1285, in the Hundred of North Erpingham, containing 31 parishes, the catalogue of crime is so ghastly as positively to stagger one." As to suicides, they were not to be wondered at; the wonder rather being that there were not more who desired to be quit of their very undesirable lives!

The various incidents from time to time already mentioned, added to what now follows, are all that remain to us of facts illustrative of life in medieval Meopham. The subjoined extracts collected for Mr. Lewis are from various Plea Rolls; and notes in elucidation of some of the entries are added:

(a) *From the earliest Placita or Assize or Plea Roll relating to Kent, temp. Henry III, 1241*

The Hundred of Toltintre comes by twelve [the jury]. Richard the son of William of Welles being charged with the death of a certain woman killed in Mepham, withdrew himself, and was attached by William the beadle of Welles, Hamo le Curtays, Mauger de Langebrugg, and William le Halte. Therefore [they are] in mercy. And the jurors say that they do not suspect him of that death, but they say that Adam de Nortwude who was outlawed for the same death in the eyre of the other justices is guilty. Therefore let Richard return if he will.

> NOTE.—"*In mercy*" or "*in misericordia,*" written, in the abbreviated Latin of the Rolls, "*in mĩa,*" signified that the offender was at the mercy of the King; the amercement, or fine, being small, and therefore merciful, in proportion to the offence.
>
> "In the eyre of the other justices." The earliest provincial courts were those of the Itinerant Justices, or Justices in Eyre (from the Norman-French word *erre*, a journey) (Cox). Their modern representatives are the Circuit Judges.

(b) *From same reference,* A.D. 1241

Henry the tailor of Mapham accused (*appellavit*) Gerold the son of Thomas of breaking the king's peace, and of robbery, and of felony. And likewise he accused of the same Robert the son of Robert Biset of Wuldeham, Thomas the son of Constance, William Coker and Johanna his wife. And now he comes and will not prosecute them. Therefore let him be taken into custody (he is a poor man) and his pledges for the prosecution are in mercy, to wit, Peter son of Wulvard of Mepham, and William his brother. And all the accused come. And the jurors say that they are not convicted, but they testify that the aforesaid Gerold, because the same Henry brought a certain writ of Novel Disseisin against him and gained nothing through the assize, took away chattels of the same Henry to the value of 20/–. Therefore Gerold is in mercy. And let him pay to the aforesaid Henry 20/– for his chattels, giving pledges for the said amount and for the mercy [amercement] of Gerold himself and Nicholas of Ore. They say also that Robert the son of Robert and all the others were with the aforesaid Gerold at the commission of that robbery. Therefore they are all in mercy by the pledges of the same Nicholas and Robert of Wudeham.

> NOTE.—"Writ of Novel Disseisin." "The *Assisa novae disseisinae*, so called because the Justices in Eyre went their circuits from seven years to seven years; and no assise was allowed before them which commenced before the last circuit, which was called an ancient assise; and that which was upon a disseisin since the last circuit, an assise of Novel disseisin."—Tomlin, *Law Dictionary*.

(c) *Ditto*, 1241

Alice of the Well, John Sutor of Mepham and Cecilia his wife, charged with associating with thieves, and with receiving, come and defend the whole, and put themselves on the country etc. And the jurors say that they are not guilty. Therefore they are acquitted.

> NOTE.—Alič de Puteo = Alice atte Well and later the surname of Attwell (*v.* Well House). John Sutor probably means John the shoemaker (of Meopham).

(d) *Ditto*, 1241

James the son of John was burnt in the fire by accident (per *infortunium*). Matilda his mother first found him. And now she does not come. And she was attached by Thomas of the Westland, the Borsholder. Therefore [she is] in mercy. And the village of Mepham buried him without view of the Coroner. Therefore it is in mercy.

> NOTE.—Two transgressions of the law occur here; the one in that the mother did not come forward to give evidence, and

the other that the body was buried without the usual inquest being held. In Furley's *Weald of Kent* it is pointed out that the "borough" in Kent was "composed of freemen or heads of families who were mutually burgh or sureties for each other . . . ten of these boroughs or tythings constituted originally the Hundred." The absence of a witness was therefore liable to be punished by fine of the county; or even the whole community, or hundred, might, as in this case, be "in mercy."

(e) *Ditto*, 1241

Agnes, who was the wife of Thomas the Carpenter of Mepham, hung herself by a certain noose in her house at Mepham. Agnes her daughter first found her. And now she comes, and is not suspected, nor any other. Judgment—*felo de se*. Her chattels 6/-, for which the same sheriff is responsible.

> NOTE.—By statute 17 Ed. ii. c. 1 the goods of felons belonged to the King, and in this case His Majesty gained 6/-! The burial of a "*felo de se*" was, until the time of George IV, required to be in a highway with a stake driven through the body (*v.* Churchyard).

From the second oldest Placita or Plea Roll of 39 Hen. III, 1255

Robert Kiterel and Letitia his wife were found killed in their house in the village of Mepham.

The first discoverer and four neighbours came, and were not suspected. No Englescherie. Judgment, murder upon the Hundred. And the town of Mepham buried the aforesaid dead persons without view of the Coroner, by William Shetelcroft. Therefore it is in mercy.

And Richard Crulle and Gilbert his brother and Robert the Tiler withdrew themselves on account of the aforesaid death.

And Richard was taken at Dover with thieves, and there acknowledged the death of the aforesaid Robert and Letitia *et falssiatus fuit.** And the aforesaid Robert was taken at Rochester, and there was hung before the Justices appointed for the gaol delivery. And the aforesaid Gilbert is suspected of that death. Therefore let him be exiled and outlawed. They had no chattels. And Gilbert

---

* "Falssiatus" is evidently wrongly written. It may mean Fossiatus; for in an old work, *The Interpreter of the Lawes*, 1684, Fossa et Furca are interpreted Pit and Gallows, the gallows for hanging male criminals and the pit for drowning female ones.

was in the "burgh" [pledge of] Gilbert Sunteyne in Westmepham. Therefore he is in mercy. And the towns of Westmepham, Ash, and Trottescliff did not come to the inquest. Therefore they are in mercy.

> NOTE.—The burg or burgh has already been explained. No Englesherie (*nulla Engleceria*) needs explanation. The word is an old one, signifying the being an Englishman. When Canute became King of England, the bulk of his Danish army returned home; but some Danes he retained, and for their protection he made a law which was not repealed till 4 Edward III, that if an Englishman killed a Dane he should be tried for murder; or if he escaped, the town or hundred where the deed was done should pay 66 marks to the King. Hence, in every case of murder, it was incumbent on the townspeople or the hundred, in their own interest, to prove that the murdered man was *not* a Dane; and this proof was called "Englecery" or "Engleschirie," and had to be sworn before the Coroner by two witnesses who knew the father and mother of the murdered man. (Abstracted from Tomlin's *Law Dictionary*.)
>
> In the case narrated the "no Englescherie" shows that Meopham failed in its duty in not proving the couple to be English, and added to its offence in burying the bodies without an inquest. Perhaps it had a suspicion that the murdered people might prove to be Danes, were the Coroner's inquest held.

(a) *From the Placita Coronae temp. 7 Edw. I, 1279. Ref. in Public Record Office,* $\left. \begin{array}{c} m \\ 2 \\ 30 \end{array} \right\}$ 1. *m* 7. 7*d* & 8

Clement Peche walking along the king's highway between Graveshend and Northflete came upon a certain stranger lying dead, in a field called Chypwode, having his throat cut. The first discoverer and four neighbours come and are not suspected. Therefore they are quiet therefrom. No Englischerie. Judgment: Murder on the Hundred. And the boroughs of Iuelde [Ifield] and Mepeham were not fully represented at the inquest. Therefore they are in mercy.

> NOTE.—This is not the first time we have seen Meopham fail in its public duty, on similar occasions.

(b) *Ditto*, A.D. 1279

The jurors present that when Adam the son of John Prestwode came to the wake of a certain Matilda la Zache with divers others, the said Adam wishing to have a game, got upon the back of a certain Richard Prestwode to play a game called 'Castel' [Castle]. But in the game he fell from the back of the aforesaid Richard and broke his neck and immediately died therefrom. And Gervase Thedon, Philip Boghurst, Richard Prestwode, William Welbe, Simon Bedesham, Gilbert atte Styghele and William the Carter were present. Therefore the Sheriff is commanded to cause them to appear. And afterwards the aforesaid Gervase and the others came and for good and ill put themselves on the country. And the jurors say on their oath that in no respect are they guilty. Therefore they are in quiet for the aforesaid death, but because they were present at the game aforesaid let them be held in custody. Afterwards they paid a fine of 40/- by their pledges John le Fynch of Leddesdon, Henry Alyfend, William atte Sole and John le Welbe of Mepeham.

NOTE.—This is interesting for many reasons. It shows that wakes of true Irish pattern were the custom at that time; and the game —apparently allied to leapfrog—was quite in keeping. From the record it is clear that this was a funeral "wake"; but in Tudor times the Dedication festivals were termed wakes. It seems rough on the spectators that having been acquitted by the Coroner's jury they nevertheless should be taken into custody till their "pledges" or "burghs" (*v. ante*) had paid a heavy fine. In some way it would seem that by their countenancing the horse-play they made themselves contributory to the fatal accident.

The names of Gilbert atte Styghele and William atte Sole are commented on elsewhere. The name Boghurst appears in our old Parish books, and at one time the "George" was kept by a Boghurst. In 1313 Richard Titche de Luddesdown was apprehended for stealing mead from Richard de Boghurst at Meopham, of the value of 10d. He was sent to prison for 15 days.

In the Meopham Subsidy Roll of 1523, containing assessment for the payment of the subsidy to Henry VIII, John Boghurst appears as the richest man in the village; he is assessed at £25, and his subsidy was 25/-.

The name Prestwode at once suggests Priestwood or Priesthood. Incidentally it disposes of the suggestion that Priesthood received its name from the lands left to endow the

Chapel of St. James de la Dene; for this endowment was not till fifty years later than the record above quoted.*

In the same year (1279) John Prestwode—presumably the father, already mentioned, of the unfortunate Adam—was arrested and sent to prison for three years as a poacher, he being found "with ferrets and nets and other instruments for taking rabbits" in the park of Lord William de Monchensi, at Swanscombe. He was traced by means of his dog, which was first captured.

(a) *From the Placita Coronae* 21 *Edw. I*, 1293. *Off. Ref.*

$$\left. \begin{matrix} m \\ \text{Kent } 2 \\ 31 \end{matrix} \right\} \quad 5. \; m \; 23$$

Alice the daughter of Hugh voluntarily set fire to her house in the borough of Mepham and burnt herself in the house, so that she immediately died. The first discoverer and four neighbours come and are not suspected. Judgment, *felo de se*. Her chattels 8/4½; for which the Prior of Canterbury is responsible.

> NOTE.—This seems a determined case of suicide, for even had she lived, nothing was to be gained by burning down the house; for fire insurance was not known in the thirteenth century. The verdict of *felo de se* was common then, and indeed until recent times; we take a more charitable view of such deeds nowadays. In this case the Prior, as Lord of the Manor, seems to have claimed her goods.

(b) *Ditto*, A.D. 1293

John the son of Emma of Meleton [Milton] hung himself by a noose in a certain garret, in the borough of Mepham. The first discoverer and four neighbours come and are not suspected. Judgment, *felo de se*. He had no chattels.

---

* The Lords of Monchensi (de Monte Canisio in the Kingdom of Naples) held the Manor of Hartley and others in this neighbourhood after Odo, Bishop of Bayeux. Lord William was one of the Barons called to the Parliament of 1265 (Henry III). He also had a gallows at Swaneschampe (Swanscombe), and three thieves were hung there, and were taken by the brothers of the Hospital to the monastery, where one of them was found to be alive! (Farley's *Weald of Kent*, vol. ii, pt. v, p. 143).

NOTE.—"In a certain garret"—*in quondam solario*. The solarium was the floor next above the ground-floor. Such would be found in only the better class of houses; so John was not one of the peasantry.

(a) *From the Placita Coronae 6 Edw. II*, 1313, *Off. Ref.* $\left. \begin{array}{c} m \\ 2 \\ 34 \end{array} \right\}$ 9. *m* 14

14*a*. 15 15*a*. P.R.O.

William the son of John Tichoun, with the concurrence of Gilbert the son of John le Maistre of Mepham, killed John the son of Waren at John Tichoun's house in the borough of Mepham, and immediately after the act fled, and the jurors suspect him. Therefore he is exiled and outlawed. No Englisherie was presented. Judgment, Murder on the hundred. He had no chattels, but was in the borough of Mepham; therefore it is in mercy; and because this happened in the daytime, and the aforesaid borough of Mepham did not capture him, therefore it is in mercy. And the jurors state that the aforesaid Gilbert is remaining in the country, therefore let him be taken. Afterwards the jurors state that the aforesaid William is dead. Therefore nothing to be required from him. And because the said William was indicted for the death, and the aforesaid Gilbert of concurrence, and the said William is dead, therefore nothing is taken from the aforesaid Gilbert.

NOTE.—John le Maistre (later Master and Masters) was at Camer at this time; it seems certain therefore that Gilbert was his son. Owing to the escape of the actual murderer, the hundred was held responsible; and the more so, since the murder was in daylight, and apparently in the minds of the jury there was no reason why he should not have been captured. Owing to the murderer's death shortly after—perhaps he committed suicide—Gilbert le Maistre, though his accomplice, was not further proceeded against.

In the following record it will be noticed that stress is also placed upon the felony having been committed in the daytime; so it seems that this was always looked upon as an aggravation of the offence of not capturing the offender.

(b) *Ditto*, A.D. 1313

Richard Eyldrech of Sevenoke, servant of John de la Dene, Chaplain, found Ralph Kynge the son of Simon Kynge in his master's room carrying off his master's goods; and the same Richard struck him on the head, so that the said Ralph afterwards died therefrom. And the aforesaid Richard immediately took flight. And the jurors suspect him. Therefore he is exiled and outlawed. He had no chattels, but was of the manupast [*de manupastu*—i.e. a domestic] of the aforesaid John de la Dene. Therefore he [i.e. J. de la D.] is in mercy, and because it happened in the daytime and the village of Mepham did not take him, therefore it is in mercy. . .

> NOTE.—The servant's master apparently would have escaped censure had the crime been at night. It is not clear why Richard need have run away; he did his duty by his master, but perhaps too vigorously.

Two other records of this time I will only briefly abstract. The first contains the name of a place in Meopham, not, as far as I am aware, now to be indentified. In one case a man and a woman were murdered at Shyngeledewelle (i.e. Single-well) and, the bodies having been scalded by the murderers (also a man and woman), presumably to prevent identification, they were carried "in a certain cart by Walter Trippe of Shyngeledewelle as far as a certain place called Gunnyldescroft in the borough of Mepham, where they deposited the bodies."

In the other case:

Roger atte Hatche of Ludesdone with another man unknown murdered the wife of John de Smalebourne at Mallyngstone in the borough of Mepham . . . Therefore he is exiled and outlawed. He had no chattels, nor was he in pledge because he was a stranger.

> NOTE.—It was discovered later that the unknown stranger was one John de Russhepol; and the reference to the pledge means that, being a stranger, no one in the hundred was acting as his surety or pledge, and therefore no pledges could be called, and placed "in mercy" or fined. Roger atte Hatche clearly lived by the hatch or bar that closed the entry to the surrounding forest.

The next case I will quote the first few lines of:

Stephen atte Wode of Mepham, John of Essex, miller, and Nicholas Adam the cowherd fought together outside the house of Edgar the Tanner in the borough of Mepham . . .

NOTE.—The cowherd was killed and the rest took flight. This record shows that in the fourteenth century tanning was a village industry. Oak-trees for the purpose were more plentiful then than now.

From Pleta coram dno Rege apud Westm de termino Sce Trinitatis anno regni Regis E filii Regis E quinto [i.e. 1331]. Public Record Office.

The following short abstract records a curious instance that occurred in 1311 under the law of Gavelkind; and also is interesting as being in the Northwode family—presumably the origin of the name of "Norwood Green" (*q.v.*):

There were three Northwode brothers: William, the eldest, then Simon, and then Henry. William married a certain Alina; and Simon (apparently at this time dead) had left two daughters who had married respectively John le Ken and John Le Mirye.

On a certain occasion Henry, with his two nephews by marriage, "burgled" the house of Alina, then a widow, and stole or took away her goods, chattels and woollen garments to the value of 40/-. For this she sued them. The defence set up was, that the three brothers had inherited from their father their property under the Kentish Custom of Gavelkind, by which the property of the parent was divided between all his children; that in regard to a widow, according to the same custom, she inherits a certain moiety of her husband's property as long as she conducts herself properly; and the defendants go on to say that the said Alina had received her moiety thus conditionally on her husband William's death. But since then the said widow had been guilty of crimes against morality, and thereby had forfeited her rights; so the moiety now reverted to the other members of the family, and to the two nephews of Simon the second brother, through their wives, his daughters. The widow, however, not seeing matters thus, had refused to surrender her share, and so the family took the law into their own hands and broke into her house as narrated, apparently in order to compel her to bring them into court, and thrash the matter out. The case was to come on just before Michaelmas; but at the last moment the lady thought better of it and declined to prosecute! The brother-in-law won the day, but the lady was not yet out of the wood; for at this time, if any one instituted a civil action, he had to find bails or pledges that he would carry the matter through, and if he failed his bails were called upon and fined, *pro falso clamore*, for having made a row about nothing. The end of the record therefore runs:

Therefore she and her pledges of prosecution are in mercy. Let the names of the pledges be ascertained.

From the Nona Rolls (14 *Edw. III* $\frac{123}{7}$ *m.* 9. *P.R.O*) A.D. 1340

Mepham. For the "ninth" in this parish are charged Henry Lomere, Alexander Northwode, John de Mildenacre, Alexander Smyth, Thomas Osbarm and Walter Hoghe, parishioners, at forty marks. And afterwards it was ascertained by the twelve jurors that the parish is not worth more than thirty-two marks and ten pence, and so does not meet the tax by seven marks twelve shillings and sixpence, as appears in the presents attested by the same jurors for the reasons stated therein.

> NOTE.—The people mentioned were clearly the substantial men of the Parish. The tax of a ninth was passed by Parliament, 14 Edw. III (1340), to help the King to carry on his wars, and was termed the Nona, from its being the ninth lamb, the ninth fleece, the ninth sheaf; and this was continued for two years. When in a parish, the value of the ninth exceeded the tax, that (as has been mentioned under the "Court") Pope Nicholas IV had already placed upon the Church, then the ninth was to be surcharged to the level of the tax (as in the case of Meopham); but if the value of the ninth were less than the church tax, then the true value of the ninth only was to be levied.
>
> The Church tax in Meopham in 1292 was £26 13s. 4d., but now (1340) only thirty-two marks and ten pence, or £21 7s. 6d.

All the foregoing records are written in the abbreviated official Latin of the time; the entry given in English under 1279 I will quote from the original as a specimen:

" Clemens le Pech ambulans in via regali int̃ Graueshend & Norfletc inuenit quemd̃ extñeum jacentē mortuū in quod̃ Campo qui vocat̃ Chypwode hẽntem gulā amputatā. Prim̃ inuentor & q̃tuor vicini vẽn & nõ malecr̃. Id̃ inde q̂eti. Nulĺ Engĺ. Iudm̃ murdr̃ sup Hundr̃. Et Borgh̃ de Iuelde & Mepehā nõ veñunt plene ad inquis̃. Id̃ in miā etc."

The following glossary will be found useful here, and for the appendices:

∼ =omission of any letter or letters : hẽntem=habentem; — =omission of m or n: n̄o=non; ℧ =omission where one letter is a: q̄tuor=quatuor; ꝑ =per or par: sup=super; ꝓ = pro ; ꞿ =præ ; ꝰ =er or re: eũꞌ =euer (ever); pꝰ =pre: pꝰ dic̃t=predicata; sꝰ ũnt=servant.

KING ATHELSTANE'S CHARTER, A.D. 939

THE following is Athelstane's Charter (A.D. 939), referred to in Chapter I.

(Ref.: Brit. Mus., Cotton MS., K 377, B. iii. 9, Aug. ii. 23.)

(Translation)

Our Lord Jesus Christ eternally reigning, and ruling in due order, from the highest heaven, all things both visible and invisible: whilst the course of our own life is daily running out, and the enjoyment of our own riches and possessions passing away: I, therefore, Athelstane, by the Divine favour King of England, and Ruler of the whole of Britain, concede freely by a perpetual donation my right to a certain portion of land to my faithful minister named Ealdulph, twelve tenements ["xii. mansas"] in that locality popularly and familiarly called Meapham. Let him enjoy and continually hold the property as long as he shall abide in this frail life: and let him, to whom we have confirmed it for ever, leave it to whomsoever he will as his heir in perpetuity. Let the aforesaid property be free from all impediment, along with all property belonging to it—fields, pasture, meadows and woods. With the exception of these three for the upkeep of the bridge and the building of the castle (or fort). Moreover should anyone (which heaven forbid) proudly attempt to cross this our will, may he suffer from icy blasts, and the winged army of evil spirits, until he make amends with tears of penitence, and true amendment. By these terms the aforesaid land is seen to be protected.

Then follow the limits of the property; from Netles-Stede (Nursted), then along a ridge of hog's back to Fearnleage geate (Fearnley Gate: ? the Cobham woods up Scalers Hill to Shepherd's Gate); thence to the boundary of Cobham ("Cobbahammes Mearce"); thence eastward to "Heorotfelda geate" (Hartfield: ? the Harefield already suggested as the same as Harvel), and so to "Stanihtan hyrst" (copse) (? Stanstead) and "Ceorla Den."

The interest in the last paragraph is in the old nomenclature of the surrounding villages.

The deed of gift is signed first by the king in these terms: "Rex totius Bryttanniae, cum sigillo sce crucis" (King of all Britain, with the sign of the Holy Cross). It is witnessed by nine bishops, the first being Wulfhelm, Archbishop of Canterbury, whose endorsement runs: "Regis donationem cum tropheo agiae crucis ✝ consignavi" (I have signed the deed of gift with the mark of the Holy Cross). The signatures of twenty-three laymen follow.

THE LICENCE GRANTED TO ENDOW THE CHAPEL OF ST. JAMES DE LA DENE

Extract from Patent Roll 1 *Edw. III* (*m* 7). *P.R.O.*

R. omĩbus ad quos &c. saltm̃. Licet de cõi consilio &c. p finem tamen quem magist Edmundus de Mepham, magist̃ Simon de Mepham et Johĩs de la Dene fecerunt nobiscū concessĩm eis et licenciam dedĩm pro nõb et heredibȝ ñris, qutu in nõb est, q̃d ĩpi vnū mesuagiū, duo molendina, viginti et quinqȝ acras t̃re, quatuor acras prati, duas ac̃r bosci, viginti et quinqȝ solidatas redditus cum p̣tin in Estmallyng, Berlyng, Northflet Mepham et Hoo dare possint et assignare cuidem Capellano diuina singulis diebus in capella Sc̃i Jacobi de la Dene in parochia eccl̃ie de Mepham pro anima Johanne de la Dene et animabȝ predcõr Edmundi, Simonis et Johĩs, ac patrum et matrū parentū et benef̃tor' ĩpor' Edmundi, Simonis, & Johĩs & omĩ fideliū defunctor' celebraturo. Hẽnd et tenend̃ eidem Capellano et successoribus suis capellanis diuina singulis diebȝ in capella p̃dca pro animabȝ p̃dcis celebraturis imp̣petuū. Et eidem Capellano q̃d ĩpe p̃dca messuagiū, molendina t̃ram, pratū bos̃cm et redditum cū pertinentiis a prefatis Edmundo, Simone et Johẽ recip̣e possit et tenere sibi et successoribus suis predcis imp̣petuū sicut predc̃m est tenore presentiū similit' licenciam dedim' sp̃alem. Nolentes q̃d predc̃i Edmundus Simon et Johẽs, aut heredes sui vel predc̃us Capellanus seu successores sui r̃one statuti predc̃i p̣ nos vel heredes ñros · inde occõent' in aliquo seu g͞uent'. Saluis tamen capitalibus dñis feodor' illor' suĩciis inde debitis et consuetis. In cuius &c. T.R. apud Westm̃ xxv die Martii.

> NOTE.—The preamble is omitted; it refers to the statutes of Mortmain, which this licence overrules in favour of the petitioners. Spãlem = specialem; r̃one = ratione; occõent' = occasionentur; and g͞uent' = graventur. T.R. = teste Rege.

LIST OF PARISH RECORDS

Churchwardens' Account-books (3)
  1612–1739 (missing since 1900).
  1739–1832, and
  1836–1843.

Vestry Books (3)
  1788–1812. This contains a loose parchment leaf: a copy of Mrs. Markland's will (1665) and also a full account of her bequest extracted from the Register of the Prerogative Court of Chancery; also a full memorandum of the Wouldham Bequest.
  1831–1857; and
  1857–1902.

Overseers' Disbursements (5)
  1774–1781; 1781–1789; 1789–1798; 1810–1811; 1818–1827.

Assessments for Relief of Poor (2)
  1752–1763; 1792–1796.

Highways (Surveyors) (3)
  1768–1781; 1803–1808; 1824–1836.

A few loose accounts showing payments to constables, John Bennett (1848), Thomas Jeal, and Thomas Crowhurst; also expenses in connection with the payment of the Parish constables.

Certificates showing certain persons to be parishioners, from 1700.
Conveyance for site of Culverstone School church, 1872.
Early English window in vestry (partially filled up with bricks), reopened and repaired, 1874.
Faculty for removing galleries and square pews and reseating the whole church and putting on entirely new roof, 1859.
Conveyance of site given by Dean and Chapter of Canterbury for National School, 1841 (*v.* Appendix K).
Copy of grant of waste land near to a place called Harvel Green to the Churchwardens and Overseers of Meopham for the use of the Poor. Nov. 4, 1833.

This list is drawn up from two supplied by the late Mr. Lewis and our present Vicar, Mr. Owen.

LIST OF CHURCHWARDENS FROM 1593

THE following is a list, compiled by Mr. Lewis, of the Churchwardens from 1593:

Sixteenth Century

Th. Hubbard (1598)	Th. Skirmer
H. Wraight	Th. Kennit
W. Cripps	

The Churchwardens' names appear for the first time in 1598, and after some baptismal entries comes the following:

All these names as are written we the Churchwardens of Mepham being in office the same year when they were written do confirm the same to be truly written out under our hands

THOMAS HUBBARD

HENRY WRAIGHT × his mark

Churchwardens

Thos Sympson
ptr. curat of Mepham.

Seventeenth Century

John Edmeds (1600)	Matthew Loft
Th. Kitridge	Th. Lysney
J. Warner	Th. Master
J. Warren	— Johnson
E. Skirmer	T. Boghurst
James Munn	W. Taylor
Gabriel Master	H. Munn
W. Middleton	H. Weight
W. Boghurst	A. Swann
W. Gardiner	Oliver Whiffin
James Taylor	J. Carnell
Robert Butcher	W. Haffenden (1647)
H. Munn	H. Masters
E. Skirmer	W. Swift
W. Warren	J. Skirmer
I. Taylor	W. Spriver
E. Bell	R. Whiffin
H. Haslyn	J. Boys
George Master (1620)	H. Haslyn

Seventeenth Century—continued

A. Butcher
W. Gamble
J. Child
N. Piggott
Th. Wouldham (1665)
N. Piggott
T. Haise
R. Taylor
H. Loft
George Masters
H. Facer
W. Boghurst
J. Bright
J. Letchford
T. Skirmer
E. Audril
J. Edmeads
Th. Masters
F. Bright
J. Scudder
W. Swift

W. Hays
T. Mercer
W. Taylor
T. Spriver
J. Alchin
J. Sharpe
J. Butler
J. Loft
Rich. Masters
J. Hills
A. Gunning (1685)
W. Swift
Hugh Knowlden
J. Nordash
S. Tiesdell
James Bright
T. Munn
W. Wood
W. Attwood
R. Gunning (1694)
W. Gibson

Eighteenth Century

Peter Gunning (1700)
John Alchin
T. Mercer
J. Swift
George Masters
N. Tiesdell
W. Swift
J. Markett (1717)
T. Crowhurst
W. Rich
W. Salmon
T. Ashby
J. Wood
J. Phillips
T. Lewton
J. French
George Masters

J. Nevill
Whiffin Salmon
E. Crowhurst
W. Masters
J. Munn
W. Rogers (1763)
D. Hunt
T. Weller
T. Edmeads
N. Reeve
J. Boorer
G. Smith (for 47 years, 1783)
T. Plummer
T. Lynds
J. Child
R. Buggs
J. Parker

N. Wane

Nineteenth Century

F. Markett (1803)

W. Best

P. Buggs

W. Masters-Smith (1831)

A. F. Bromley

W. Andrus

J. Poltick

J. Munyard

R. Barnett (1857)

Rev. Alan Smith-Masters (1862)

H. Mungeam

J. Evenden

J. Ashdown (1874)

J. Barnett

George Bliss (for 15 years)

Capt. Jackson

W. A. Smith-Masters

Dr. Griffiths

Jesse Garratt

C. H. Golding-Bird

W. A. Smith-Masters

Captain R. Arnold

John Pinches

J. Edmunds

LIST OF BURIALS IN THE CHURCHYARD

THE following is the list compiled by the late Vicar, Mr. Lewis, of all the names still legible upon the tombstones of the churchyard. The list was first published in the *Parish Magazine* for July 1898.

South of Church

1.	H. Nordish	1821	30.	John Allchin	1760
2.	T. Nordish	1814	31.	Mary Edmeades	1800
3.	Ann Nordish	1830	32.	John Phillips	1741
4.	Hannah Buggs	1815	33.	Thomas Phillips	1789
5.	Elizabeth Johnson	1815	34.	Margaret Phillips	1790
6.	W. Johnson	1836	35.	John Phillips	1807
7.	Sarah Parker	1796	36.	Robert Munday	1809
8.	Joseph Parker	1823	37.	Joseph Munday	1798
9.	John Parker	——	38.	Mary Munday	1794
10.	John Johnson	1870	39.	Jane C. Rich	1808
11.	Thomas Cox	1701	40.	Jane Rich	1815
12.	Uridge Cox	1704	41.	Thomas Hart	1829
13.	Edward Markett	1714	42.	Hannah Hart	1809
14.	Elizabeth Cox	1717	43.	Mary Langford	1831
15.	Ann Spratt	1717	44.	Joseph Langford	1839
16.	Elizabeth Markett	1719	45.	John Nevill	1771
17.	Mary Markett	1724	46.	Jane Shesdell	1801
18.	Thomas Markett	1728	47.	Whiffen Salmon	1791
19.	George Markett	1733	48.	William Salmon	1796
20.	John Markett	1750	49.	Elizabeth Gunning	1736
21.	Ann Markett	1750	50.	Catherine Gunning	1783
22.	Mary Reeve	1776	51.	Richard Masters	1689
23.	Susanna Reeve	1800	52.	Joan Edmeades	1717
24.	Nicholas Reeve	1817	53.	Elizabeth Shepherd	1814
25.	Rickeby Tiesdell	1737	54.	Richard Sutherden	1780
26.	Nicholas Tiesdell	1766	55.	Sarah Sutherden	1763
27.	Elizabeth Tiesdell	1769	56.	Catherine Salmon	1781
	Thomas Munn	1766	57.	William Salmon	1785
28.	Sarah Munn	1727	58.	Eliza Salmon	1726
	William Munn	1766	59.	Richard Harwood	1710
29.	Elizabeth Swift	——	60.	Thomas Harwood	1710

South of Church—continued

61.	Eliza Harwood	1710	75. Richard Snelling	1819
62.	Joseph Munn	1788	76. Sarah Snelling	1871
63.	Margaret Munn	1805	77. David Hunt	1801
64.	Hannah Munn	1745	78. Edward Saunders	1720
65.	Isaak Blissett	1799	79. David Hunt	1801
66.	John Munn	1777	80. Nicholas Piggott	1701
67.	R. H. Tweddell	1895	81. Mary Edmeades	1808
68.	Elizabeth Salmon	——	82. Thomas Edmeades	1832
69.	John Salmon	——	83. Rebecca Edmeades	1830
70.	Alfred Johnson	1877	84. Robert Edmeades	1819
71.	Mary Nevill	1822	85. Catherine Edmeades	1822
72.	Elizabeth Nevill	1849	86. Esther E. Edmeades	1833
73.	John Nevill	1859	87. Kate Edmeades	1833
74.	Richard Snelling	1833	88. Robert Edmeades	1865

89. Ann Edmeades   1881

South-East

90. Thomas Crowhurst	1750	93. William Crowhurst	1718
91. Thomas Crowhurst	1768	94. William Dalton	1797
92. Mary Crowhurst	1711		

South-West

95. Sarah Terry	1763	104. James Killick	1889
96. Lydia Terry	1766	105. Thomas Killick	1891
97. David Terry	1777	106. Samuel Meakin	1892
98. John Wood	1750	107. Ada Tong	1898
99. Richard Wood	1714	108. Richard Barnard	1837
100. Harriet Killick	1861	109. Hannah Barnard	1856
101. Susannah Killick	——	110. James Barnard	1815
102. Thomas Killick	——	111. George Hone	——
103. Amelia Killick	——	112. Robert Hills	1813

113. Mary Hills   1820

East of Church

114 John Bachelor	1760	121. Robert Norris	1751
115 Mary Bachelor	1797	122. Elizabeth Salmon	1789
116. Caroline Williams	1857	123. Rev. John Hooper	1875
117. Mary Smith	1830	124. Frances Hooper	1887
118. Ellen Pett	1848	125. Alice M. Hooper	1897
119. Sarah Tomlyn	1837	126. Peter Gunning	1747
120. William Tomlyn	1844	127. Jane Gunning	1767

East of Church—continued

128.	Sarah Gunning	1702	151. John Child	1778
129.	Peter Gunning	1714	152. Frances Child	1766
130.	Robert Barnett	1872	153. Timothy Child	1797
131.	Jane F. Barnett	1890	154. Sarah Edmeades	1728
132.	Reginald Barnett	1870	155. Thomas Edmeades	1723
133.	John Barnett	1887	156. Mary Tilden	1744
134.	Benjamin Cogswell	1891	157. John Alchin	1825
135.	M. H. G. Elwyn	1885	158. Mary Alchin	1796
136.	Capt. C. Elwyn	1888	159. John P. Alchin	1808
137.	Walter Nelson Leeming	1897	160. Thomas Alchin	1854
138.	Ann Copper	1878	161. William Best	1833
139.	Mary Ann Killick	1887	162. Mary Best	1855
140.	Rosa S. Baber	1883	163. Frederick Andrus	1835
141.	Dr. Baber	1894	164. John Charlton	1867
141a.	Emma Baber	——	165. Laetitia Charlton	1849
142.	Robert A. Jackson	1878	166. Elizabeth Ann	1839
143.	Ann Cooper	1797	167. Sarah Charlton	1839
144.	Sarah Young	1887	168. T. Alchin Charlton	1840
145.	Ann Rushton	1838	169. John Charlton	1817
146.	John Rushton	1839	170. Ann Charlton	1832
147.	John Child	1799	171. Edward Beaumont	1821
148.	Elizabeth Child	1838	172. William Beaumont	1806
149.	William Andrus	1846	173. Thomas Loft	1888
150.	Mary Ann Andrus	1862	174. Joseph Cleverley	1884
			175. May Russell	1881

176. Alma Ashdown 1894

North of Church

177.	Rev. J. Thompson	1851	190. Richard Langford	1834
178.	W. Mungeam	1846	191. Richard Langford	1845
179.	Catherine Mungeam	1848	192. Sophia Langford	1843
180.	Frances Mungeam	1850	193. Norah Constance Dryland	1893
181.	Glover Mungeam	1791	194. Rev. Allan Smith-Masters	1875
182.	Ann Mungeam	1821		
183.	Frederick Hollman	1897	195. W. Masters Smith	1861
184.	Grace Manley Smith	1818	196. Edith Edwards	1873
185.	William Smith	1830	197. George Smith	1831
186.	Catherine Smith	1839	198. Rebecca Smith	1843
187.	James Langford	1852	199. Alban Dorrington	1855
188.	Thomas Lynds	1799	200. Elizabeth Dorrington	1849
189.	Sarah Lynds	1762		

North of Church—continued

201.	Alban Dorrington	1870	232. Arthur Goodwin	1862
202.	Alban Dorrington	1876	233. Ellen Oliver	1863
203.	John Poltick	1846	234. Mary Bartlett	1866
204.	Ann Poltick	1867	235. Jane Jeal	1876
205.	Thomas Nordish	1842	236. G. R. Jeal	1872
206.	Sarah Chayney	1839	237. Florence J. Jeal	1874
207.	W. Taylor	1856	238. Richard Waterman	1884
208.	Albert Taylor	1854	239. Barbara E. Waterman	1878
209.	Eleanor Lynds	1866	240. Edwin Johnson	1875
210.	Percy M. Gibb	1873	241. Beatrice A. Johnson	1884
211.	Maurice H. Gibb	1870	242. James F. Stone	1859
212.	Isabella Mason	1877	243. F. J. Stone	1857
213.	Mary T. Johnson	1869	244. Franklin Light	1871
214.	Louisa Taylor	1867	245. William H. Light	1876
215.	George French	1848	246. Alfred Light	1879
216.	Rebecca French	1872	247. Frances Ann Light	1879
217.	John Wells	1868	248. Thomas Leeming	1886
218.	Mabel Lewis	1888	249. John Body	1888
219.	Richard Scoons	1817	250. Rachel Body	1892
220.	Elizabeth Scoons	1825	251. Charles Dunch	1896
221.	W. Noakes	1844	252. John D. Dunch	1868
222.	Mary Noakes	1844	253. Maud M. Dunch	1894
223.	W. R. Wells	1836	254. George Griggs	1895
224.	W. Wells	1852	255. Ann Esther Ashdown	1874
225.	Edward Noakes	1877	256. Jane Hills	1872
226.	W. Jury	1844	257. Henry Hills	1865
227.	Martha Jury	1848	258. Henrietta Scott	1888
228.	Charlotte Jury	1849	259. Josias Scott	1898
229.	Thomas Goodwin	1866	260. James Hartopp	1896
230.	George Goodwin	1867	261. Haiselders & Lofts	——
231.	Thomas Goodwin	1859	262. James Loft	1894

263. Eliza Loft   1889

North-West

264.	Clara French	1874	272. Mary Ann Brownfield	1878
265.	Thomas French	1875	273. Hester Martin	1895
266.	James Maton	1890	274. William Martin	1896
267.	Frances C. E. Stevens	1896	275. Jane Thompson	1862
268.	Elizabeth Durling	1878	276. Caroline Thompson	1878
269.	Ambrose Mercer	1895	277. Thomas Thompson	1884
270.	Chas. Brownfield	1891	278. Clara A. Blackman	1883
271.	Wm. Brownfield	1862	279. Robert Butcher	1706

North-West—*continued*

280. Robert Butcher, jun.	1706	
281. Matilda Parker	1858	
282. Sarah Parker	1856	
283. William Atwood	1714	
284. Philip Buggs	1858	
285. Edward Coombes	1858	
286. Sarah Coombes	1861	
287. Eliza Evenden	1876	
288. Ann Evenden	1855	
289. Eliza Taylor	1874	
290. Thomas Lathan	1846	
291. Ann Lathan	1879	
292. John Figgess	1851	
293. Rebecca Figgess	1854	

West

294. John French	1811	
295. Mary French	1836	
296. Robert French	1802	
297. Margaret French	1870	
298. John French	1875	
299. Sarah Beney	1839	
300. Harriot French	1871	
301. Emma French	——	
302. Ann French	1762	
303. John French	1777	
304. Ann French	1806	
305. Thomas French	1810	
306. Sarah French	1849	
307. William French	1818	
308. Mary French	1874	
309. Ann French	1851	
310. Edward French	1876	
311. Emily Lynds	1868	
312. Martha Lott	1818	
313. Mary Blackman	1820	
314. Edward Bell	1724	
315. Charles Jeal	1878	
316. Mary Lane	1872	
317. Mary Buggs	1804	
318. Thomas Buggs	1804	
319. Thomas Scudder	1810	
320. Elizabeth Scudder	1831	
321. Robert Scudder	1832	
322. Sarah Scudder	1846	
323. Richard Scudder	1852	
324. Thomas Laurie	1808	
325. Thomas Laurie	1859	
326. George Buggs	1860	
327. Mary Buggs	1818	
328. Richard Buggs	1808	
329. Mildred Buggs	1786	
330. Sarah Fairman	1785	
331. Mary Buggs	1831	
332. George Barkaway	1875	
333. Alice Cuckow	1821	
334. Thomas Cuckow	1821	
335. Henry Buggs	1846	
336. Harriot Buggs	1856	
337. William Buggs	1823	
338. Ann Barkaway	1830	
339. Henry Buggs	1826	
340. Richard J. Buggs	1834	
341. Harriot Buggs	1834	
342. Elvira Buggs	1868	
343. Julia Buggs	1870	
344. James Buggs	1890	
345. Henry Buggs	1894	
346. E. Warne	1896	
347. F. Warne	1890	
348. Arthur Bale	1894	
349. Thomas Edmeades	1820	
350. Anne Edmeades	1832	
351. Eleanor Edmeades	1802	
352. Eliza Salmon	1770	
353. Elizabeth Plummer	1752	
354. Thomas Plummer	1764	
355. Sarah Salmon	1832	
356. Thomas Salmon	1822	
357. Catherine Salmon	1810	
358. Eliza Plummer	1712	
359. William Buggs	1756	

GIFT OF DEED OF LAND BY GODFREY TRAUNCEYS IN 1240

TRANSLATION of the deed of Godfrey Traunceys, giving rent of lands to the Prior and Convent of the Holy Trinity at Canterbury (Hen. III, 1240).

Know all people present and to come that I Godfrey Traunceys have given, conceded, and by this deed have confirmed to the Prior and Convent of the Holy Trinity at Canterbury, and to their successors xii^d of annual rent on their Manor of Mepeham, in free, pure and perpetual charity—which Richard de Lomere has been accustomed to pay annually—that is to say:—On the festival of St. Michael vi^d from certain land which lies lengthwise between the field called Pirifeld and land (held by) Robert the Miller: and is in breadth (bounded by) land of the aforesaid Godfrey, and land of Peter de Westdun; and at the festival of the Blessed Apostle St. Thomas, vi^d from certain land which lies lengthwise between the field called Brominghame, and the land of the aforesaid Godfrey, and in breadth between the land of Thomas de Westlonde and the land of Peter de Westdun. To have and to hold the aforesaid rent from me and my heirs by the aforesaid Prior and Convent and their successors freely, quietly, peaceably for ever. And I the aforesaid Godfrey and my heirs will guarantee and maintain the aforesaid rent to and for the Prior and Convent and their successors against every man and woman for ever as a free, pure and perpetual charity.

Hiis testibus—Willō de Dodemere. Reginaldo de Mildenekere—Waltō de Isebere—Waltō de Norwode—Johē de la Dene—Simon de la Dene—Roberto de Northwode. Thom: de Westlonde. Godefr' de Westld: Rico de Lomere—Hug̃ Colome et multis aliis.

THE MANOR OF DUDEMERE

A TRUE and perfect Rental of all the Quit Rents payable by the free tenants of the said Manor, renewed, made and perfected at a Court Baron there holden for the same on Wednesday, 17th April, 1861.

Richard Wilson Shepherd Wilson

One parcel of land called Pierce lying at Hedge, near Culversole Green.

2/2   Formerly belonging to Sir Charles Sedley, Bart., since to Catharine Smith, then to her son William Smith by fealty suit of Court.

Yearly Rent of 10d and two hens (value 16d), total 2/2.

Charles Gustavus Whitaker

1/6   A parcel of land called Gulpreed or Culpreed, late Whiffins formerly purchased of David Polhill, Esq., and belonging to Whiffin Salmon, since to Thomas Salmon.

Thomas Johnson

6d   A parcel of land called Menewether croft—formerly by Richard Kipps of Edward Peckham, Gentleman.

Edward Coombes and Mary Buggs

Three parcels of land on which stood formerly a house called Usbarnes, formerly John Cod's.

6d; and two Hens (1/6) and 32 eggs at 16 a groat, total 2/6

Edward Coombes and Mary Buggs

A parcel of land called Carpenter's Croft, containing about 3 acres, lying at South Street, formerly Thomas Salmon's; rent 3d and one hen (8d).

1/½   *Also* a piece of land called Forge, *alias* Frogcroft— about 2 acres and 3 yards—formerly Frankwells.

John Samuel Evenden

½   One parcel of land called *Whites* Croft.

1/8½   *Also* a parcel of land called *Gyles Bushes*, formerly Edward Fowle's, then W. Mungeam and late Glover Mungeam.

Alban Dorrington

1/8½   One messuage—*slaughter-house*—Meopham Street. Late John Parmiter's and since Bicknell's—afterwards the Rev. W. Mansfield.

William Masters Smith

19ᵈ   One messuage and several parcels of land lying at Pitfield Green and one piece of land, Goldalls and Cripps Croft, purchased by George Masters, of Mr. Smith and Ellen his wife, daughter of Mr. Cox.

Thomas French

5ᵈ   One parcel of land lying near the dwelling-house heretofore of Thomas Taylor, called *Longland*, at yearly rent of 3ᵈ.

        Also a moiety of a parcel of land called *Gyles Bushes*—formerly belonging to Thomas Taylor in right of Constant his wife, daughter of Thomas Crowhurst, then to Hannah Elgar, and since to Sarah French.

Benjamin Worthy Horn

3ᵈ   A piece of land called *Angel Croft* lying at Pitfield Green (now occupied by H. Langford), belonging formerly to Thomas Plummer, then Edward Stoneham, Sarah Stoneham, Major Kirkham, Francis Markett, Isabella Markett, William Philip Snell, B. W. Horn.

John Samuel Evenden

6ᵈ   One messuage or tenement lying at Leading Street, belonging formerly to Sarah Stoneham, Catherine Stoneham, W. Mungeam, Rev. Glover Mungeam, Glover Mungeam, J. S. Evenden.

1/–   *Also* a parcel of land called *the Thole*.

Amos Fletcher

2^d   *Gyles Bushes* (*occupied* by J. Bennett, John Borer, Jeremiah Chenes, W. Mungeam, Senr, W. Mungeam, Henry Nordish, *James Loft*), formerly belonging to Richard Whiffen, Elizabeth Whiffen, Ed. Russell, J. Wade, C. Whitehead, W. Mungeam, Senr, W. Mungeam, Amos Fletcher.

Robert Barnett

1/2   A piece of land called *Wheatfield* and 3 acres more. W. Tankards, Francis Markett, Isabella Markett, Robert Barnett.

Edward Coombes

½   One moiety of a parcel of land called *Gyles Bushes Wood.*

Smith

½   One parcel of land called *Bakers Croft* (formerly occupied by W. Wheatley, Esq., Robert Hills, Thomas Nordish, W. Mungeam, Leonard Hawley, Ed. Coombes, John Coombes, jun^r, W. Coombes.)

3^d   *Durrant Croft*

2^d   *Hemphaugh Croft*, occupied for many years by Mr. Wheatley, now by *W. Coombes*. Formerly belonging to Thomas Skinner, lately to W. Wheatley, G. Wheatley, Leonard Lewin Wheatley, and now *Smith*.

William Stevens

4^d   *Little Wood Reeds* occupied by James Vain, James Hawley, Leonard Hawley, now H. Langford: *belonging* to Mary Turner, W. Pawley, Thomas Stevens, W. Stevens.

Edward Coombes and Mary Buggs

4½^d   *Blacklands*

10½^d   A croft of land whereon a house stood, *belonging* to John Codd, Christopher Dobson, Richard Buggs, Philip Buggs and Mary Buggs—now Edward L. Coombes and Mary Buggs.

Amos Fletcher

$4\frac{1}{2}$d   *Blacklands*, belonging to Thomas Wood, George Masters, W. Masters, Catherine Smith, W. Masters Smith, Capt. Fletcher, Amos Fletcher; now occupied by James Loft.

Francis Andrus

6d   *Bean Croft*, belonging to E. Chapman, George Masters, William Masters, Catherine Smith, George Smith, William Masters Smith, Francis Andrus.

Benjamin W. Horn

$\frac{1}{2}$ *Pipers*, belonging to Gabriel Masters, John Markett, John Markett, Junr, Francis Markett, Isabella Markett, W. P. Snell, B. W. Horn (occupied now by John Goodwin).

Robert Barnett

2d   *Bereges Acre*, belonging to John Baynard, Allen J. Markett, Francis Markett (grandson), John Markett, Isabella Markett, Philip Snell, R. Barnett.

William Masters Smith

8d   *Liplome* or *Innfield*, belonging to Lady Barrett, T. Copland, George Masters, W. Masters, Catherine Smith, George Smith; occupied now by Alban Dorrington.

John Usher

1/-   *Downfield*, one acre and half, adjoining a lane at corner of Fowlerstone; belonging to Ed. Hodsoll, Isaak Tomlin, Robt Crowhurst, E. Argles, Rosher, Hopper, John Usher.

Robert Barnett

$8\frac{1}{2}$d   *Little Millfield*, boundary to Merryhaugh. For many years in the *occupation* of *John Allchin*. Belonging to Laurence Holker, Potts, Esq., —Potts, — Potts, Robt Barnett.

TOTAL OF THE MANOR—19/3$\frac{1}{2}$.

SUBSIDY PAYERS, *TEMP.* HEN. VIII

Assessment of the first payment of the subsidy granted 1524 Hen. VIII. on the inhabitants within the hundreds of Toltyngtrowe, Wrotham, Axton, Hoo, and Sharnell in the County of Kent.

$\frac{124}{187}$ (From Official Catalogue of Lay Subsidies)

Mepeham.		Subsydy.
Richard Bokly in goods	C.s.	ij.s. vj.d.
Water Wells in wag̃s	xxvj.s. viij.d.	iiij.d.
John Clode in wagis	xl.s.	xij.d.
Richard Barre in wagis	xl.s.	xij.d.
Richard Cost in goodis	vj.li.	iij.s.
Iohn Kede in wagis	xl.s.	xij.d.
Thomas Germen in londs	xx.s.	xij.d.
Thomas Barre in wagys	xl.s.	xij.d.
Iohn Sedkobe in goodys	xl.s.	xij.d.
Iohn Peers in londys	xxvj.s. viij.d.	xvj.d.
William Peers in goodys	xl.s.	xij.d.
Robert Peers in goodys	xviij.li.	ix.s.
Willm Gyllam his s̃unt in wag̃s	xx.s.	iiij.d.
Iohn Dolder in goodys	xl.s.	xij.d.
Richard Bocher in landys	xl.s.	ij.s.
Iohn Typpyng in goodys	x.li.	v.s.
Richard Roger thelder in goods	xl.s.	xij.d.
Richard Roger yonger in goodys	xl.s.	xij.d.
Herry Hewe in londys	xx.s.	xij.d.
Iohn Miller in goods	xl.s.	xij.d.

John Hastelyn in goodys........ C mrc .... lxvj.s. viij.d.

Herry Hyllys al Ellys his s͠unt in

   wags...................... xl.s. .... xij.d.

Iohn Mason hys s͠unt in wags.... xxx.s. .... iiij.d.

Nicholas Elder his s͠unt in wags . xxiij.s. iiij.d. .... iiij.d.

Iohn Brown his s͠unt in wags ... xxiij.s. iiij.d. .... iiij.d.

William Chapman in wags...... xx.s. .... iiij.d.

Nicholas Hamon his s͠unt in wags xx.s. .... iiij.d.

Iohn Collyn his s͠unt in wags .... xl.s. .... xij.d.

William Collyn his s͠unt in wags. xl.s. .... xij.d.

Iohn Dobynson his s͠unt in wags xl.s. .... xij.d.

Thomas Collyn his s͠unt in wags xxxiij.s. iiij.d. ... iiij.d.

Richard Tayllour in londys...... vj.li. .... vj.s.

William Bocher his s͠unt in wags xxvj.s. viij.d. .... iiij.d.

Thomas Callew his s͠unt in wags xxij.s. iiij.d. ..... iiij.d.

Robert Batman in goodys....... xxiiij.li.vj.s.viij.d. xxiiij.s.iiij.d.

Nicholas Fesaunt in goods...... xl.s. .... xij.d.

Herry Hyllys in goodys......... x.li. .... v.s.

Iohn Fox his s͠unt in wagis..... xx.s. .... iiij.d.

Nicholas Fynytre in goodis ...... vj.li. .... iij.s.

Robert Wylcoke in goods .... xl.s. .... xij.d.

Andrewe Rysden in wags .... xl.s. .... xij.d.

Iohn May in wags .... xl.s. .... xij.d.

Richard Skyrmar in wags .... xl.s. .... xij.d.

Richard Heyward in goods ...... vj.li. .... iij.s.

Richard Marshe in goods .... lx.s.............. xviij.d.

Iohn Leke in wags .... xl.s.. .... xij.d.

Iohn Smyth in londs .... xx.s. .... xij.d.

Robert Pollys in wags.......... xl.s.. .... xij.d.

Iohn Chapman in wags . . . . xl.s. . . . . xij.d.

Thomas Launce in wags . . . . xl.s. . . . . xij.d.

Thomas Coke in wags . . . . xl.s. . . . . xij.d.

William Ifte in wagis . . . . xl.s. . . . . xij.d.

Willm Sybbyng in wags . . . . xl.s. . . . . xij.d.

Richard Spreuer in londs . . . . xl.s. . . . . ij.s.

Richard a Deane in londs . . . . ix.li. . . . . ix.s.

Iohn Bogherst in goods . . . . xxv.li. . . . . xxv.s.

Iohn Geppe in goods . . . . xl.s. . . . . xij.d.

Thomas Leston in wags . . . . xl.s. . . . . xij.d.

Iohn Gylmen in wags . . . . xl.s. . . . . xij.d.

William Chepard in goods . . . . . . iiij.li. . . . . ii.s.

Richard Brynson in wags . . . . xl.s. . . . . xij.d.

William Warren in goods . . . . x.li. . . . . v.s.

Thomas Greuell in goods . . . . xl.s. . . . . xij.d.

Robert Master in londs . . . . xl.s. . . . . ij.s.

Iohn Baker in wagis . . . . xl.s. . . . . xij.d.

Thomas Fuller in goods . . . . x.li. . . . . v.s.

Edwarde Wayte in wags . . . . xl.s. . . . . xij.d.

Robert Chasemore in wags . . . . . . xl.s. . . . . xij.d.

Simon Tymber fled for ffelony
  before the settyng by the me-
  moryall, in wags . . . . xl.s. . . . . viij.d.

Thomas Power in goods . . . . xij.li . . . . vj.s.

John Bullyn in goods . . . . xl.s. . . . . xij.d.

Laurens Eldre in londs . . . . xx.s. . . . . xij.d.

Thoms Care in wags . . . . xl.s. . . . . xij.d.

Thoms Rusell in goods . . . . lx.s. . . . . xviij.d.

William Myxson in goods . . . . xl.s. . . . . xij.d.

Iohn Hills in wagis............. xl.s. .... xij.d.

Sm of Mepeham —xj.li.xvi.s. ij.d.

Sm of the Hundred ⎫
                  ⎬ —cxvij.li. ix.s. iij.d. ob.
of Toltyngtrowe ⎭

This list gives 76 names. Multiplying by 5 we have 380 as the population; or if we first subtract the thirteen servants, who can hardly be looked upon as heads of families, we have 315 as the approximate population.

The tax on land is invariably 1/– in the pound, or one-twentieth, and is paid by ten persons.

The tax on goods is 6d. in the pound, or one-fortieth; but if the goods are over a certain amount in value, only one-twentieth is charged; e.g. this is paid by John Hastelyn, Robert Batman, and John Boghurst, whose goods were valued at more than £20.

The tax on wages seems to be one-fortieth if they are £2 in value, but if less the sum of four pence is charged. The felon gets off cheap.

EXTRACT FROM HEARTH TAX ROLL IN 1673

(Lay Sub. Kent, $\frac{129}{746}$. 25. Car. ii)

East Burr? in Meopham Parish

	Iohn Edmeads .	.	5		Henry Henfield	.	1
	Nicholas Edmeads	.	1		Thomas Smith	.	1
	William Terry .	.	2	"n."	Alexander Ashwood		1
	Thomas Watts	.	3	"n."	Len Bullen. .	.	2
	Fran: Twisden, Esq.		2	"n."	Thomas Bennett	.	1
	Iohn Boyce	.	4		William Tayler	.	2
	Richard Horsey	.	3		William Nordash	.	3
	Iohn Wellerd .	.	2	"n."	James Lotter .	.	1
"e."	Henry Maisters	.	3		Robert Tayler .	.	1
	Thomas Cooke	.	1	"e."	William Walker	.	2
	William Fryer .	.	1	"n."	John Acresse .	.	1
"e."	William Fenn .	.	1		John Easden .	.	2
	John Hills .	.	2		Edward Everrell	.	1
	John Scudder .	.	1		Edward Atwood	.	2
	Jonas Pilcher .	.	2		John Acresse .	.	3
	George Wellerd	.	1	"n."	Arthur Ginings.	.	2
	Richard Whiffen, two				Mathew Loft .	.	1
	houses .	.	6		David Whiffen .	.	2
	Edward Loft .	.	2		Oliver Whiffen	.	4
	Richard Harwood	.	1	"n."	Widow Gamball	.	1
	Robert Rutland.	.	1				—
	John Round	.	2				82
"n."	Widow Weels .	.	2				

Viewed by

{ Roger Parsons, Collect^r.
{ Jonas Pilcher Boshold^r"

West Burrough

	Thomas Woulding	3		William Spruer	2
	Robert Tayler	5		William Swift gen.	10
	John Litchford	3		Thomas Munns	1
	Henry Higgins	1		Christopher Copland	3
"n."	Abraham Hackett	2		John Butler	2
	Thomas Mace	2		Henry Fater	3
"n."	John Loft	2	"e."	Robert Ginnings	3
	Henry Kerby	2		John Butler	3
	John Bennett	2	"n."	Gabriel Reave	1
	John Henvill	2		John French	3
	Richard Whiffen	5		Henry Ifield	2
"n."	Abraham Edwards	1		Dorothie Tayler	2
"n."	Richard Rumney	1		James Munn	2
"n."	Widow Gransden	1		Henry Reve	1
	Thomas Wooldham	2		David Nearn	3
	Thomas Skearmore	1	"new"	George West	3
	Edward Best	1		Thomas Skeamore	4
	William Higgens	1		Henry Bell	2
	Richard Rabson	1		Thomas Mun	2
"n."	George Vane	1		Fran: Bright	2
	Nicholas Piggott	6		Edward Gray	1
	Henry Loft	3		Nicholas Pullen	4
	George Maisters	2		John Reeve	1
"n."	Thomas French	1		Thomas Ifield	2
"n."	William Foucks	1		Gabriel Haselby	1
	William Boghurst	2		Widow Bright	2
	John Childe	4		Thomas Hayes	1
	Nicholas Butcher	5	"n."	Widow Holeman	1
	William Turner	1	"n."	Widow Scudder	1
"n."	Nicholas Gibson	2	"n."	Christopher Downes	1
	Widow Johnson	2	"n."	Widow Johnson	2
	William Johnson	1	"n."	Martyn Kettle	1
	Thomas Boghurst	2	"n."	Nicholas Muns	1
"n."	Thomas Pearsh	1			
	Edward Best	4			149

Viewed by

{ Roger Parsons, Collect^r
{ Henry Loft, Constable.

(m.32d. and m.33)

The Hearth Tax is mentioned in Chapter XIV, and this list gives 550 as the population of Meopham in Charles II's time; it also shows the magnitude of the two boroughs, East and West. The letter "e" specifies empty houses, of which there are but four, and three of these are in the East Borough; "n" signifies new houses, of which there are no less than twenty-six; and as nearly all have but one hearth, they were of the humbler sort. The Court Lodge (Wm. Swift) contained ten hearths, and the Parsonage (Rev. C. Copland) three, whilst the house at Camer (Henry Maisters) only appears to have had the same number.

THE DEED OF GIFT ON THE AUTHORITY OF THE ACT OF 6 WILL. IV "TO FACILITATE CONVEYANCE OF SITES OF SCHOOLROOMS"

The Dean and Chapter of Canterbury grant bequeath and sell to the Vicar and Church Wardens the north east corner of a field called Merry Hearth for the purpose of erecting thereon Schools and Schoolhouses to be used for the education of the Poor children in the Principles of the Christian Religion according to the Doctrine and Discipline of the united Church of England and Ireland and that this grant bargain and sale is on condition that the above shall be used according to the intent of this act otherwise it shall be void.

The area of the ground amounted to 1 rood, 5 perches, and was valued at £13 10s.

LIST OF MEOPHAM RATEPAYERS IN 1648
THE YEAR OF THE KENT ROYALIST RISING

Name	Amount
Henry Haslen } Rich: Haslen }	12/
Nicholas Butcher	14/
Thos: Swift	£1. 10. 0
Will: Taylor	17/
Thomas Plumer	18/
John Cooke	4/
Thomas Skirmer	3/
Widow Nordash	4/
Will: Hassell	1/
James Warren	4/
Robert Warren	2/8
Robert Gunnings	1/8
Geo: Rookes	1/
Will: Watson	0
Antony Swan	2/
Thos: Piggott gent:	0
James Reeve	3/
John Carnell	14/
Will: Sprever	6/
Henry Masters sen:	4/
Walter Salmon	/6
Abraham Kittle	/8
Thos: Hayse	1/8
Rich: Knight	2/8
Nicholas Tayler	2/8
Will: Warren	4/
Will: Alands	1/
Roger Kittlewell	2/8
John Standen	2/4
Thos: Lissone	1/
Thomas Eatonbury	/8
John Bennett	1/
Edward Dines	0
Robert Whiffen	1. 0. 0

Name	Amount
Thos: Wouldham	3/4
Thos: Munn	/4
Will: Tomson	1/6
Thos: Edmeades	12/
Nicholas Middleton	2/8
John Bright	1/8
Geo: Masters	2/8
Widow Loath	3/
Will: Hoffenden	9/4
John Hutchford	18/
Thomas Hayse	4/
Thomas Hulke	2/
Will: Gamble	1/
John Roberts	/4
John Boyce	2/
Matt: Loath	2/4
John Skirmer	3/
Will: Middleton	3/4
Widow Nordash	2/4
John Biggs	2/8
John Munn	4/
Henry Waite	4/
Thomas Hills	3/4
Olliver Whiffine	14/
Thos. Masters	3/
Thos. Johnson	1/
Martin Gudborough	/6
Henry Boghurst	1/4
Henry Sprever	1/
Henry Masters jun^r.	1/
Iohn Rounde	0
Harbert Snepp	1/
—— Bance	1/
Steven Pemble	2/
John Stapleton	4/

OUTBORDERERS

John Philpot	2/8	Edmund Attwood gent.	1/
John Chrowhurst	12/	Robert Page	1/
Robert Child	2/8	Thos: Wellards	/4
Robert Edmeades	1/	James Edmeades	/4
Walter Salmon	2/	Sibbin Rolphe	2/
James Taylor	2/	Matt: Wiburne	1/
Henry Stacy (min:)	1/		
Thos Harmon	/8	Total, 84 payers = £17. 14. 8	

DOCUMENT *TEMP.* EDWARD I, REFERRED TO IN CHAPTER IX

THE following is a copy of the document referred to under the "Court." It deals with the enfranchising of the land from certain customs and services. Each service had its special name when rendered by a tenant in Gavelkind. Thus Gavelearth = tillage or ploughing. Gavelcorn = corn paid for rent. Gavelwood = carting the Lord's wood. Gavelwork = general farm or labourer's work, etc. The "inland" consisted of "Lands holden in Demesne and designed to the furnishing of the Lord's board or table, and the maintenance of him and his family." The original Latin document is taken from Somner's *Gavelkind*, ed. 1726. I add a translation of it:

Relaxatio servitiorum et consuetudinum Tenentium de MEPHAM pro annuo redditu solvendo.

Universis pateat per presentes quod in festo Nativitatis Domini, Anno ejusdem Mcccvi Regni vero Regis Edwardi filii Henrici xxxv, Henricus Prior et Capitulum ecclesiæ Christi Cantuar: remiserunt et relaxaverunt hominibus et tenentibus suis de MEPHAM quasdem consuetudines et servitia pro annuo redditu quinquaginta septem solidor: trium denarior: et unius oboli eisdem Priori et capitulo in prædicto manerio suo de MEPHAM in festo Apostolorum Petri et Pauli annuatim solvend: in formâ subscriptâ, viz.
Tenentes de GAVELLOND de octodecim jugis pro cariagio triginta et sex carectat: feni de prato de REDHAMME apud Clyve usque MEPHAM quindecim solidos viz pro qualibet carectat: quinque denarios. Et unum dimidium jugum est in Dominico. Item pro averagiis tredecim solid: et quatuor denar: Item pro clausura circa blada duos solidos undecim denar: et obolum. Item pro clausura circa Curiam qua decitur BURGHYARD viginti duos denar: obolum et quadr: Item Tenentes de sex jugis et dimid: de INLAND pro trituratione et ventilatione triginta et quinque quateriorum frumenti novem solidos quinque denar:

obolum et quadr: viz pro trituratione cujus libet summæ tres
denar: et pro ventilatione unum quadr: Item pro trituratione et
ventilatione septemdecim grossarum summarum et dimid: avenæ
tres solid: tres denar: et unum quadr: viz pro trituratione cujus
libet summœ duos denar: et pro ventilatione unum quadran:
Item pro opere sarclandi octo decim denar: Item pro opere tassandi
in autum pro tredecim denar: Item pro fimis spargendis sex denar:
et obolum. Item pro xviii cladibus faciendis ad ovile sex denar:
Item pro cibo Prioris querend: et pro servitio quod dicitur WOR-
DERINDE et pro pomis fragendis duodecim denar: Item pro
clausura circa blada qua dicitur SWINHEY duos solidos decem
denar: et quadr. Item pro clausura xvi perticarum et quinque
pedum muri infra Curiam ab ostro Aulæ versus Portam Curioe
XVI denar: et obol: Item pro Grangia cooperienda duos solid:
et sex denar:—

In quorum omnium testimonium sigillum commune prædictorum
Prioris et capituli et sigilla Walteri de NORTHWODE. Johannes
de ISEBERGH. Johannis de HALIFELD. Henrici de MILDEN-
ACRE Petri de MILDENACRE et Johannis de PRESTWODE
pro se et omnibus aliis tenentibus de GAVELLOND ad requisitionem ipsorum: et Johannis de PETTESFELD, Johannis de la
Dene, Capillani, Henrici de LOMERE. Alfredi de NORTH-
WODE Henrici de NORTHWODE et Walteri IVE pro se et
omnibus aliis tenentibus de INLAND ad requisitionem eun-
dorum huic scripto chiroraphato alternatim sunt appensa. Acta
sunt hæc anno supradicto.

TRANSLATION

Commutation of services and customs of the Tenants of Mepham
for payment of an annual rent.

Be it known to all men by these Presents that on the Festival of the
Nativity of our Lord in the year 1306, the 35th year of the reign of
King Edward (the 1st) son of Henry (the iiird), Henry the Prior
and the Chapter of Christ Church, Canterbury, released and quit-
claimed to these men and tenants of Mepham certain customs
and services for an annual rent of £2 17s. 3½d., to be paid annually
to the Prior and Chapter in their aforesaid Manor of Mepham, on
the feast of the Apostles Peter and Paul, in the following manner,
viz.

Tenants in Gavellond of 18 yokes for the carriage of 36 loads of
hay from the meadow at Redhamme near Clyve to Mepham 15s.
viz. for any load 5d. And one half yoke is in the Demesne. Item for

carriage by horse* 13s. 4d. Item for fencing round corn 2s. 11½d. Item for fencing round the Court which is called Burghyard 1s. 10¾d. Item Tenants of the Inland of six and a half yokes for grinding and winnowing thirty-five quarters of wheat 9s. 5¾d. viz. for grinding any seam (quarter) 3d. and for winnowing ¼d. Item for grinding and winnowing seventeen and a half gross seams† of oats 3s. 3¼d., viz. for grinding any seam 2d. and for winnowing ¼d. Item for labour of weeding 1s. 6d. Item for labour of stacking in the Autumn 1s. 1d. Item for spreading manure 6½d. Item for making xviii hurdles for the sheepfold 6d. Item for providing meat for the Prior and for the service called Worderinde and for mashing apples 1s. Item for fencing round corn called Swinhey 2s. 10¼d. Item for fencing xvi perches, and for five feet of wall from the entrance of the Hall down towards the gate of the Court 1s. 4½d. Item for roofing the Grange 2s. 6d.

In witness of all of which the common seal of the aforesaid Prior and Chapter and the seals of Walter de Northwode, John de Isebergh, John de Halifeld, Henry de Mildenacre, Peter de Mildenacre and John de Prestwode and for all others the tenants of Gavellond at their request; and of John de Pettesfeld, John de la Dene, chaplain, Henry de Lomere, Alfred de Northwode, Henry de Northwode and Walter Ive, for themselves and for all other the tenants of Inland at their request, have been respectively affixed to this chirograph (written document). These acts have been done in the above-named year.

* "Averagium," according to an old dictionary, is derived from "averia, cattel, and consequently signifieth service which the tenant owes to the Lord, by horse or carriage of horse."

The following extract from an Inquisition held in Edward III's time and given by Somner (*Hist. of Gavelkind*) clearly has the same meaning.

"Inquisitio de terris et tenementes quae Isabella de Monte alto tenuit de Priore Ecclesiae Christi Cantuariae."

. . . "et per servitium faciendi duo averagia de Orpington usque Mepham per annum et valet opus viii denar:"

† A seam = 8 bushels or one horse-load.

MAKING OF THE TURNPIKE ROAD FROM GRAVESEND TO WROTHAM

THE following explanatory paragraph I owe to Mr. A. A. Arnold:

Towards the end of the eighteenth and in the early part of the nineteenth centuries numerous Acts of Parliament were passed for making Turnpike Roads in Kent, and among them was an Act, 6 Geo. IV, c. 50 (1825) for making a Turnpike Road from Gravesend to Wrotham. Trustees were appointed by these Acts with large powers for taking over the existing roads, and for improving, enlarging, and diverting them. They were empowered to put up Toll-bars and Gates and to levy tolls on all animals and on all wheeled conveyances according to a table which the Act authorized. The Toll-Bars and Gates were let by public auction—usually for one year only, and the system continued till toward the close of the nineteenth century, when the Highway Boards and afterwards the Rural District Councils took over the duty of looking after the roads.

CLAIM OF TRADESCANT FOR MONEY FOR WORK DONE

DOCUMENTS relating to Tradescant, Sen.:

i   *By vertue of an Ordinance of both Howses of*
Parliament of the xxist daie of Septem., 1643.
these are to will & require you Out of such threasure
as now is, or shall be in your hands, to paye unto Mr.
John — Tredescant the sume of Fortie pownds
to be issued upon Accompt for Worke to be don for
amending the Walks in the Vineyard Garden, &
for Worke to be don to the Gardens at Oatlands,
& for repairing the Bowling Greene there. And for
soe doing, this together with his Acquittance for the
Receipt thereof, shall be your Warrant, & discharge.
And allso to the Auditor generall to Allowe the
sume upon your Accompt. Dated at the Comittee of
Lords & Commons for his Ma^{s} Revenue sitting
at Westminster the twelf daie of Aprill. 1648
         Pembroke & Mont:

                     Salisbury
                  W. Say & Seale
   ? J. Young

                Tho: Hoyle
To our verie Loving freind Thomas Fauconbridg Esq -
         Receiver generall of the Revenue
Mr. Tredescant

ii   *Vicesimo primo die April 1648*
Received by mee John Tredescant
     of Thomas ffauconberge   *li*
Esqre Receiv^{r} Gen'all of the —   *xx*
Revenue the Sume of Twenty
Pounds in pt of ffourty pounds
According to the Warr^{t}. wthin
written I say rec^{d} —

            John Tredescant

Endorsed

                              —li

   Mr. Tredescant   *40/.*

An interesting point is that nowadays Tradescant's name is not written as he did; for he himself always spelt it Tredescant. The originals are now deposited in the Ashmolean Museum at Oxford—photographed copies have been hung in our vestry.

REFERENCES TO OUR CHURCH IN THE MS. ROOM
OF THE BRITISH MUSEUM

To the courtesy of Mr. Hodgess Roper of Strood I am indebted for references about our church to be found in the Manuscript Room of the British Museum. I give them with their library numbers, so that anyone can refer to them.

ADDITIONAL MS. 32368

Folio 86

Is an etching of the church by R. S. Miles, dated July 25, 1840. It appears as at present, but if the churchyard paths are correctly indicated, there was none at that time along the south side of the church. There is also carefully drawn the figure of an old copper key with wards and an hexagonal pipe; the bow forming the handle is square: one corner being attached to the pipe, the other three having copper knobs the size of large peas. The total length is five inches. There is nothing to show to what it belonged: could it possibly have been the key of the aumbry?

Folio 87

A sketch of the church, without date, but as it shows the churchyard to have a rustic wooden fence with a swing gate at the south-east corner, where the tunnel now is, it must have been drawn prior to 1859.

On the east gable of the nave is clearly shown a line of worked stone, let into the flint wall, indicating that the present chancel roof has been rebuilt at a steeper angle than formerly. It is still to be seen.

The tracery of the east window is as at present, showing that when the tracery was replaced in 1874 the old pattern was exactly followed.

Folios 88 *and* 89

Are two tinted sketches of the exterior of the church, without date, but both clearly by the same hand. One is of the north-east angle and shows the old stone water-drain with its still open mouth for the discharge of rain water. It also indicates the altered roof of the chancel as mentioned above. The other is of the south side of the Chancel and shows everything as at present except that both the "High Side" window, and the one next to it are bricked up from below to half their height.

Folio 90

This is a view by R. S. Miles, dated September 15, 1838, from the north-west, and with the exception of the nave roof having large square shingles on it at its eastern half, the rest being tiled, the view is as at present.

Folios 91 and 92

These are architectural drawings (from Brand's *Analysis of Gothic Architecture*, 1847) with full measured details of the east window, confirming the conclusions arrived at under Folio 87 above.

Folios 93, 94 and 94A

Are full-sized coloured drawings of some of our old church glass. One drawing, dated August 13, 1836, represents a three-quarter figure of a smooth-faced saint with halo, of sad countenance, and with hands crossed over the breast. It measures 10 inches by $5\frac{1}{2}$ inches, and probably is the figure of St. John. Another is of a "quarry," as may still be seen in the window at the west end of the south aisle. What remains of the old glass described in Chapter IV is now restored to the church in the form of an *omnium gatherum* memorial window in the south aisle.

Add. MS. 35211. K. I., Vol. I, P. 144

This is a full-sized coloured drawing by Winston of the figure of St. Thomas of Canterbury. A similar drawing (with others of figures in the old glass) now hangs in our vestry.

DEEDS RELATING TO MEOPHAM AND DEANE

(i) A deed in Latin, dated September 6, 1597 (Queen Elizabeth), whereby Christopher Poole, of Bromley, Kent, yeoman, for £41 sells to Robert Child, son of William Child, of "Mepham," yeoman, a messuage or tenement, one garden, two orchards, two pieces or parcels of land known as St. Chaplains, in all two acres, more or less, situated in the parish of "Mepham," "near the Common called Hooke Green," of which property the house, garden, and one orchard, known as Chamberlaine's, are thus bounded: on the north by the King's Highway, on the south by the lands of Christopher Pooer, on the east by the common way, *ad puten* (? to the well), on the west by the other orchard.

The boundaries of the "other orchard" are on the north by the King's Highway, on the west by the lands of Robert Butcher, on the east and south by the lands of Christopher Pooer.

The two pieces of land are known as Woodcrofte. One of these is bounded on the north by Christopher Pooer's house, on the west by the lands of Robert Butcher, on the east by the way *ad puten*, on the south by the lands of Salomon Cooper. The other is bounded on the north by a private land way, on the south and east by the lands of William Sprever, and on the West by the lands of Robert Butcher.

Though the boundaries are given, it is not possible to locate the property now. All that can be said is that since the northern boundary was the King's Highway, the only road now near Hook Green and running east and west, so forming a north boundary, is Norwood Lane; no other could form a north boundary, and if this is so, the land must have lain between that road and the Camer Road.

Both William Sprever of Dartford, in 1525, and Robert Sprever, 1604, were benefactors to the Parish. The William Sprever of this document (1597) may have been a son of the former, and Robert a grandson. Robert Butcher figures largely in the deeds relative to Deane.

(ii) Deed dated June 1, 1611, by which Henry Godden, of Milton, Gravesend, sells to his brother, Jacob Godden, of Woldham (Wouldham) for £30, a part of a five-acre wood in the parish of

Meopham, known as Ludgate or Lybgate Wood. There is nothing to indicate its position in the Parish now, nor does the name survive.

(iii) An indenture dated April 17, 1691 (William and Mary), by which John Whiffen of Ridley, Joan his wife; Oliver Whiffen of Stanstead and William Tomlyn of Wrotham, agree to let to John Edwards of Meopham, yeoman, one messuage or tenement, one barn, one stable, one garden, one parcel of land of about 7½ acres called Broadfield, in the parish of Meopham, now occupied by John Edwards and John Goddin, alias Goodwin, at the yearly rent of one peppercorn, if so demanded: and 5/- to be paid down before the sealing of the deed.

A property of this name no longer exists, though the field in "Leading Street," in which "Broadview" is situated, is called Broadfield. A tradition of a farm having been at or near there long ago is still extant in the village.

It may be noted that Godwin: Goodwin: Goddin: Godden, are all forms of the same name; and indeed the name Goodwin, still extant in the Parish, is always locally pronounced Good'in.

(iv) An indenture dated September 16, 1714 (Queen Anne), by which a family of the name of Peckham makes over to a relative, John Williams, for £50 "the messuage or tenement called Merry Weathers," with its garden, orchard, one close, and one parcel of arable land in all one acre, more or less, in the parish of Meopham "at or near a certain streete commonly called or known by the name of Culversole and formerly occupied by Richard Romney and later by—Ffrench." It was still earlier in the hands of one Johnson, of Tonbridge.

There is nothing given by which this property may now be identified; but there was a homestead consisting of an old cottage with garden, orchard, etc., in all about the size mentioned in the deed, and occupied half a century ago by Richard Bennett, a wheelwright, which lay where now is the "Wilderness." The cottage was burnt down about forty-five years ago.

(v) The will, dated 1799, with probate, of John C. Markett (who held Meopham Court from 1789 to 1801). He had married Ann, daughter of John Hooker of Tonbridge Castle, and their daughter Elizabeth became the wife of Sir John Bayley. The will directs that only £30 shall be spent on the funeral.

To his son Augustus the testator leaves £3,000; to his daughter Ann £3,000; and to his married daughter Elizabeth, £1,000 over and above her marriage portion. He makes his son-in-law, John Bayley, trustee of the annual sum of £50 to be paid to his other son Frederick Markett, at the discretion of the trustee, in order that Frederick shall not have it in his power "To sell or dispose of the same." There is one legacy of £50 to Thomas Goodwin his servant.

Everything else, real and personal, he leaves to his son Francis, who succeeded him at Meopham Court and who, with the brother-in-law John Bayley are the Exors. Probate was granted October 7, 1801. Besides the property of Meopham Court and lands, there were £37,000 in the Funds.

The Will is witnessed by Thos. Walker, William Mungeam, and Alban Dorrington.

The Marketts were of Huguenot stock, and the name really was Marquette. Of the witnesses, Alban Dorrington was doubtless the father of the man of the same name already mentioned, and William Mungeam was Master of the Meopham workhouse and Clerk to the Vestry.

DEEDS RELATING TO DEANE MANOR OR FARM

(vi) An indenture, dated June 15, 1627, by Adrian Evans, citizen and clothier, of London (of the first part); Samuel Harfleet, of Bromleigh, Wiltshire, gent., and Joane his wife (of the second part); Sir Christopher Harfleet, of Wollands, in the parish of Ashe, next Sandwiche, Kent (of the third part); Walter Harfleet of Beastsbourne (? Bekesbourn), Kent, gent., and John Harfleet his son and heir (of the fourth part): Henry Austyne, gent., and Henry Questenbury, both of Rochester (of the fifth part), whereby the above-named in consideration of £400 due to Adrian Evans from Samuel Harfleet, and of £110 due from the same to Sir Christopher Harfleet, and of the £125 due from the same to Walter Harfleet, do make provision for Joan Harfleet by letting Deane Manor for £50 per annum, and in the event of certain conditions not being carried out by Adrian Evans, certain benefits are to accrue to Henry Pigott, son of Thomas Pigott, clerk of Meopham.

The surmise may perhaps be allowed that this reversionary gift to Henry Pigott shows appreciation of the family of the Vicar, Rev. Thomas Pigott, who was afterwards "sequestered".

(vii) A deed of "bargain and sale," dated June 14, 1650, of the "Manor of Deane Place," with all appurtenances, for £600 to Francis Twisden, by Nicholas Butcher, of Meopham, yeoman, by Joan Holmeden, of Meopham, widow, and Edward Dane, or Deane, of Deane, husbandman. The property is described in full, amounting to about 500 acres, in the parishes of Meopham and Luddesdown. At the time of sale, Deane was in the occupation of John Chapman and Edward Deane.

(viii) This is the actual deed of sale of Deane, dated July 4, 1650, and attested before His Majesty's Judges at Westminster, in which the sellers mentioned above agree to part with the property by Michaelmas Day, on receipt of £600.

In this deed Joan Holmeden appears as Joane Homeden: she was the sister of Nicholas Butcher, mentioned below.

Robert Butcher was Churchwarden early in the seventeenth century.

(ix) The acknowledgment of the £600 of Nicholas Butcher, from Francis Twisden, for Deane, as per the deeds above quoted, dated July 4, 1650 (Staple Bond).

(x) Deed, dated August 16, 1650, of surrender of the lease of Deane Manor to John Twisden, of Peckham, Kent. Deane had been previously held by Samuel Harfleet, who had leased it to Robert Butcher, father of Nicholas Butcher, in "the 12th year of King Charles I," i.e. 1637, for 21 years.

As this deed is dated 1650, the surrender covered eight years.

(xi) A document in Latin, known as a "fine," executed September 3, 1650, at the Court of Westminster, before the Justices Sir John Puliston, Peter Warburton, Edward Atkins, and others, showing that the sale of certain lands had been completed by Nicholas Butcher and Edward Dane (Dene) to Sir Francis Twisden. The property is in the parishes of Meopham and Luddesdown, and consists of 450 acres of land: 73 acres of woodland, various messuages, tenements, and one "Columbarium" (Dove-cote) valued at £280.

This deed is of peculiar interest for these reasons. It is beautifully written on parchment, or rather, in duplicate on two strips of parchment. It was the custom at that time, and for long after, when the sale of a property was concluded, that a statement to that effect should be drawn up in court in the following way. An oblong skin of parchment had the deed written on it in triplicate; two copies being written, one under the other, on, say, the left-hand end of the parchment, the third being written across the end, at right angles to the others. The three were then cut off with scissors, in a wavy line (hence "indenture"); the two former were for the seller and buyer to keep, the third was retained by the Court, and was called the "foot of the fine"; "fine" here meaning, not a money payment, but "finis" or end, because it was the actual and irrevocable end of the business. The Record Office which guards the old Court documents must have many of these "feet of fines," but to have all three together is very unusual; in the museum of the Record Office may be seen a complete "fine" with its three parts. The two that I hold are the horizontal ones, the seller's and buyer's. The "foot" would be in the Record Office, if anywhere.

The object in not cutting them apart in a straight line was a preventive against forgery, as the wavy lines could be fitted accurately together if the documents were genuine.

(xii) A deed dated May 12, 1676, is one releasing Sir Thomas Twisden of Deane Manor from certain payments that he was required to make under the will of his father, Francis Twisden. Francis made his will April 1, 1675, and by it he gave all Deane Manor, in the parishes of Meopham and Luddesdown, to his brother, Sir Thomas, for life, and then to his wife Jane, for her life; and after her decease he appointed Sir William Twisden, of East Peckham, and Francis, Sir Thomas's son, trustees for twenty years to hold all rents from Deane Manor and divide them equally among all the younger children of the said Sir Thomas Twisden, and after the twenty years, "Did give or devise" the same to Roger Twisden, eldest son of Sir Thomas Twisden, for ever. The deed then states that Sir Thomas Twisden, his wife Jane, and the younger members of the family do now, May 12, 1676, in consideration of the sum of £320 paid down by Sir Thomas, release him from the obligations put upon him by the will, so as to avoid all disputes, suits, etc., that might arise in time to come, and to the end also that, "there may be maintained, cherished, and nourished amongst us the same Amitè, Affection and Love, as now (Blessed be God) there is. . . ."

The deed bears the signatures and seals of the ten beneficiaries.

All the above documents are now in the custody of the Kent Archæological Society.

RESTORATION OF THE OLD CHURCH GLASS

At the morning service on Sunday, January 7, 1923, the restored glass in the south aisle was dedicated "to the glory of God and in memory of His servant Florence Marion Golding-Bird." The gift of one who by his published writings has already shown his interest in, and love for our ancient Parish Church, remains of the old glass, dating from the fourteenth and fifteenth centuries, have been most carefully and artistically arranged in the best way possible by Messrs. Powell of the Whitefriars Glass Works, without the addition of a single piece of new coloured glass.

With the exception of four figures at the top and of three quatre-foils at the bottom of the three lancets, it has not been found possible to follow any orderly pattern; yet the various broken fragments of glass have been so arranged as to form, on the whole, a very pleasing effect.

The following is a description of the more recognizable portions; but the odd pieces dotted about everywhere each provide a study for the archaeologist. Starting from the east or left-hand side, the four top panels contain: (1) a figure of St. George, helmeted, and holding his shield with the Cross upon it; (2) St. Thomas of Canterbury, a figure which at one time was thought to be that of Simon de Mepham, but this is disproved by two circumstances: one, that he wears a corona signifying canonization; and the other that there is in Farningham Church an almost identical figure, about which there has apparently never been any doubt of its representing St. Thomas of Canterbury.

(3) Shows St. Catherine, with her wheel; and (4) is a composite one containing three heads, the middle one being beautifully drawn. Whom they represent it is not possible to say.

In the three large lancets the following can be traced. The first or left-hand one is, in its upper third, largely composed of fragments, but in the right-hand lower corner is the part of a figure of the devil, very hairy, brown in colour, and with a very evil eye. In the middle third is a disc with "Ladie" on it: it is part of an invocation to the Virgin Mary, completed in the last lancets by a similar disc, inscribed with the word "helpe." These are known to have been in the east window as late as the year 1854. The lower third has a perfectly arranged quatrefoil in blue and red, the only regular pattern that could be made out of the old glass. Similar quatrefoils are seen in the other two lancets.

The middle lancet shows in its upper third a panel representing an angel blowing a trumpet, and the head of another angel, of most sorrowful countenance, below. Curious spike-like rays shoot across this panel, the meaning of which is not clear. In the middle third is a draped figure, but without a head, and bearing a palm branch in the right hand; very suggestive of the angel of the Annunciation. Below this is a single inset which shows a half-draped leg. The lower third has the quatrefoil mentioned above, and in the lower left-hand corner is a curious fragment of a finger and thumb holding a plectrum or striker, with which the strings of a harp or similar musical instrument are being sounded.

The third lancet shows in its upper third the figure of a smooth-faced saint with halo—possibly St. John—and on either side is a head with curly golden hair: these are probably the heads of angels. Below this is the body and arm of a figure, with the remains of flowing hair descending on the shoulders, possibly representing St. John the Baptist. The rest of this lancet is similar to the above.

It is impossible to speak of the many individual small fragments, though each deserves a careful study, but it will be noticed that in the trefoil at the top of the middle lancet are two very good representations of the Royal (nowadays called Tudor) Rose. The plain white diamonds of glass that fill in the interstices, and the short memorial inscription below, are the only new glass employed in this window.

It is evident that we have here only a very small portion of the coloured glass originally in the church; nor is it known in which windows it was placed. There is a record, however, that in 1846 there was coloured glass in the east window, and some must have been in the perpendicular windows of the nave, since the figures of St. Catherine and of St. Thomas exactly filled the small panels of the present window without any alteration.

Much of the old glass, it will be noticed, is covered with black specks: this is due to the weathering, in course of centuries, of the outside of the glass: and the reason that all of it is not so affected is that in olden times church glass was sometimes made with a potash silicate and sometimes with a soda silicate; the former became pitted as mentioned above, the latter remained unaffected.

At a meeting of the Society of Art Technology, held at York, on October 19, 1922, in two papers communicated by Mr. J. A. Knowles of York and by the late Mr. H. J. Powell of the Whitefriars Glass Works, it was pointed out that "the most defective glass belonged to the fourteenth century" whilst a "good deal of the twelfth- and thirteenth-century glass was perfectly sound." The presence of potash in fourteenth-century glass was insisted upon as the cause of decay.

In the vestry may be seen drawings of some of the panels described, made in the middle of the last century.

METHOD OF TOWER-BUILDING IN OLD TIMES

THE skilful and harmonious repair of the buttresses is due to the personal care of Mr. Percy Martin of Meopham, and he furnishes the following note on the building of the tower:

When old buildings are being repaired, rather interesting things are sometimes found.

As the men were erecting the scaffold to the church tower in 1930, the method of scaffolding used in its construction was revealed by their finding holes, about 8 inches square and about 4 feet apart vertically, left in the walls, with one stone covering the hole on each face of the wall. So we deduce that the builders raised the walls as high as they could reach from the ground-level, and then laid on the walls a row of 8 inches by 8 inches oak putlogs reaching over about four feet on each side, with a cantilever brace to each. On these putlogs were laid the scaffold boards, and the process was repeated each time the men had raised the walls as high as they could.

They were careful not to 'pinch' the putlogs when building round them, and carefully selected stones long enough to form a bridge over the top of each, so that when it was required to take them out it was easily done. The 'tunnel' formed in the wall for the putlog, was never filled in when the latter was taken out; only closed on each side by a single flint, having a larger flint over it.

This suggested that it might come out easily for our own putlogs to be inserted—which proved to be the case, and a lighted candle on a stick proved the 'tunnels' to be intact.

The probable reason for scaffolding in this manner would be the difficulty of obtaining home-grown timber straight and small enough for poles, and it was probably out of the question to import from Norway in those days.

APPENDIX T

THE PETITION OF REV. WILLIAM GIBSON

To the Worshipful Deane & Chapter of Canterbury the humble petition of William Gibson, Minister of Meopham, sheweth that whereas your petitioner, Master of Arts standing 28 years, ordained Deacon of a Bishop An.Do. 1634 and afterwards Minister An.Do. 1637, formerly legally presented to a living and in these late divisions by a malicious and factious people sequestred from the same, and since the Act of re-entrance resigning the troublesome place, having liberty to officiate where I am, your petitioner was the second that succeeded Mr Pigott, legall incumbent of the vicarage of Meopham, not without his consent, duly and truly paying fifth for as long as he lived.

Now seeing all the revenues appertaining to the vicarage of Meopham to the utmost and upon record amounts to noe more than 15£ per ann., your petitioner humbly desires that it may be made a competency out of the Rectory of Meopham according to the King's Majestie's gracious declaration.

And your petitioner shall ever etc.

William Gibson.

ADDENDA AND CORRIGENDA

SINCE the publication of the second edition of the book in 1934 there have been a number of events which have a direct bearing on some of the topics in the book, and it seems useful to mention them here. There has also been the opportunity for further documentary research, which has revealed a limited number of inaccuracies in the original work. All these items are listed below in page order.

p. 21: Several archaeological digs in the area south of the George have revealed the existence of a Roman farmstead dating to the lst and 2nd centuries A.D.

p. 24: The Perambulation of Kent was re-published in 1826, and the reference is to be found on pp. 442-449.

p. 40: As noted later (p. 203) the charter was granted in 1447, some 13 years *before* the will of Hugo Chiddingstone. It is possible that the church was re-dedicated to St. John between these two dates.

p. 46: A further reference is to Glynne's *Churches*, 1877, at p. 277.

p. 68: The pulpit in Trottiscliffe Church (given in 1824.) is illustrated in *Smetham's Rambles*, Vol. I, p. 129.

p. 80: The reference to Glynne's *Churches of Kent* should read p. 277.

p. 82: The reference in paragraph 2 should be to Appendix R (not S). Mrs. Golding-Bird died in 1919.

p. 100 et seq.: Two more bells were added in 1949. They were both cast by Gillett & Johnston, of Croydon, and bear the inscription: "*To the Glory of God. Presented by Mrs F. E. Worthington, Easter 1949" Vernon S. Nicholls, Vicar. F. Worthington and H. E. Ruffell, Churchwardens.* Bell No. 1 is tuned to F# and weighs 4 cwts, 2 qrs, 8 lbs. Bell No. 2 is tuned to F, and weighs 4 cwts, 2 qrs, 20 lbs. The entire cost of the augmentation and restoration was given by Mrs F. E. Worthington.

p. 108: The reference to Robert Scriver should be "Spriver".

p. 127: Against the entry for 1550 delete the name "Cranmer".

p. 128: For further information about John Folsham and the accounts of the Manor, see *Archaeologia Cantiana* Vol X, pp. 316-317

p. 129: William Gibson's petition is now included as Appendix T on p. 312. The reference to Martin Huggard is apparently taken from Cranmer's Register, p. 412.

p. 140: The correct reference to the *Gentleman's Magazine* should read "Vol 79, part I, p. 513".

p. 143: The living once more became Rectorial when the parish of Nurstead was amalgamated with Meopham in February 1979,

p. 151: The lordship of the Manor of Dodmore has now been acquired by Dr D. Adamson, of Dodmore House.

p. 165: Considerable research into the story of the Tradescants has been undertaken in recent years, and readers are referred to *The Tradescants* by Prudence Leith-Ross.

p. 181: The Post Office has now returned to its former home, Elizabeth House.

p. 191: The Frances Smith and the Clay Cottages trusts have now been amalgamated, and are run by trustees appointed by the Parish Council.

p. 203: The charter was granted on 5th February 1447. This date rules out the reason for the grant suggested on p. 204. In fact the charter also granted to the prior and convent of Christchurch the right to hold fairs and markets at Hollingbourne, Eastry, Monkton and Chart. (The latter a market only).

p. 207: The various village greens came under the legal ownership of the Parish Council in February 1949, when they acquired the rights of the Lordship of the Manor from the Church Commissioners for the sum of £25.

p. 211: The map deposited with the Turnpike Act of 1825 makes it quite clear that the road to be improved was the same as the one now in use, and it shows no road at all on the line suggested, via Lomer. It would seem that Mr. Golding-Bird relied on incorrect information supplied by Mr. A. A. Arnold.

p. 227: The Cricketers took its present name in 1735, and moved to its present building in 1794. (*The Cricketers Inn at Meopham*, by W. Gunyon).

p. 228: On the evidence of field names and other documents it can be established that Meopham has had at least 7 mills since 1240, when Robert the miller was mentioned in the Geoffrey Trauncey deed (Appendix F).

p. 232: Leading Street—see the note above regarding p. 211.

p. 238: Owls Castle is a 16th century farm, originally called Cooks Farm, after the family who had lived there from that time. Their 16th century aisled barn still survives.

p. 244: For *Memoirs of Malling* read *Memories of Mailing*, 1893.

p. 253: The Parish Crouche. A document of 1598 concerning the George Inn and other adjacent properties refers to them as being "situate at and being the parish crouche". It probably stood, therefore, at the junction of The Street and Wrotham Road.

p. 273: Parish Records. The documents listed, and many more besides, are now deposited at the County Records Office, County Hall, Maidstone.

p. 274: The following churchwardens should be added:

17th Century, Thomas Grinnell (1616), Wm. Child (1613)

18th Century, John Salmon (1773-4), John Jewiss (1773-4). There may well be others not documented.

p. 277: The list of burials appears to have been prepared by Rev. T. S. Cogswell (see p. 115).

THE AUTHOR

Cuthbert Hilton Golding-Bird was born in London on 7 July 1848, fourth son of Dr. Golding-Bird, eminent medical scholar and Assistant Physician at Guy's Hospital until his sudden death in 1854. The younger "G.B.", as he came to be called, was educated at Tonbridge and King's College, London. He began his medical training at Guy's in 1868 and his rise to academic distinction was almost meteoric: first prize at the end of his first and third years and, in 1873, the Treasurer's Gold Medal for Surgery, followed in 1874 by success in both Primary and Final F.R.C.S. examinations. In 1875 he was elected Assistant Surgeon, subsequently attaining the Lectureship in Physiology. His opinion was constantly sought on orthopaedic and spinal deformities and his exceptional manual dexterity and unusual mechanical flair enabled him to demonstrate with apparent simplicity the most complicated surgery. He took endless trouble with his students and his Tuesday round of the wards became legendary as the educational highlight of the week. He was regarded with deep affection by dressers, ward clerks and house surgeons for his accessibility, kindly humour and total absence of self-importance. He liked simply to be known as a "Guy's Man". He was appointed Full Surgeon in 1893 and, before retiring in 1908 as Senior Consulting Surgeon, he was also acting as Consulting Surgeon to Gravesend Hospital and to the Royal School for Deaf and Dumb Children in Margate.

On his retirement "G.B." settled permanently in Meopham. He had married Florence Baber of "Leylands", then known as "Deodars", in 1870 and bought Pitfield Cottage on Meopham Green as a holiday home in 1884. In 1897 the cottage was pulled down and Pitfield House was erected on the site of the old barn adjacent to it. Florence died in 1919 and there were no children, but "G.B." lived there until his death in 1939 at the age of 90. He involved himself in many village affairs, becoming a trustee of the Village Hall, a churchwarden and inaugurator of the Meopham and Nurstead Nursing Association of which he remained President for life. He also served for many years as Chairman of the Kent County Nursing Association. His personal interests were wide, ranging from photography to gardening and archaeology, but his over-riding passion was clocks; he collected rarities, whatever their condition, repaired them and restored their chimes and tunes. He was always ready to help those in need, including the local doctor in any difficult surgical case; his diagnostic acumen came to be seen as almost uncanny! His first book on Meopham: *The Story of Old Meopham* (1918) and the later edition: *The History of Meopham* (1934) were both published at his own expense and sold for the benefit of local charities; he bequeathed the copyright of the latter to the Kent Archaeological Society of which he was a long-standing member. His generosity continued to be exemplified in the bequest of his house and its grounds to Guy's Hospital, in the hope that it might become a convalescent home for nurses, though that wish never came to fruition.

PITFIELD COTTAGE IN 1887

"PITFIELD" AFTER 1897

INDEX

Index is arranged alphabetically, in word-by-word order, where a space precedes a letter (e.g. 'de Woldenham' comes before 'Deane'). Page locators in bold denote material of major relevance; locators in italics denote illustrations; *n* after a locator denotes footnote; entry headings in italics denote a document title; 'St.' is filed as though spelt out; numbers are also filed as spelt, with the exception of dates qualifying headings (e.g. Subsidy Rolls, 14th Century), where filing is chronological.